# THE SECOND CHANCE CLUB

Hardship and Hope
After Prison

## JASON HARDY

Simon & Schuster
New York   London   Toronto   Sydney   New Delhi

Simon & Schuster
1230 Avenue of the Americas
New York, NY 10020

First Simon & Schuster hardcover edition February 2020

SIMON & SCHUSTER and colophon are registered
trademarks of Simon & Schuster, Inc.

For information about special discounts for bulk purchases,
please contact Simon & Schuster Special Sales at 1-866-506-1949
or business@simonandschuster.com.

The Simon & Schuster Speakers Bureau can bring authors
to your live event. For more information or to book an event,
contact the Simon & Schuster Speakers Bureau at 1-866-248-3049
or visit our website at www.simonspeakers.com.

Interior design by Lewelin Polanco

Manufactured in the United States of America

1  3  5  7  9  10  8  6  4  2

Library of Congress Cataloging-in-Publication Data

Names: Hardy, Jason Matthew, author.
Title: The second chance club : hardship and hope
after prison / Jason Hardy.
Description: New York : Simon & Schuster, 2020. |
Includes bibliographical references and index.
Identifiers: LCCN 2019035155 (print) | LCCN 2019035156 (ebook) |
ISBN 9781982128593 (hardcover) | ISBN 9781982128609 (paperback) |
ISBN 9781982128616 (ebook)
Subjects: LCSH: Parolees—Louisiana. | Parole officers—Louisiana. | Prisoners—
Deinstitutionalization—Louisiana. | Ex-convicts—Rehabilitation—Louisiana.
Classification: LCC HV9305.L8 H37 2020 (print) | LCC HV9305.L8 (ebook)
| DDC 364.6/20922763—dc23
LC record available at https://lccn.loc.gov/2019035155
LC ebook record available at https://lccn.loc.gov/2019035156

ISBN 978-1-9821-2859-3
ISBN 978-1-9821-2861-6 (ebook)

*For Kristin*

# AUTHOR'S NOTE

This is a work of nonfiction. I have described real people but changed names and certain details. My accounts would fairly reflect any number of cases, in New Orleans and elsewhere, which is just to say that as unsettling as much of this is, it happens every day.

# CONTENTS

## PART THREE – harm reduction

# INTRODUCTION

The summer heat in New Orleans drove most drug dealers inside by noon. By one o'clock, only the addicts remained on the street, resigned to waiting for the market to reopen at dusk. The Landry brothers usually spent most of the day inside, but the air at their house was out. The two brothers and the three big dogs were seated on the front steps when I showed up. I was the probation and parole officer—the "PO," as we were known—to both brothers. I was new to the job, but probation and parole visits were old hat to the Landrys, and they let me know with a nod that they were in the middle of something and would be with me in a minute.

Javaron, the older one, had just turned thirty. He was short and stout like a college wrestler, with small, serious eyes. Ronald was as thin as a picket and covered in scars incurred during the violent epileptic fits he'd been having since he was a teenager. Ronald was twenty-five but could have passed for forty.

The brothers both had cigarettes lit and beer bottles in hand. Between sips and drags they exchanged pages of a police report given to Ronald by his defense attorney. According to the report, Ronald had been the passenger in a car that was pulled over for speeding. Ronald and the driver had been drinking, and the car smelled like weed, which gave the police cause to conduct a search. The weed was already smoked, so the cops didn't find any. The cops weren't all that interested in weed anyway. They were looking for guns. They found one under the passenger's seat.

The gun was registered to the driver's uncle, and the uncle had given the driver permission to take it. The driver had no permit. In Louisiana, that wasn't a serious problem, but when paired with alcohol, the gun became a misdemeanor offense for the driver. Ronald had two prior drug convictions and one prior gun conviction and was forbidden from being within arm's reach of a firearm. For Ronald, riding in a car with a gun in it was a felony.

"You're sitting right on top the motherfucker," Javaron said. "Can't believe they gave you bail."

"The uncle came in and vouched for us," Ronald said. "He's got that big church on the West Bank."

Javaron side-eyed his brother. "He's got votes is what he's got. Don't think those judges don't know it."

Judicial allotments were pure luck. Political connections or not, there was only one judge in town that Javaron could see letting a probationer walk out of jail with a pending gun charge. "One-in-twelve shot," Javaron said, "and you fucking hit." He laughed and raised his beer bottle to his brother's good fortune.

"I didn't know he had a gun," Ronald told me.

I told him I believed him. It was little consolation. A good report from a PO might convince a judge to go easy on a drug charge, but guns were another matter. Both Landrys knew it. Ronald was lucky to be free now, but he would likely lose his freedom when the case went to trial.

Javaron wagged his beer bottle at me. "You want one?"

Technically, probationers and parolees weren't supposed to be drinking, but no sensible PO bothered enforcing this restriction. "Little early for me," I said. "Let me do my thing and I'll get out of your hair."

Javaron drained the beer bottle, flicked the cigarette into his overgrown yard, and led the way inside. It was a small three-bedroom house, at most twelve hundred square feet. The Landrys' mother had the front bedroom. She was at work answering phones at a doctor's office.

Neither of her sons was employed. Ronald's seizures had gotten him sent home from the few jobs he'd managed to get. Javaron had spent his twenties in and out of jail, mostly on felony charges related to his work for the local crack dealer, and he considered himself unemployable. I got the impression Javaron was more of an enforcer than a dealer, but he'd had a lot of product on him during his last arrest and was sent to prison. Most drug charges, like the one Ronald pleaded guilty to the year before, were resolved with probation—in other words, without jail. Javaron served the first two years of his five-year sentence "upstate" in prison. As long as he didn't get in trouble again, he'd spend the next three years under my supervision on parole.

In Louisiana, the probation rules and the parole rules were functionally identical. When conducting a home inspection, it wasn't necessary for me to remember which of the two forms of community supervision the guy I was visiting was on. Most POs referred to probationers and parolees collectively as "offenders."

The home inspection had two purposes, and even a rookie could see that they were an odd match. Purpose one was to look for contraband: drugs, guns, stolen property. If I found any, I was supposed to confiscate it, write a police report, and charge the offender with a crime. Purpose two was to make surface-level observations about the health, socioeconomic status, and pattern of life of the offender and the home's other residents and use the data to help the offender turn his life around. In simple terms, purpose one was to put the offender back in jail. Purpose two was to keep him out.

Most of the floor space in Javaron's room was occupied by rows of large black kennels. The three dogs I'd met outside on the steps were the product of a breeding tree Javaron had kept going for the better part of a decade, with Ronald stepping in to run things when Javaron was in jail. The bedrooms were small and clean, with twin beds and TVs on wicker nightstands. I spent no more than five seconds in each of the three bedrooms and another five in the kitchen and living room.

It was all the time I needed. Home inspections were "plain view" only. I couldn't open closets or go into drawers unless I developed reasonable suspicion that something illegal was on the premises. Reasonable suspicion, sometimes referred to in law enforcement circles as an "educated hunch," was easy enough for a PO to articulate. A long delay in opening the door during daylight hours (early mornings you got more leeway), an overly anxious or combative demeanor on the part

of the offender, weed smoke—any of these could be cited in a police
report as legal justification for a more thorough search.

Quick, courteous inspections were a small but important way of
showing offenders that I didn't want to put them in jail. I believed
America should get out of the business of punishing people because
they had a drug problem, or because they were broke, or because our
city's failing schools hadn't prepared them for college or employment.

I'd found this job during a late-night Internet dive into the topic of
mass incarceration. The third or fourth mass-incarceration article mentioned probation and parole as part of the problem and, potentially, part
of the solution. Most of the articles critical of probation and parole as
institutions argued that offenders were set up to fail. POs asked too
much of them and tried to solve every problem with jail. The answer
seemed obvious enough. If reasonable people filled PO positions, outcomes would improve.

It didn't occur to me—or, as far as I could tell, to most of the people weighing in on probation and parole matters on the Internet—that
POs used jail because jail was the only tool they had. It was all taxpayers
were willing to spend money on. It's not hard to understand why. Most
people see jail as an investment in public safety. When we think about
public safety, we don't think about the costs. As soon as incarcerated
people are released, we tend to reclassify them as receivers of social
services. Investing in them stops feeling like investing in a less violent,
less addicted America. It feels like a handout for people who probably
don't deserve it.

During my four years as a PO, I learned that "deserving" really has
nothing to do with it. Probationers and parolees who go without housing, health care, drug treatment, and reliable income reoffend at alarm-
ing rates. Offenders paired with services tailored to their needs suffer
fewer relapses and go back to jail far less often. They cost taxpayers less
money. Some become taxpayers themselves.

There are about 4.5 million people on probation and parole in
America, more than twice the jail population. For most of my time as a
PO, my caseload contained more than two hundred offenders. It would
be impossible to include all of their stories here. Reporting on only the
hardest cases would give a false impression of the pluck and resiliency

I so often observed in the probation and parole population. Ultimately I settled on seven offenders whom I considered representative of the whole, in both the challenges they faced and the way they responded to them.

Most of the events described in this book occurred between 2013 and 2015. I'm sorry to say that not much has changed since then, either nationally or in New Orleans. Our failure to provide adequate probation and parole programming remains the single greatest missed opportunity in the entire criminal justice system, and possibly the entire American safety net.

Since Hurricane Katrina, my hometown of New Orleans has become emblematic of institutional decay in America. New Orleans places in the top five cities for murder rate almost every year. Until 2018, when Oklahoma edged us out, Louisiana was the world's leading incarcerator. New Orleans continues to send more people to prison than any other city in the state. The New Orleans school system consistently ranks at or near the bottom in Louisiana, always in the running for the worst-educated state in the nation. Only Mississippi does worse.

In New Orleans the two Americas coexist side by side. Central City, the most violent neighborhood in town, with the highest density of offenders, adjoins the richest parts of the Garden District, where almost no one on probation or parole lived during my four years on the job. The oak-lined mansions of St. Charles Avenue stood a little more than ten blocks from the Landry residence.

About a third of the houses on the Landrys' block contained offenders. Many of those houses also contained guns. When, about a year later, the one in the Landry house went off, I got the call that every PO in New Orleans fears.

The homicide detective's questions started off small and clinical—questions about drug tests and patterns of life. He saved the big one for later. Was there more we could have done to intervene? And if so, why weren't we doing it?

# PART ONE

## need

# ONE

# emergency

Probation and Parole was my second attempt at public service. When I got out of college, I taught high school English. My mom and dad were the kind of teachers approached years later at restaurants and movie theaters by former students who could still remember the lesson that changed their lives. I taught for three years before I admitted I lacked my parents' aptitude for the work. The next fall I enrolled in the creative writing graduate program at LSU. I graduated three years later with a degree that did nothing to improve my job prospects and a three-hundred-page novel that not even a mother could love. Mine, the English teacher, advised me to find a day job.

I spent the next two years working in restaurants, bartending, and, most recently, selling watches at JCPenney. In the twelve-week period between my last bartending job and my first day at JCPenney, I moved in with my girlfriend, Kristin, who did a heroic job of hiding her misgivings about my prospects. JCPenney was paying me $10 an hour. I covered utilities while she paid the rent.

The probation and parole position seemed like my best chance to make myself useful before I turned thirty. Kristin agreed that unwinding mass incarceration was a worthy cause. It didn't hurt that the barriers to entry were low. A bachelor's degree and a clean record were the only requirements.

The interview was conducted at the New Orleans probation and parole headquarters, known simply as the New Orleans District. The building was long and gray in the Eastern Bloc style. Probation and Parole had the third floor. Other state agencies occupied one and two. I didn't get to see much of the office that day. I was whisked to a small brown conference room and seated at a table with duct tape over the holes in the particle board. I was told that this would take no more than an hour.

The POs who interviewed me were in their late forties, with skinny arms and big guts. They wore faded polos and cargo pants with holes in the seams. They read the interview questions from laminated legal sheets. When they got to the one about why I'd applied, I said I wanted to make the criminal justice system more just and New Orleans a safer place to live. By the next question I'd figured out that the interviewers were mainly interested in determining whether I was willing to work for thirty grand a year, and I shifted from trying to appear excited about the job to trying not to appear too excited about the salary.

The next day I worked the evening shift at JCPenney. I was hunkered down in the food court, savoring the last five minutes of my dinner break, when I got the call. The guy on the phone introduced himself as Dan. He told me he was the regional manager, which clearly translated to *boss*. "There weren't a lot of applicants," he said. "You seemed like you had the easiest job to get out of."

The Louisiana Division of Probation and Parole—"P&P," Dan called it—ran only two academies per year, three if they got really lucky with the budget. They hadn't gotten lucky with the budget in a long time. The way things had been going, the next academy could be the last one for a while. For reasons unknown, the bosses in Baton Rouge, where all the state offices were headquartered, had given the regional managers only five days to fill slots. The job was mine if I could make it on time.

Dan didn't mention the interview or my résumé, and I was left to assume that what he'd said about my selection was the whole truth. He'd gone with me because he thought my current job would be easy to quit.

He was right. I had the worst numbers in the watch department by far. My boss didn't care that I wasn't giving two weeks.

---

D uring working hours at the academy, we shot guns and memorized obscure Louisiana statutes like *Theft of an alligator.* Our instructors were senior POs taking a break from the grind. They weren't like the academy instructors in police movies. They told us that the districts were starved for manpower, and every one of us needed to pass this thing. No one had to worry about getting weeded out, especially by the firearms portion.

The instructors assured us that shootings on duty were exceptionally rare. Many of the districts had never recorded one. The New Orleans District had only one shooting in the last twenty years.

Half of us had never held a gun before the academy. We came from all over the state and would be deployed to every corner of it. I was the only cadet going to New Orleans, but I seemed to have a lot in common with my classmates. At twenty-nine I was right at the median age. We had all applied to P&P after washing out of another profession, or two or three.

By the second week we'd figured out that our stints at the academy were mostly meant to fulfill the training requirements of the state law enforcement commission. There wasn't much time for instruction on our actual jobs. Between classes we sometimes coaxed our instructors into telling us a few things. We learned that while probation and parole were functionally identical, many states allotted them to separate agencies. Louisiana kept both under the same roof, that of the Department of Corrections.

Louisiana led the US in incarceration, and the US led the world. The Department of Corrections used to take pride in this. Lately there had been some ambivalence. The racial disparities in incarceration were a problem. The state was about 30 percent black, but African Americans made up more than 60 percent of the inmate population.

Louisiana spent more than half a billion dollars annually on prisons and had the highest murder rate in the country to show for it. We'd held the title since 1989. There were people in the legislature who felt that it was time to try something else. P&P was it. We were the future. The academy director said this about ten times during her graduation speech.

"You're coming aboard at an historic moment," she told us. "Prison is the past. Community supervision is the new model for corrections in America."

I showed up early for my first day as a fully commissioned PO and walked the halls in the new boots I'd bought myself as a graduation present. The carpet at the New Orleans District was balding. The ceiling was flecked with mold. It was exactly the kind of place where I'd always imagined social justice was made.

At around nine o'clock Dan, the regional manager, took hold of me. Later in the day I would learn that the staff referred to him exclusively as Dan the Regional Manager. He was short and trim, with a big chin that bobbed as he shook hands, and a black mustache carved thin. He wore a constant, nervous smile, as if he'd gotten good news but was holding off on believing until he saw the proof.

"You can't imagine how happy people are gonna be to see you," he said.

The New Orleans District was allotted forty-five positions, but lately there had been funding for only forty. Pay was frozen, benefits were getting more expensive by the year, and caseloads were the highest they'd ever been. A fresh body showed the troops that the state hadn't forgotten about "little old P&P." It was an unconventional welcome speech, nothing like the academy director's, but I didn't have time to parse it. We'd arrived at my office. There was my name on the door. The name above mine was Charles Lewis.

He looked to be about forty but was as fit and lean as a high-school distance runner. He had a heavy beard and a hometown ball cap pulled low across his brow. I would learn later that Charles was one of only ten African American POs at the New Orleans District, but if he was put off by the news that the bosses had hired another white person, he didn't let it show.

"New guy," Dan the Regional Manager said by way of introduction, and he clapped me once on the shoulder and continued down the hall.

"Good timing," Charles said. "We're just getting started. This is Vincent."

He pointed at the person seated across the desk from him, a man about twenty or twenty-one with a Colt .45 tattooed laterally across his neck. Vincent's chair had cracks in the two rear legs and yellow foam spilling from the ripped cushion. Vincent pressed the balls of his feet to the carpet and eased the chairback into the wall. "Anyway," he told Charles, "I'm glad you locked me up. Another week at the pace I was going, and I would have been fish food."

"That's good to hear," Charles said. "You didn't seem all that glad at the time."

"At the time I was a junkie. Now I'm clean. It was destiny, you finding me when you did."

"Destiny, huh?"

It was all a lot more candid than I'd expected. Thirty seconds in, and they were already broaching the mysteries of the universe.

"They wouldn't call it the second chance club," Vincent said, lifting his hands to providence, "if they didn't expect you to fuck up."

P&P had accrued a lot of nicknames over the years. According to academy lore, this one was meant to be sarcastic, a joke at the expense of the state's longstanding austerity. Vincent sounded sincere when he invoked it. That an offender truly believed the New Orleans District was in the second-chance business reflected well on my office mate, and I was eager to gain his favor.

"Might as well get comfortable," Charles told me. "This could take a while."

He pointed me to the second desk, located barely two feet past the one he was sitting at. While I opened drawers and logged onto my state-issued laptop, Charles read Vincent the conditions of probation. Vincent said he remembered the conditions from last time, but Charles had to read them anyway, for liability reasons.

He began with the fines and fees, one of the few probation- and parole-related topics I'd been briefed on at the academy. Parolees owed the state $63 per month. Probation went for $60 per month. What the extra $3 were for, no one seemed to know or care. The state couldn't penalize probationers and parolees for refusing to pay. Fees went ignored by most POs. Charles reminded Vincent that the rules that mattered were the Big Three: Don't do drugs, don't get arrested, and keep showing up.

Parolees who violated the rules answered to the parole board, a panel of upstanding citizens appointed by the governor. Probationers in violation were subject to a hearing before the judge who sentenced them. The PO stood before the judge and reported the violations on the record. Then the judge decided whether to give the offender another shot or revoke his probation. Post-revocation, the offender was shipped "upstate" to prison. Sentence lengths depended upon the severity of the offense. Most offenders would be sentenced to serve between two and five years on a probation or parole revocation and be released after they completed 40 percent of it. A single conviction could produce multiple parole periods and multiple revocations, each a little less than half as long as its predecessor. According to Charles, the current New Orleans District record for revocations on a single conviction was seven.

"I don't think we'll ever see it broken," he told me after he finished with Vincent. "But you're welcome to try."

He was kidding, but I sensed he was also sizing me up, trying to figure out what my expectations of the job might be. I was eager to share. "I came to get people out of jail," I said, "not put them back in."

I had assumed that not everyone at Probation and Parole would feel the same. Many of my older coworkers had joined up in the mid-nineties, when draconian sentencing was at its peak. Charles didn't officially declare a side just then, but his conversation with Vincent suggested that the PO wouldn't go out of his way to put the offender in jail as long as the offender didn't go out of his way to get put there.

He didn't tell me anything more about Vincent except that he was young and dumb and had a rich uncle, a big-time drug dealer who could pay for the kind of attorney who could get you sentenced to two probations in eighteen months—that is, to two felonies with no jail time—even though the first probation nearly ended in a fatal overdose. Charles spoke of these things without affect. If anything, he seemed to find them mildly amusing. I was careful not to ask too many questions or otherwise give away so soon that I had no prior experience ministering to addicts or felons.

When it came time to share our personal histories, I tried to sound like a person who had committed his twenties to gathering valuable life experiences, and forgot that the man I was talking to spent most of his waking hours asking people about their choices. He had a big, generous laugh, with no hard edges.

"Same here," he said. "Didn't know what else to do, so I came to P&P."

If this didn't fully absolve me of my inexperience, it induced me to be a little more forthcoming about my other limitations. "White guy from the suburbs. I'm gonna have some proving to do."

African Americans made up about 60 percent of the city's overall population but nearly 80 percent of the offender population. Charles agreed that whiteness was a disadvantage for a PO in the early going, but most offenders would give me a chance to win them over. The best thing I had going for me was that I was local. I knew about the murder rate, the poverty, the rampant addiction. Out-of-towners who signed up to be POs in New Orleans rarely lasted more than a couple of months. "People come here from California," Charles said. "They think it's nothing but tits and beads."

Charles grew up in New Orleans but had lived all over the South. He'd been on the job fourteen years. If he wouldn't commit to loving it, he was past the point of imagining he could do anything else. He mentioned feeling optimistic about the new political momentum to get away from using jail to fix every problem, but he was withholding judgment on just how different this new era was really going to be.

One thing that had not changed since Charles came aboard was the department's attitude toward new PO development. What I'd received at the academy was all the formal training I was going to get. Everything else I would learn by tagging along with other POs. Dan the Regional Manager would tell me to seek out as many of them as would have me, but the bulk of this tutelage usually fell to the rookie's office mate.

The New Orleans District was a maze that day, the corridors narrow and dimly lit. Every office had the same brown door splintered at the corners and around the knob, and in the middle the same black name tags with white block lettering. Charles and I took three turns before we found the lobby. There was a receptionist behind a glass wall—"Not bulletproof," Charles said—and eight rows of plastic folding chairs. About two-thirds of them were occupied. A couple of offenders sat cross-legged on the floor. One guy pressed his forehead to the lobby's lone window and watched a green streetcar rattle by.

The office was located on a good block in the Central Business District, walking distance to the Superdome and the French Quarter.

A less ratty building would have been prohibitively expensive, but our landlord was apparently content to lease to the state at half the market rate provided we didn't hassle him about the leaks and the mold.

A metal detector separated the lobby from the processing room where offenders had their fingerprints taken during their first trip to the office. There was an old ink-and-paper rig in the corner for POs to turn to when the digital scanner crapped out. Charles had a couple of veteran offenders waiting in the lobby. He called his second new guy of the day first so that I could watch him operate the fingerprint machine and get another look at the intake procedures.

He shook the offender's hand as he stepped through the metal detector and told him they would save the getting-to-know-you stuff for the office. The offender said he was good with that, and Charles took him by the wrist and rolled his fingers one at a time across the glass panels of the fingerprint machine. It looked like a Xerox, squat and sharp-cornered, and smelled of the antiseptic wipes applied to its surface after each session. It gave a little beep when you submitted a good print and a little hiss when you gave it something it couldn't read. Charles got only one hiss and looked pleased with himself for it.

The offender appeared to be no more than half-awake. He was about forty-five, in tan work boots and a gray T-shirt with holes in the pocket. He followed us down the corridor to our office and sat in the chair across the desk from Charles, which Charles referred to as "the offender chair." It was the offender's first time on probation. Charles read the conditions slowly, emphasizing the Big Three and going into detail about the nature of the questions he was asking about the offender's work history, his living situation, his history of drug abuse, and his mental health. He spun his laptop around so the offender could see the rows of multiple-choice questions included in the intake questionnaire. "They call this a risk/need assessment," Charles said. "The idea is that if we know what your needs are, we can decrease your risk of getting in trouble."

He gave me a quick glance to let me know that this was for my benefit, too. I nodded along eagerly. The risk/need assessment seemed to be built on the vision of criminal justice that had drawn me to this job in the first place: The best way to discourage most antisocial behavior—most risk—was to provide for the needy.

The offender said his needs had been few until recently. He'd worked construction, blown out his back, gotten a prescription for Oxycontin, and woken up sixty days later a junkie. Charles told me that "Oxy offenders," as they were known at the New Orleans District, were a relatively new breed. Whereas most offenders used drugs to escape lives of poverty or depression, Oxy offenders used drugs so that they could keep their lives as they were. They weren't looking for a high. They were looking to get their pain under control so that they could go back to work.

When the pills ran out, the Oxy offender started buying heroin. He had his withdrawal period in jail and vowed to self, family, and God that he wasn't going through that hell again. Orleans Parish Prison, known as OPP, had an inmate death rate four times the national average. The federal government had come in and instituted a consent decree, but progress so far had been slow. You didn't have to work in the criminal justice system to know this. It was all over the news.

The offender vented a little more about his four days as an OPP inmate, but in the end he doubled back to his original position that he didn't need anything from his PO except to be left alone. He'd gotten his job back, his job provided health insurance, and his health insurance provider covered addiction counseling. He hadn't used heroin in eight weeks.

A paycheck combined with health insurance to provide counseling and, if necessary, anti-withdrawal medications like Suboxone and methadone were the most effective cures for addiction currently known. By probation and parole standards, the employed Oxy offender's needs were few, and the risk assessment gave him its lowest possible rating. According to the assessment, Charles didn't need to see the Oxy offender again for six months. Charles gave the offender a business card and sent him on his way.

We ate a quick lunch in the break room in the rear of the New Orleans District. There were a few folding tables, a rusty refrigerator, and a white Mr. Coffee labeled BROKE. Charles introduced me to everyone who came in. The office looked to be about 75 percent white and 60 percent male. I put the median age right at forty. As Dan the Regional Manager predicted, all my coworkers agreed that a new guy was good news for the office. Everyone invited me to tag along anytime I wanted, and my overall impression was of a group of people who enjoyed their work and believed it was worth doing.

By the time our lunch hour was over, Charles had six people waiting in the lobby. The first five had all been on probation or parole for at least a year. They sat in the offender chair and told their PO very different stories than the Oxy offender's. As Charles had predicted, the prevailing theme was need. None of the five offenders had a job. Four were in custody battles with former wives and girlfriends. Three were recovering from recent relapses. Two were literally homeless, another two functionally so. Only one of the five, crashing with his grandmother, had what could be described as a stable living situation.

Charles didn't take notes. He opened his laptop only to document changes in home address or telephone number. He proposed adjustments rather than solutions. He talked to the addicts about their triggers—the toxic ex, the shit-stirring aunt or uncle—and told them that in many cases the answer was just to walk away. He had a degree in social work but assured me that the best listeners got that way by repetition rather than training. I could be one, too, if I put in the time.

The therapeutic value of simply being heard is well-documented, and anyone who passed by our office could plainly see that offenders left with cooler heads and clearer eyes than they came in with. The service my office mate provided here was invaluable. It was also insufficient. These people needed more than a sounding board, but Charles hadn't offered any substantive assistance, no housing or health care or employment, nor had he suggested places in town where offenders might go looking for it.

The sixth offender of the afternoon was an old woman in blue pajamas and glasses held together with masking tape. She muttered to herself all the way from the lobby to the offender chair. I took her for senile.

Charles drew a different conclusion. "How long since you smoked crack?"

"This morning," the old woman said.

Charles nodded slowly. "I'll try Odyssey House. But if there's no beds, I have to take you in. Can't let you leave like this."

"I know."

Odyssey House, Charles would inform me later, was the only free detox clinic in the city. There were usually only a handful of beds available at a time. Getting an offender in on short notice, the only kind of notice I supposed addicts ever gave, was at best a one-chance-in-twenty-five proposition. The screener who answered the phones told Charles her next available opening was on Friday.

"Friday's too late," Charles told the old woman. "We both know that."

He pointed at the wall behind the offender chair. The old woman got up and turned around. Charles pulled his handcuffs from his belt and snapped them around the old woman's wrists.

"I know it sucks to detox in jail," he said. "But if I don't take you, and you go out and OD, that's on me. I think you knew that when you came in here. You weren't due for a visit this month."

"I know," the old woman said again.

I'd heard heroin and crack withdrawals compared to the worst flu of your life. Charles told me later that nobody at the New Orleans District had figured out how to tell the difference between a person who needed medical assistance to get through withdrawal symptoms and a person who could quit on his own. Most addicts would need clinical detox at some point. Most wouldn't want to admit it. I guessed the old woman's decision to come to the office that day put her somewhere in the middle. We walked her slowly down the back corridor and out onto the roof, where a row of Crown Vics were kept for jail transport purposes. We loaded the old woman into the back seat.

You could make the trip from the New Orleans District to the jail in seven minutes if you got lucky with the lights. The gray towers of OPP looked down on one of the busiest stretches of I-10. We parked behind the jail and walked the old woman up the exterior stairs. Charles pressed the get-in button and said who we were and what we were doing there. There was only one thing we could be doing, but Charles said you had to say it or they wouldn't let you in.

The buzzer went off. Charles shouldered the door open, and I gave the old woman's elbow a gentle tug. It was early May and sweltering, but the sky was bright and blue. The old woman had a last look up at it and stepped across the threshold.

The intake area wasn't much bigger than a walk-in closet. The deputy at the counter wrote down the old woman's name and date of birth and rang for a second deputy—"Female!"—and a nurse. It smelled like shit—literally. A grated wall separated the intake area from the much larger room where arrestees waited to be brought into the bowels of the jail. There were TVs and rows of chairs. Some of the men in the chairs slept against the shoulders of other men. Some laughed and talked trash. Far off in the corner, someone shrieked. A deputy told him he had better quiet down, or else. Another deputy asked who the shitter was, and what he'd had for lunch, and why.

The nurse and the female deputy entered the intake area through a grated door. The deputy told the offender to grab some wall. She ran the backs of her hands along the offender's arms and legs and waist and crotch. She told the offender to kick off her shoes. They were slippers, really, brown with shredded lace trim. The deputy looked inside them, slapped them against the floor, and handed them back. The nurse strapped the blood pressure band to the old woman's arm, filled it with air, and took the reading. She asked whether the old woman had taken any drugs.

"Crack," the old woman said.

"How much?"

"Couple of hits."

"When?"

"Couple of hours."

The nurse looked in the old woman's eyes and felt along her wrist and dragged a sigh from the old woman to Charles and back again. "We'll take her."

Air could be heard pushing through unseen vents, but the interior of OPP felt no cooler than the pavement we'd walked to get here.

"You'll be out in a week," Charles said.

The old woman nodded but kept her eyes on the ground. The deputy gave Charles his handcuffs back and told us to have a good day.

Charles pressed the get-out button. The door buzzed again. Charles pushed it open. We went down the stairs and got back in the Crown Vic.

He turned on the AC but didn't take the shifter out of park. "That was an emergency," he said. "Nothing else we could do."

I believed him. By sheer luck I'd landed an office mate I trusted implicitly.

"It doesn't get easier," he said. "Sometimes the job's talking and listening, trying to make people feel like they've got somebody in their corner. But sometimes it's this."

I couldn't figure out how to explain what I was thinking. That I mustn't have really thought things through? That I'd known the jail would be part of the equation, but I'd hoped to get through my first day without having to take the ride?

"I guess," I said, "I thought there would be more of an in-between."

"You're feeling how you're supposed to be feeling right now. The POs who walk out of that place like it's nothing—those are the ones I worry about. We'll pick her up in a few days, get her into sober living. This is a temporary stop."

That was the end of the pep talk. He turned on the radio and drove me back to the New Orleans District parking lot, where a Crown Vic of my own was waiting to be driven home for the first time. It was twelve years old and had more than 150,000 miles on the odometer. It had probably made the drive to OPP hundreds of times, and it was safe to assume that most of those trips were taken for lack of a more sensible alternative.

Nothing I'd learned about my office mate that day gave me any reason to believe he or any other of my new coworkers had made their peace with OPP lightly. They seemed, quite in contrast to my expectations, like reasonable people. If the heart of the problem at P&P was POs who were bigoted, incompetent, or just plain lazy, then an infusion of better people—people like me—stood to transform the system overnight. If the POs already on the job were people like Charles—that is to say, people as good as or possibly better than me—then the answer was a lot less clear.

I wasn't the only PO who wanted to provide offenders with social services. I wasn't the only PO who wanted to keep offenders out of jail. Most of the rest of the staff of the New Orleans District had felt what I was feeling after their first day, and they'd stayed in the job anyway. Tomorrow I would try to figure out why.

# TWO

# a max case

I spent the rest of that first week shadowing Charles. The following Monday, as promised, we picked up the old woman from jail and drove her to a sober-living facility called Grace House. We were allowed only as far as the front door. The facility was housed in a gorgeous old home uptown with a big porch and a wrought-iron fence. The caseworker to whom we handed off the old woman appeared excited to see her.

On our way over, the old woman told us that the medical care at the jail, or at least the detox services, were every bit as lousy as she remembered—"Consent decree mustn't have gotten around to that part yet"—but she did feel better now. "You saved my life," she told Charles.

"*You* saved it," he said. "You made the choice to come in. You knew what was gonna happen. You look ten years younger, by the way."

I would have said fifteen. The woman I'd met a week earlier lurched around like a crone and spoke in whispers. Today she was bright-eyed and confident. She told us she'd been a schoolteacher before she found crack in the early nineties.

After we dropped her off, Charles told me that Grace House would keep her at the facility for about a month before transferring her to a larger and more dilapidated building across town. She could stay there a few more months, provided she pitched in with housekeeping and cooking and the like. If, a few months after that, she hadn't gotten a job or disability benefits, she would have to move on. There were only so many sober-living facilities and so much space in each. The people in greatest need of help—the people fresh off a detox—got priority.

We didn't make any arrests that week or the week after. Our office visits remained mostly listening sessions. As I watched Charles work, I picked up on a few of his little tricks: the quiet sighs when an offender was feeling a little too sorry for himself, the firm corrections when an offender took more than his share of the blame for his current situation. Mostly, Charles communicated with nods and facial expressions. He'd trained his chin to transmit sympathy at one angle and exasperation at another. He could stop a conversation cold with a flick of his right eyebrow.

When Charles entered an offender's home, he never gave the impression he was conducting a shakedown. He framed his inspections as social calls. He knew the names of aunts and grandmothers and nieces and nephews. He noticed when a troublesome member of the household moved out or came back in. He remembered birthdays, pets, favorite television shows.

If very few offenders were delighted to see a PO at the door, no one treated us as anything worse than a nuisance. In the poorest and most distressed homes Charles brought me to, where the power had been turned off and the temperature was well over 100, he pretended not to notice. He flipped on the flashlight he kept in his pocket and passed through the rooms in the usual fashion, making casual conversation and moving rapidly enough to give the impression that he wasn't looking for anything in particular.

It was another trick. He noticed everything. Every time we left a house, he pointed out all the little details I'd missed: an offender more receptive to his grandmother's advice than his father's, and whose girlfriend was his primary substance abuse trigger, and who put a stick of gum in his mouth every time he told a lie.

We spent most of our time in Central City, Hollygrove, and Gert Town, neighborhoods I knew only from news coverage of murder scenes. Statistically speaking, they were dangerous places, but I never felt that I was in any danger when I passed through them. The gun at my hip had nothing to do with it. I felt safe because the people whose houses I entered were used to us. They lived in neighborhoods where police encounters were extremely common, if not always pleasant.

Like the jail, the city police department was operating under a federal consent decree. Although more than half of NOPD officers were African American, many black New Orleanians viewed the consent decree as the federal government's official declaration that the police department was not to be trusted. P&P was an entirely separate outfit, our black polo shirts impossible to mistake for the blue NOPD button-down, and people in New Orleans's poor neighborhoods knew the difference. They knew that POs wore guns and bulletproof vests but also spent two days per week at the office serving as counselors, and they knew that counseling often took the form of teaching offenders how to stay on the right side of law enforcement—that is, how to avoid police encounters entirely.

Charles had figured out how to play the dual role to his advantage. When we walked in on offenders smoking marijuana, Charles reminded them that weed was still illegal and that smoking it in a car was a good way to get pulled over for Driving While Black. Smoking it on a street corner all but assured you would get patted down by every passing squad car. "I want them to think I'm enough a part of the system that I know all the tricks," Charles explained to me, "but I can bend the rules when it suits me."

The ideal PO could help offenders navigate the system and avoid getting locked up over petty nonsense. At the same time, Charles reminded offenders that while half of his obligation was to them, the other half was to the general public. If he believed an offender was putting another person at risk, Charles had the authority to step in.

In the lunchroom at the New Orleans District, POs talked a lot about discretion. There was some friendly disagreement about where exactly the lines ought to be drawn. There were rules everyone agreed we couldn't bend, violations we couldn't look away from: firearms, acts of violence committed in our presence, large quantities of drugs. Misdemeanor offenses like weed possession we were free to ignore.

Headquarters emails, of which we seemed to get about three per hour, encouraged us to use our discretion to make the point that P&P

was about transforming a punishment-based system into a rehabilitation-based one. In practical terms, this often meant letting things go that would have been seen as serious violations a decade ago. As late as 2010, POs were still instructed to bring offenders to jail if weed was discovered during a home inspection. Less than five years later, POs who locked people up for marijuana were almost certain to get overruled by the parole board and reprimanded by Dan the Regional Manager for wasting valuable jail space on a minor infraction.

I was halfway through my third week on the job when I used my handcuffs for the first time. In the academy we'd learned that every successful cuffing turns on the moment when metal touches flesh, known as "first contact." Pre–first contact, the arrestee has been told where to stand and where to place his hands. If he hasn't been told he's going to jail, he's probably figured it out. But incarceration and freedom are abstractions, subject to interpretation, negotiation. First contact is physical, steel on skin.

A weak grip on the part of the officer or an imprecise application that misses the "cuffing notch" between palm heel and wrist lets the arrestee know that the officer can be gotten over on. In video after video, we saw half-assed handcuffers get the shit kicked out of them. We saw a few lose their lives. At the academy, we practiced handcuffing until our wrists bled.

When the time came to do it for real, I focused all my attention on first contact, on preventing the offender from running or fighting and thereby making his situation that much worse. This offender, an old man whose PO had deemed him an overdose risk, didn't flinch. Neither did I. The academy had made a once-complex process completely automatic.

I didn't disagree with the other PO's assessment that the offender was probably going to keep using heroin until we intervened. I felt, as I had when I watched Charles arrest the old woman, that even if jail wasn't the long-term answer to the addiction problem in America, it was the only tool I had to save the particular life for which I was responsible that afternoon. I felt I was using my authority wisely, but the physical act of taking away another person's liberty was just as unnerving as the academy instructors had warned me it would be.

The PO who'd put me up to the arrest reminded me after the fact that jail runs were last resorts—"emergencies," to use Charles's term—and while I shouldn't expect them to get any less unpleasant as I grew into the job, I could train myself to remember that we spent the vast majority of our time trying to find some other tool, any other tool, to keep our people out of trouble.

By my third Friday on the job, I believed that P&P really was, as the academy director had promised, trying to form a safer, saner justice system. I believed I'd underestimated the value of office visits that first day and overestimated the horrors of the jail, or at least the frequency with which I was likely to subject offenders to them. I was glad I'd decided to stick around.

Kristin, my girlfriend, took me out to dinner to celebrate the end of my first three weeks at P&P and my thirtieth birthday, which had fallen a few days before. Kristin is one of the rare truly green-eyed people. The eyes were all I saw the first year I knew her, but there was also that beautiful skin, as fair as a river birch, and a lone freckle on her upper lip that made her smile a playful thing even when she ran some heat through it.

She'd had plenty of options but, for reasons that remain unclear, had chosen to see me through the worst year of my professional life. My bartending career had ended abruptly after I threatened to throw a drunken customer in the lake. I'd been out of work for nearly three months before I got the job behind the watch counter at JCPenney. Kristin knew I was eager to believe I'd found my place at last, and she listened patiently as I rattled off all the things I was excited about: the chance to help people who really needed it, and an office mate who seemed willing and able to show me how. We were eating dessert before I got around to admitting that my initial reservations were still with me. "Resource-wise," I said, "there's the jail and the office and not much else."

Kristin was a lawyer by profession, and I could always count on her for unsentimental analysis. "You kind of knew that, though, right? I mean, you applied there because you knew it was fucked-up." She wore her red hair long and pushed it behind her ears when she was transitioning to a word of caution. "I know you're tired of starting over.

But this doesn't have to be it. If it's a bad fit, you can try something else. I'll float you."

I knew she meant it, and I could feel myself flushing as I assured her that her days of sponsoring me were over. Charles had warned me about the dangers of spending too much weekend time talking—or, after really bad weeks, venting—to your partner about the job. The best way to be fresh for offenders on Monday was to forget all about them on Friday night.

After dinner we met friends for drinks for my birthday. Most of our friends were people I'd known since first grade. We'd all gone to Catholic school together. In New Orleans, the decision to send your kids to Catholic school often had nothing to do with religious affiliation. The Catholic schools were priced for the middle class but often outperformed the five-figures-per-year private schools that served the city's ultrarich. The Jesuit priests who ran my high school understood that the best way for middle-class kids to afford college was to get a good score on the SAT. Our junior year was nothing but standardized-test prep. A fifth of my graduating class were National Merit Scholars.

If you could afford Catholic school in New Orleans, you could afford to give your child the greatest privilege there is: the chance to choose his own path. I was the only one of my circle who'd chosen poorly. At thirty I was surrounded by doctors, lawyers, accountants, and computer scientists, and through various channels since I'd shipped off to the police academy, they'd all expressed their concerns that I'd taken a job that should have gone to someone who had trained as a counselor or who had grown up in the inner city and could speak with authority to the challenges people faced there.

The only defense I could think of was to lean in. "Of course they shouldn't have hired me," I said. "But nobody good wanted the job."

The joke got a laugh, and it changed the subject, but later that night, alone with the prospect of a new decade, the first one in which it was no longer acceptable to be anything but a functioning, contributing adult, I didn't see the humor, and I struggled to take Charles's advice about keeping my apprehensions from Kristin. I wanted to tell her that I had no way of knowing whether I would be of any assistance to any of my offenders, and I was terrified that if I flamed out again, there would be real consequences. A year ago I was working for tips. Now I had human lives in my hands.

The fact that I was hired for this job was more than a punch line. It was a microcosm of the very problem I hoped to helped solve. Nobody who mattered gave a shit about probation and parole.

I got through Saturday and Sunday without bringing any of this up with Kristin. I showed up early on Monday, but the clerical staff had beaten me by at least an hour. My caseload, in the form of 220 brown manila folders, was stacked eye-high on my desk and chair and the narrow pathway to the file cabinet. Probationers got a blue label, parolees yellow. The ratio looked to be about two-to-one—standard for the New Orleans District, according to Charles, who'd looked on with amusement from his desk as the case files were wheeled in ten at a time.

"I guess I should read them?" I asked.

He grabbed one of the larger volumes and paged through. "This one would take you about four hours. And he's just a three-timer. You've got six-timers, seven-timers in here. The sooner they go in the file cabinet, the sooner you get your desk back."

Some of the folders were graying with mildew. Some bore the old-school aroma of ditto paper. I examined a brittle police report that included such racial demographics as "NEGRO" and "ORIENTAL." The file cabinet was seven feet tall and broad as an NFL lineman. The last ten files wouldn't fit. I stacked them under my desk, where I was sure to knock them over often enough to keep me from forgetting they were there.

An email informed me that I now had an account of my own in our case management system. I double-clicked on my name, and there they were, my 220 souls, ranked by their scores on the risk/need assessment. We were told that best practices recommended about fifty cases per PO, but caseloads varied widely by jurisdiction, and most studies of PO burnout appeared to be reluctant to name an ideal offender-PO ratio. For our purposes, it was enough to know that 220 was a ludicrous number. Charles admitted that there were guys on his caseload whom he couldn't pick out of a lineup.

Forty-five of my 220 were in warrant status, meaning they'd abandoned their known addresses and stopped showing up at the office. You weren't supposed to get a warrant for an offender until you'd exhausted opportunities to track him down. Most warrant cases had probably skipped town. If they got arrested in another state, Louisiana rarely paid to extradite them back. As long as they weren't causing trouble on home turf, the Department of Corrections was happy to be rid of them.

Another twenty offenders were in administrative status. These were people whose probation or parole had been declared inactive—"in other words, turned off," Charles explained—usually because the offenders came down with a terminal illness or were grievously wounded in a knife- or gunfight, and the judge or parole board had deemed further supervision a waste of time and resources. Like the warrants, these files would stay in my cabinet until their terms expired. On the date of expiration I would attach a closure notice to the front of the file and return it to the clerical room, and Dan the Regional Manager would assign me the next new case that walked through the door.

The other cases—the active ones—fell into one of three categories: maximum risk, medium risk, and minimum risk. The minimum risk cases, of which I had eighty-one, needed to be seen only twice a year. Medium-risk cases got four visits per year. Only maximum-risk cases had to be contacted every month.

A fifteen-question multiple-choice test designed for POs with caseloads well above the national average, the assessment tool had done a far better job of predicting risk than anyone had expected when the state rolled it out a couple of years before. No one fully understood the tool's math, but its logic was simple. The neediest people were at the highest risk of getting back in trouble. We should spend most of our time on them.

My caseload was mostly inherited from the PO I'd replaced. He'd left for a better-paying job in the private sector. This had come as quite a shock to my colleagues, all of whom had held my predecessor in extremely low regard. Charles suspected that even my maximum-risk cases had probably gone unseen for several months. He suggested we spend the next couple of field days trying to get an accurate head count of who was still around and print warrants for the rest.

---

W e began the first field day of the week in the Lower Ninth Ward, the impoverished downriver neighborhood leveled by Hurricane Katrina in 2005. Nearly a decade later, many homes remained abandoned. Lawns had returned almost completely to seed. Vacant lots were jungles of cattails and briars. Kendrick, the first offender on our list, lived in the nicest house on the block, a white two-story with green shutters yet to see a hurricane season.

"Somebody bought it cheap, fixed it up," Charles said. "Guarantee the tenant's Section 8."

The federal government's largest rental-assistance program, Section 8 was designed to allow poor people to get housing in neighborhoods where poverty wasn't as concentrated as it was in housing projects. The Lower Ninth Ward probably wasn't what the architects of Section 8 had in mind. People who fixed up and leased properties there and in other poor neighborhoods could recoup their investment in five years. Properties bought for low five figures could easily bring in $900 per month in rent.

Probationers and parolees couldn't collect Section 8, but then again, neither could most poor people. In New Orleans, 17,800 families received Section 8 vouchers. As long as they didn't report earnings of more than 80 percent of the median household income in New Orleans—about $48,000 for a family of four—they could collect Section 8 forever. Only about 1,000 families left the Section 8 program annually, meaning only 1,000 wait-listed families got on. The overwhelming majority of poor people in New Orleans never got off the waiting list.

The lessee at Kendrick's house was a middle-aged woman named Tina. The young men who lived with her referred to the house as Tina's Place. Tina opened the door for us that morning and confirmed that Kendrick was on the premises. "Let's get one thing straight before you come in," she said. "He's crashing. Not staying."

Veteran Section 8 recipients knew that housing a probationer or parolee could cost them their voucher, at least in theory. Charles had never heard of anyone's losing a voucher for this reason, but he couldn't fault Tina for being cautious. She was small and gaunt, with pockmarked cheeks and bloodshot eyes. The marijuana smell from inside the house was so strong the Charles let out a yip when he caught his first whiff of it. Tina promptly told us she had errands to run, and she scampered down the street, leaving the front door wide-open. I followed Charles in.

Weed smoke hung as thick as swamp fog about the living room. Six men slept on sleeping bags on the floor. The guy on the couch was the only one who woke up when we walked in. I recognized him immediately as Kendrick, the offender from the mug shot in my case file. His teeth and hair were as gray as oyster shells. The circles beneath his eyes looked like they'd been drawn on with a charcoal pencil. He was supposed to be thirty-four but he looked fifty.

"Yo!" he shouted. "Parole people are here."

The guys on the floor bolted up. The open doorway provided the only light in the room. The windows had been blacked out with cardboard and masking tape.

"Clear the fuck out," Kendrick said.

Mumbling as they went, the other men dragged their sleeping bags with them down the dark central hallway and out of sight. Charles found a light switch beside the door and flipped it.

Kendrick yawned and reached for the big white T-shirt balled up between two couch cushions and pulled it over his head. He grabbed a pair of jeans off the floor and stepped into them.

"Must be time for a new PO," he said.

"This guy," Charles said, and gave me a whack on the back.

I stuck out my hand and introduced myself. Kendrick had a much better grip than I'd expected, given his physique. He was about five foot eight but couldn't have weighed more than 120 pounds.

"These young bucks are always smoking in here," he said. "I don't fuck around with that shit. I can piss if you want."

I saw my first chance to show I wasn't that kind of PO. "I'll take your word for it."

Kendrick tipped an imaginary cap in my direction. "Y'all want the tour?"

He walked us back to the kitchen, the only room on the ground floor with any daylight in it. The rear window was open, and the six guys we'd woken up were smoking cigarettes and opening the day's first beers. Kendrick was the oldest person at Tina's Place by a decade at least. Most of the other guys looked no older than eighteen. Kendrick rattled off their names, and they waved to us without interest. As we turned to make our way back to the front of the house, one of them muttered "Faggots," and everybody laughed.

In the thirty-odd houses I'd entered with Charles, we'd never been subject to epithets, at least not to our faces. Before I could look to him to see whether we should address the remark, Kendrick shoved the guy who said it into the counter. The guy lost his grip of his beer but managed to catch it before it hit the ground. When he looked up again, Kendrick was standing over him with his fist cocked.

"No need for that," Charles said. "We're done here."

The guys in the far corners of the kitchen snickered as we went. The guy who'd make the remark didn't. He'd looked genuinely shaken when Kendrick stood over him, and he looked shaken even as Kendrick walked away.

Kendrick followed us out of Tina's Place and pulled the door shut behind him. Charles gave me a nod that said that this was *the field*, this was the kind of stuff that happened. Now was as good a time as any to practice dealing with it. "Don't worry about that," I told Kendrick, and decided that surviving my first on-the-job insult entitled me to tell my first on-the-job lie. "We've heard worse."

"That wasn't for y'all," Kendrick said. "That was for that dumb fucking kid in there. That mouth is gonna get him in trouble. Better he gets his ass kicked by me than his head shot off by some dude on the street."

"You the boss around here?" Charles said.

Kendrick laughed. "You're talking about Tina."

"What's she charging you?"

"Half my food stamps. Guys that get a check throw in another fifty."

Kendrick estimated that Tina, whose Section 8 voucher paid two-thirds of the rent, was receiving more than $1,500 in food stamps in return for opening her doors. Kendrick believed Tina spent about a third of the food stamps on food and sold the rest for fifty cents on the dollar to poor families in the neighborhood. For a personal investment of about $300 per month, Tina got back about $500 in food and another $500 in cash.

Because people on probation and parole couldn't collect housing assistance of any sort, people like Tina provided a valuable service, especially for young offenders who were still keeping late hours and not looking to answer to a landlord at any price. The "check" Kendrick had referred to was a monthly payment of $674 in Supplemental Security Income, or SSI. Funded by the US Treasury, SSI was established in the early seventies to cover basic living expenses for people too disabled to work. Blind people got it. So did people with acute bipolar disorder.

"I got a check when I was a kid," Kendrick told us. "But they cut it off."

"What for?" Charles said.

Kendrick shrugged. "They sent a letter. I don't read. Eighth grade's as far as I got."

I'd learned from Charles that remarks like this one were known in the P&P universe as "gates." *Ask the right follow-up question,* he told me, *and a person down on his luck will tell you his whole life story.*

I kept it simple and asked Kendrick where he went to school. Kendrick lit a cigarette and told me that the trouble started long before that. His mom got in on the early days of the crack epidemic. People who remembered her before she was an addict said that the drug rewired her from the ground up. She kept up the habit throughout Kendrick's gestation, and teachers as far back as kindergarten noticed developmental issues.

Conduct was the bigger problem. He was in first grade when he learned that if you hit a guy hard enough, he thought better of making another crack about how you were always behind in class or how your mom was always passing out in the lawn. Kendrick could keep the kids at school from talking about his mother, but he couldn't shut her boyfriends up. They were addicts like her, and a couple of them were small-time dealers. He heard them call her every kind of bitch, and he saw them beat her with belts and frying pans and bare fists and wander out to the street and sleep it off in an alley somewhere and come back the next day and do it all over again. Kendrick got to where he recognized the warning signs and knew to slip out the door before the first blood was drawn.

He was supposed to feel bad for his mother. He knew it, even as a small child, but sometimes after he fled when she got a beating, he wished he hadn't. He wished he'd stayed and "watched the show." Once in a while he even imagined he was the one wielding the belt, or he imagined that the boyfriends were punishing his mother on his behalf. He was far too young to understand addiction. To him, his mother was faced each day with a choice—to be a parent or to get high—and the days when she tried to be tender to him or any of his three siblings felt all the crueler when she relapsed. Over time, Kendrick came to hate his mother's attempts at parenting more than he hated the days when she didn't seem to know he was there.

Like everyone he grew up with, he knew that this was no kind of life. He wanted better, but he didn't know how to get it. "Out the hood" stories were fairy tales. He never met an adult who got a real middle-class job and a good, clean home to raise his children in. All the money in the Lower Ninth Ward was in the drug trade. Kendrick never saw anybody get anywhere doing anything else.

By middle school he was friendly with the teenagers who worked as runners for the drug dealers who supplied his mother with crack and his next-door neighbor with heroin. When his third or fourth big brawl of the year got him expelled from eighth grade, his mother didn't reenroll him in the fall. She "let the streets have me," Kendrick said.

It seemed like his first time smoking crack should have been some kind of mindfuck. He should have had a degree of self-awareness about going from trying to break the cycle to accepting that he was going to be a part of it, but, in Kendrick's telling, addiction never started out like that. You tried getting high because you were curious, or you were hungry, or because some girl told you she was a better lay when she was a little messed-up. You planned on being the exception to the rule. You believed that the very firsthand experiences that should have scared you off the stuff would make you more resistant to its disagreeable side effects. You figured people who had seen what crack could do would be better equipped than anybody to quit while they were ahead.

As far as Kendrick knew, his father had been more of a dealer than a user. The relationship between Kendrick's parents was over by the time he was born. Kendrick was ten when his father was shot dead in a turf war. Kendrick didn't know him well enough to miss him, but he set off on the same career path, or at least he tried. He had no mind for numbers and was never going to hack it as a "corner boy," whose job was taking customers' money and making sure the payments were counted correctly at the end of the day.

He had a short run as a muscle guy. He had a talent for violence but didn't look the part. The smart dealers didn't really want bloodshed. They just wanted the threat of it. A 120-pounder had to be seen in action to be believed. By his mid-twenties Kendrick had given up the drug thing and become a professional thief. He stole small, mostly household goods he could gather into trash bags in a thirty-second run through a home. In time he learned that the best money was in shoplifting diapers and laundry detergent from a gas station or Dollar General and selling them for thirty cents on the dollar on the street. The gas stations were tricky because the clerks sometimes waved their guns at you as you ran away. The Dollar Generals didn't put up a fight. They seemed to have written shoplifting losses into the corporate strategy. On the rare occasions when you got caught, if you had no more than a hundred bucks' worth of goods on you, the worst you were looking at from the police was two nights in jail and a misdemeanor fine.

Kendrick had never paid a fine. He'd never paid a parking ticket. The deterrents the criminal justice system set up for minor offenses served their purpose only for "civilians": people worried about their credit or about making rent. Kendrick didn't have bills and he didn't have income. He lived off his $150 in monthly food stamps, which became $75 after he gave Tina her share. Everyone at Tina's Place except Kendrick worked part-time for neighborhood drug dealers, and a portion of that revenue went to weed and groceries for the group. I assumed Kendrick wouldn't have told me about his housemates' activities if he thought I would feel duty bound to report them to the police. He seemed to think I was there for him and him alone, and he wanted me to know the whole story, which for the moment included the men he was living with.

Kendrick and his mother still saw each other from time to time. They weren't friendly, but after all these years Kendrick knew he had nothing to gain by getting into a confrontation with her. He understood addiction now. Understanding wasn't the same as forgiving, but the old rage about his childhood had faded. Kendrick had been on and off crack for twenty years. His longest period of sobriety—the one he was in the middle of now—had lasted four months.

His mother still lived in the Lower Ninth Ward, just a few blocks from Tina's Place. She still smoked crack sometimes but was more of a drunk these days. Kendrick had one son, about seven years old now. He hadn't seen him or heard from his mother in five years. They were supposed to be in Texas. Kendrick had never been out for a visit. He had never left New Orleans.

He told Charles and me all of this over the course of three cigarettes. He was lighting his fourth when his young housemates emerged, wincing in the sunlight, and lit cigarettes of their own and opened fresh beers and joked around with Kendrick as if the thing in the kitchen hadn't happened. If they noticed that Charles and I were still on hand, they didn't let our presence interfere with the conversation.

They wanted to know whether Kendrick had seen a certain drug dealer's new car and his new girlfriend, and it occurred to me for the first time that most of these men were the same age I was when I shipped off on my full ride to the University of Florida, and they wanted exactly what I wanted at that age: to get drunk, to get laid, to get nice things and show them off. At eighteen, the path to all my dreams had run through my school. Getting good grades on tests and papers were my only responsibilities. I didn't have to worry about where I would sleep or what I would eat. I didn't have to choose between hiding from violence and addiction or giving in to them. I didn't have to be tough or resilient. I grew up ten miles from Kendrick, but in our two lives you had the broad strokes of modern American life. While middle-class kids were training to be better off than their parents, poor kids were training to survive.

I remembered before we took our leave to remind Kendrick to come to the office next month for a drug test. I gave him a business card with my phone number and told him to let me know if he had any changes to report. When we were back inside the Crown Vic, Charles laughed and said, "Well, there's a max case for you."

I waited until we'd made the first turn to admit what I was thinking. "What the hell am I supposed to do with him?"

"He's probably never gonna be able to hold down a real job. GED's out: he's not a reader, we know that. Your goal now is straight disaster prevention. He told you he can be violent. Safe to assume getting high increases the risk. You'll want to be on the lookout for that."

I had just heard the answer to my initial question about my co-workers. This was why they stayed in the job. To prevent disasters. If they couldn't address need, they could get to know it so well that they could track peaks and troughs. They could predict risk.

The next day I called the Social Security office to see about getting Kendrick reevaluated for SSI benefits. The woman on the phone asked me what kind of disability Kendrick was claiming.

"I think he's just slow," I said. "Learning disabled, maybe."

"And who are you to him?"

"Parole officer."

"Did you talk to his doctor?"

"There isn't any doctor."

"He needs to see a doctor. You get a diagnosis first, then we can start the paperwork."

"I'm saying he's not someone I can send to a doctor."

"Which is why you want him on SSI. I get it. But like I said, you've got the order wrong. Doctor first. Then fill out the paperwork. Then we'll talk."

Charles had already told me that enrolling in Medicaid, the government health care program for poor Americans, was a complex process. Fraud was rampant, if more on the billing side than the application side, and the people who determined eligibility went to great lengths to ensure that applicants were as poor as they said. "If you want Medicaid," Charles said, "you've gotta be able to fill out forms, show up on time for appointments, that kind of thing. You need somebody in your corner."

"I could help with the applications."

"It's not just the applications. It's the follow-up. You don't have time. You're in the disaster-prevention business, remember?"

The irony was as tragic as it was laughable. The people who most needed social services were often the people least able to run the gauntlet required to receive them.

# THREE

## the idea

Over the next two weeks Charles and I managed to track down sixteen of my twenty maximum-risk cases. He said it was an excellent haul, far better than we'd had any right to expect of a crew of maxes who'd gone unsupervised for nearly three months. For the four "absconders"—P&P-speak for people who quit showing up—Charles helped me fill out warrant requests in our case management system as well as the violation paperwork I would submit to court for the probationers and to the parole board for the parolees. The parole board paperwork got put in the mail. We never interacted with the parole board. It met behind closed doors and rendered decisions to the P&P districts in writing.

Where violations were concerned, probation cases were a lot more labor-intensive. You had to deliver your paperwork in person to the courthouse. You had to see a judge and be prepared to answer follow-up questions if he or she had any.

Next on the agenda were my medium-risk cases. Charles was supposed to help with them, too, but on his next field day something came up at the last minute and he arranged to have me meet Beth, one of his closest friends in the office. Charles and Beth were as far apart politically as any two Americans could be, but they were that rare pair who seemed to like each other better after a disagreement. Charles told me that Beth cared about her caseload just as much as he did. She just had a different way of showing it.

She was in her mid-thirties, short and slim, with arms like a tennis player's. She wore her hair in a long, black ponytail so aggressively knotted that it seemed to pull her eyes open just a little wider than a normal person's. The eyes were like that all day, even at six in the morning, when we met in the New Orleans District parking lot. She told me that anyone who didn't get out into the field before the traffic picked up couldn't be all that serious about making contact with the people the state was paying us to make contact with.

We started our day in New Orleans East. As the name implied, it was the city's easternmost region, running along Lake Pontchartrain's south shore and dissolving into the brackish waters of St. Tammany Parish. "The East," as it was commonly known, was diverse and middle-class into the eighties. By the mid-nineties much of the middle class, especially the white middle class, had moved out to suburban Jefferson and St. Tammany Parishes, where taxes were lower, schools were better, and violent crime less common. The East fared as badly in Katrina as the Lower Ninth Ward, and its recovery had been just as slow. The siding of many houses was still tagged with "Katrina crosses," the once-ubiquitous spray-painted X marks flanked by rows of letters and numbers indicating what living or once-living things had been discovered inside when the first responders made their inspection.

The first offender of the day was Travis, a twenty-three-year-old white guy on probation for heroin possession. A decade out from Katrina, half of the houses on Travis's block in the East were abandoned. He and his mom were the only white family left in their neighborhood, a fact Travis reported more as a point of interest than a complaint, although he did remark that the neighborhood "isn't what it used to be."

The assessment had him as a medium-risk case, but Charles, in the room for the duration of Travis's and my first office visit, encouraged me to keep a closer watch on him. For one thing, he'd been conspicuously eager to take his drug test. Most offenders, especially those who weren't required to report monthly, knew that passing a drug test all but ensured they wouldn't get another one for six months. Heavy drug users had been known to dry out for seventy-two hours, just long enough to piss clean, only to run out and overdose over the weekend.

Even if you beat the traffic, it was a twenty-minute ride from the

New Orleans District to the East, and Beth and I had plenty of time to get to know each other on the way over. Beth had been on the job a little more than three years. "First in a series of questionable choices related to my divorce," she told me.

She'd taken the P&P position and moved herself and her twelve-year-old kid into a small apartment in the city while she got her affairs in order. She had a law degree and used to make good money and figured she could make good money again if she wanted to, but P&P had gone and stirred something in her, and she hadn't, as of yet, been able to bring herself to walk away.

"These people," she told me, "are the most fucked people you're ever gonna meet. They need an army."

"So why do this?" I said.

She shrugged. "That's the mystery. My theory is we all suffer from a rare brain disease. If you've lasted more than a week, you probably already have it."

Beth obviously took a more combative approach to new-PO development than Charles, but she promised to accompany me anywhere I wanted to go today, and a little abuse was a small price to pay for another person's undivided attention. I'd been through worse hazing in the bar-and-restaurant industry and had learned to take it as evidence I was part of the team. In the brain-illness remark I was sure I heard a touch of approval, or at least an acknowledgment that I'd survived the first of what I assumed would be several weeding-out periods.

By the time we pulled into the driveway in the East I'd told Beth everything I knew about Travis, which wasn't much. A recovering heroin addict, Travis had a history of committing burglaries when his supply ran out. He'd told me during the office visit that he'd been clean for eight weeks, but Charles didn't believe it.

Beth and I knocked for a couple of minutes before Travis answered the door. This wasn't unusual early in the morning, and as long as we didn't hear toilets flushing or closets slamming shut or a lot of furniture moving around, we didn't have reasonable suspicion to believe anything illegal was hidden inside.

My first thought when I saw Travis in the doorway was that he was even younger and smaller than I remembered, with thick glasses and hair the color and consistency of dead grass. In the office he'd been shockingly pale, but he'd gotten some sun since then. His cheeks were as red as plums and strips of sunburned skin fell from the tip of his nose. He lingered there in the doorway for a moment, twisting his fingers through the frayed ends of his hair and saying he wasn't usually a very early riser, and neither was his mom.

She was in the kitchen in a bathrobe. She had the same thick glasses as her son, and the same thinning hair. Her eyes jumped around the room and her teeth chattered as Beth and I sweated through our shirts. A rusty window unit in the far corner could be heard making a fruitless effort.

Charles had trained me to look for the most anxious person in the room. I was sure I'd found her. She tried to be friendly, fussing with the coffeepot and telling us she would have had fresh cups ready for us if she had known we were coming,

"We don't call ahead," Beth said. "We show when we show."

"She knows," Travis said. "She just got off paper"—meaning off probation or parole.

Beth asked Travis's mother who her PO was. The name didn't ring a bell for me, but it clearly meant something to Beth.

"He's not around anymore," Beth said. Later she would inform me that he was second-laziest PO she'd ever met, after the guy whose case-load I'd inherited.

"I haven't used in ten weeks," Travis's mother said. She pointed at Travis. "He's clean for four."

This was half as many weeks as he'd claimed in the office, and I got the feeling that duration of sobriety was the sort of detail Beth wouldn't have been able to resist unpacking. I decided to overlook it for now. I accepted a cup of coffee from Travis's mother and told Travis I was ready for the tour.

The house had two small bedrooms and a single bath. The tub was rimmed in grime. There was a crack down the center of the mirror and standing water in the sink. Roaches scattered when we entered the bedrooms and took refuge in discarded pizza boxes and fast-food bags. In the kitchen, dishes were piled neck-high in the sink. Swarms of black flies orbited the trash can.

"When you're trying to get yourself clean," Travis's mother said, "you don't have time to clean house."

"What have you been up to since you got clean?" Beth asked her.

"I don't have to answer that," Travis's mother said, and she slammed her coffee cup on the edge of the kitchen counter, sending a little chip of porcelain flying across the room.

Beth looked surprised that Travis's mother had heard an accusation in the question, but I gathered that it wasn't in Beth's nature to apologize for being misunderstood. "You're right," Beth said. "You and I don't have to say a single word to each other ever again." She turned to Travis. "Probation shouldn't take up more than an hour of your time a month. You don't cause any trouble, we won't give you any."

"It's not the time," Travis's mother said. "It's the idea."

Beth kept her eyes on Travis and forced out a smile. "You can't tell me we're worse than jail. If you tell me I'm worse than jail, I'm gonna take it personally."

Travis's mother smiled, too, just a little, at the corners of her mouth before she swallowed it back and reiterated her point, which Beth finally conceded was a valid one. An hour of probation per month was a far lighter burden than thirty days behind bars, but the prospect that the knock could come at any hour, and could result in your being handcuffed and driven away, was more than enough to make a person feel less than free. You could tell yourself that people who were in compliance had nothing to fear, but we lived in a town where police reforms were new and as yet untested. I assumed most people in New Orleans East didn't have to travel far to meet someone who'd encountered an unscrupulous law enforcement officer.

Then again, a PO didn't have to be unscrupulous to catch an offender doing something illegal. If you were an addict recovering from her tenth relapse, you knew you were at risk of having another. If you had it on a day when the PO came by, and the PO found the stash, you could be looking at a whole new felony charge. Your supervision could get revoked, and you could find yourself back in prison.

"The idea" was stressful by design. Knowing an authority figure was watching was supposed to deter relapse and all manner of other dangerous activities. I expected Travis's mother to go on to say that the stress actually had the opposite effect of the intended one, and that addicts who felt they were being watched acted out more often, and more destructively, than addicts who never came under the thumb of the criminal justice system. Instead she told us that "the idea" had, in fact, prevented some drug use on her part. She could specifically remember planning on getting high only to beg off at the last minute when she remembered she was due for a piss test. Being on parole probably didn't save her life, but it saved her a couple of bad relapses. While she felt she would be a fool to deny it, she also felt that there was something horribly un-American about the whole setup.

"It's my fucking vein," she said. "If I want to put a needle in it, who are you to tell me I can't?"

Charles had a policy of staying out of the civil liberties debate. If pressed, he admitted that he'd never been able to arrive at a coherent view of US drug policy. Overdoses were as high as they'd ever been, and the Internet had so democratized distribution that anyone who didn't have easy access to a drug dealer could buy much of what he was looking for online and have it shipped via the US Postal Service. On the one hand, the drug war seemed like a disastrous waste of time and resources, especially when you added the incalculable social costs of mass incarceration to the scale.

But was letting every man and woman decide what to put in their veins an abdication of our responsibility to the poorest among us— the people whose circumstances put them at greatest risk of looking to a needle for relief? Widespread distribution of drugs like the ultra-concentrated opioid fentanyl, designed to ease surgical pain and fatal in quantities not much bigger than a teardrop, further complicated the question of what the government should do about substances that couldn't be used safely without the assistance of an anesthesiologist. Regulation alone had been unable to control the flow of fentanyl, or even the marginally less toxic MD-prescribed opioids like oxycodone. Of course, neither had law enforcement.

I'd been undecided on the drug issue when I got the job. I'd wanted to keep addicts out of jail but believed fully legalizing all narcotics was probably an overcorrection. I had hoped that working firsthand with the issue would bring clarity, but I felt as muddy now as ever.

"That just means you're paying attention," Charles told me, and he reminded me that they hadn't hired us because of our policy chops. We weren't getting paid to solve macro-level problems. In fact, P&P was as micro as it got. The disasters we were getting paid to prevent occurred on a case-by-case basis. The micro-ness of the work was what made it so challenging and, to people who kept doing it, what made it worthwhile. You didn't have to approve of the system to do disaster prevention. You just had to understand how it worked.

I fully expected Beth, whom Charles had described as a "strong civil libertarian," to weigh in on the legalization question, but she shrugged off Travis's mother's remark and said that if she'd wanted to be employed by an outfit that made sense, she sure as hell wouldn't have applied to P&P. "You're talking," she said, "about an institution that wants to cure addiction but won't spring for a detox."

Disparaging remarks about our employer were the most reliable icebreaker I'd seen. Travis and his mother laughed and said that any-body who expected his PO to put him anyplace other than OPP after a relapse was probably in serious need of a piss test. They said this without apparent resentment, as if it were a fact of life as ancient and intractable as mosquitoes in summer, and by the second cup of coffee we were get-ting what we came for, Travis's and his mother's version of how Travis came to be the responsibility of the New Orleans District of Probation and Parole.

Travis's father was in prison when Travis was a kid. He made his way west when he got his parole, and Travis never saw him again. Tra-vis grew up in trailer parks in Jefferson, St. Tammany, and St. Bernard, the three majority-white parishes that border New Orleans. Travis was fourteen when he and his mother moved to the East. They knew the neighborhood was bad, but they could get a whole house for what they were paying for the trailer in Jefferson. They lived off food stamps and whatever money the boyfriend of the week left on the nightstand. Tra-vis's mother was on and off probation for heroin charges until the third PO convinced the judge to ship her upstate for eighteen months. Travis lived with aunts and uncles of similar means until his mother got her parole and they returned to the East, to the house they were in now. It was the nicest one they'd ever had.

The best job Travis's mother could get with a ninth-grade education and three convictions was cashiering at the Dollar General. Eventually she got on Medicaid and found a doctor willing to diagnose her
with acute depression, and she was approved for SSI. It paid her half of
what she was making on the job. She quit anyway.

It was the latest in a long line of bad decisions. She'd always hoped
her life would serve as a cautionary tale for her son. Instead he seemed
to mimic her every move. He started shooting up in high school. He
got weekend jobs but feuded with bosses.

"He's barely there a week and he's bitching about the schedule," she
said. "Bitching about other people getting the best shifts."

Travis nodded along as his mother listed his faults. If he felt she was
being unfair, it didn't show. "People always think because I'm small and
I've got these fucking Coke bottles on my face, they can just roll over
me," he said.

Like addiction, the phenomenon Travis was describing appeared
to transcend race, age, and gender. People who got the least respect in
this world felt the greatest need to demand it of bosses, friends, even
strangers on the street. They felt slights more acutely than the rest of us.
And the impulse to right the wrong frequently cost them what little
opportunity they got.

In low-wage jobs where the labor pool was fungible, bosses saw no
reason to tolerate employees like Travis. If Travis didn't like the schedule, he could find someplace else to work.

Travis's probation charge began as a traffic stop and ended with
the cops booking him with driving recklessly and without a license or
insurance—and being in possession of three heroin foils, a day's dose
for a serious user. His girlfriend was in the car at the time and twice as
high as he was, but the drugs were in Travis's pocket, and he alone was
charged with a felony.

"They say being white keeps you from getting pulled over," Travis
told us. "And it must be true, because I drove high about four hundred
times through the hood before anybody stopped me. But when they do
stop you, man, they turn you the fuck out. Like they want to make you
pay for all those free passes."

Several white offenders on my caseload had told me some version of this story, and it was easy enough to write it off as sour grapes on the part of people who'd rode an unfair advantage as far as it would take them. White offenders could always be counted on to point out that once they got convicted and showed up at our office, the playing field leveled out, and not because POs were free of the prejudices that caused cops to give white guys a pass.

P&P treated everyone equally—that is to say, poorly—because we didn't have the resources to treat anybody well. White or black, male or female, everybody got the same two treatment options: talk or jail. And putting someone in jail was such an unpleasant experience that it was hard to imagine a bigotry powerful enough to induce a PO to take that ride any more often than he had to.

When you booked someone into OPP, you had to breathe the air in there. You came out reeking of the place. It could take two days to wash the jail out of your hair. If the offender was on probation, you had to go to the courthouse the day after the arrest and tell the probation judge what you'd done and why. If the offender was on parole, you had to do a stack of paperwork and send it to the parole board, which in turn sent paperwork back that had to be filed in a manila folder and submitted to our clerical staff.

We had plenty of disincentives to make arrests, and no incentives. Unlike cops, we couldn't cite arrest stats in our applications for promotion. If anything, the legislature's newfound enthusiasm for trimming jail costs meant that POs with the highest arrest rates were the employees least likely to get promoted. The last thing you wanted to do if you were trying to get ahead in the department was put people in jail.

According to Charles, Travis's previous PO has been known across the district for his reluctance to make the drive to OPP. Despite several positive drug screens, Travis hadn't been behind bars since the night of his arrest for the probation charge. His girlfriend came from money and got him bailed out of jail and paid for both of them to go to a doctor and get prescriptions for Suboxone.

Opioid "inhibitors" like Suboxone and its cousin, methadone, made the body believe it was getting heroin, when really it was getting a look-alike. Suboxone and methadone staved off withdrawal symptoms but produced no euphoric effects—no high—if taken as prescribed. Ideally, Suboxone and methadone were "downward dosed" until the addict was fully weaned. For some addicts, Suboxone and methadone were lifesavers, albeit expensive ones. A month's supply could run four hundred bucks. Travis's girlfriend was picking up the tab for that, too.

Many New Orleans District addicts found downward-dosing an inhibitor just as challenging as downward-dosing the real thing, and Travis was no exception. He'd been on Suboxone a little over three months when he double-dosed, which left him a dose short, which took him back to the dope man. His previous PO had drug-tested him the following week and let him off with a warning. If he wasn't clean the next month—the month I took over—he was supposed to get a weekend in jail.

Charles told me that a fuzzy sobriety timeline didn't necessary indicate dissembling on the part of the offender. "Some people have been going through the cycle so long," he said, "they can't keep track of where the last loop ended and the next one began."

More often than not, there were two cycles at play at Travis's house. I had to wonder what condition the place was in when mother and son were getting high at the same time. Generational addiction was so common among offenders on my caseload that I was surprised when an offender told me that neither of his parents was an addict. Like Kendrick, Travis had believed as a teenager that his early exposure to addiction had inoculated him. He would be able to walk away before the disease took hold.

Suboxone and methadone registered as opioids on the P&P piss test, and the department's official position was that offenders weren't allowed to take them. Dan the Regional Manager had never gone on record on the matter, and the feeling around the New Orleans District was that opioid inhibitors fell under the broad umbrella of PO discretion. If we wanted to allow offenders to use them, we were free to do so as long as we were willing to accept the risk.

It was a big one. Because the P&P drug test couldn't tell the difference between Suboxone and heroin, a Suboxone prescription gave an offender all the cover he needed to go back to the real thing. POs who had once tolerated inhibitors tended to change their policy after the third or fourth offender believed to be "downward dosing" came back in the coroner's report dead of an overdose.

Opioid inhibitors produced good results in clinical trials, and there was plenty of research suggesting that they could be effective if properly administered. They didn't garner more lunchroom debate at the New Orleans District for one simple reason. Almost none of our offenders could afford them.

Since his last relapse Travis had gotten clean without detox and without Suboxone. He'd used only once during the relapse and believed that if he'd used a second time, he would have needed medical assistance to get back to his baseline. He'd been attending Narcotics Anonymous meetings five nights per week. Like its better-known counterpart, Alcoholics Anonymous (AA), NA was first and foremost a community-building apparatus. People sitting in church basements or hotel conference rooms told their life stories, with special emphasis on the bad parts, and developed quick and often lasting bonds. One night a young guy at a meeting who'd grown up in the same trailer parks as Travis told him he was never really going to get free until he had something to lose, something cleaner and more sustainable than a high.

It wasn't the first time he'd received this advice, but it finally registered. Travis knew why. A few weeks before, his girlfriend had told him she was pregnant. He went home from the NA meeting and told her he wanted her to have the child, and he wanted to provide for it.

The girlfriend's uncle worked in the oil business and was willing to help. He offered Travis a job on an offshore oil rig making more than twice the minimum wage, plus overtime, plus health care benefits. Travis shipped out on Thursday.

"Proud of him," his mother told Beth and me.

"I'm gonna move the family someplace nice," Travis told us. "Three checks at what they're paying me and we're out of this dump."

I told Travis I looked forward to seeing his first pay stub. We thanked Travis's mother for the coffee, and she told us she hoped that the next time we all saw each other, she and Travis would be out of the East.

No one else I was hoping to see in the East that morning was home. By the letter of the law, offenders were supposed to stay in the same place every night, but this provision was as unenforceable as the one forbidding alcohol. An offender needed to deactivate his last known phone number and fully vacate his last known address before we considered him an absconder and filed for a warrant. I made a note in my laptop of the failed attempts to make contact, and tried again later in the week.

Beth took me out three more times over the next few weeks. She happened to be with me again when Travis returned from his first stint on the oil rig.

His mother wasn't home. He opened the door only a crack. When he saw who it was, he said, "Oh, fuck."

He was still a little loopy from the dope but managed a coherent explanation of what had happened. Rig work was usually two weeks on, two weeks off. The "on" weeks were killers. You climbed ladders and turned wrenches. If you were small of stature and not accustomed to manual labor, when you got back onshore you probably felt you'd earned yourself a good time, and followed most of your rig mates to the French Quarter.

Men who'd lived the rig life for years, and who were free with their money during shore time, knew where to draw the line. They could get as drunk as they wanted. They could leave half their check at the strip club. But they couldn't get high. They knew they had to pass drug screens if they wanted back on the rig. Travis had been warned. He hadn't planned on getting carried away. He was excited about the paycheck, and excited about the baby, and around hour thirty of the bender he called up his old dealer and asked if they could meet in an hour.

The oil company called him in for a piss test the next morning. His girlfriend tried to talk to the uncle, but it was out of his hands. Travis lost the job. He turned the rest of the check over to the dealer. By then he'd been high for three days. When I showed up at his house, detox was the only answer.

I called Odyssey House to check for beds, but Travis didn't get his hopes up. He turned around and faced the wall. I applied the handcuffs, and Beth and I put him in the back of the Crown Vic and took him to jail. The following week, I would pick him up and deliver him to a monthlong stay at Bridge House, the male counterpart of Grace House, the sober-living facility where Charles and I took the old woman we arrested on my first day on the job.

I'd always assumed that addiction hunted mostly at night. It came for you when you were at your most desperate, when you weren't seeing clearly and your defenses were low. Travis's relapse had come at arguably the best time of his life. He'd been living in squalor long enough to comprehend the magnitude of the opportunity presented by a job with benefits and good pay, and gone and traded it all for dope anyway.

At my most starry-eyed—before I complained to Charles about the lack of in-between sanctions, and long before he told me about disaster prevention—I'd never imagined that a PO could provide an offender a ladder like the one Travis had been handed. It stood to transform not only his own life but his mother's and his girlfriend's—and his unborn child's. If the opportunity of a lifetime wasn't stronger than the disease, how was I supposed to supply a cure?

There would be 72,000 overdoses in America in 2016, most of them from opioids, but the drug sucked up plenty of other things before it made off with your life. Heroin, once a distraction from poverty and dysfunction, now seemed to ensure that Travis would stay poor and dysfunctional forever.

# FOUR

# ride or die

Once Charles was satisfied that my missing-in-action maximum-risk cases couldn't be found, he took me to the courthouse to get my warrants signed. Most locals referred to the building by the name of the intersection it inhabited, Tulane and Broad. The blocks immediately surrounding the courthouse retained the bondsmen's huts, chicken shacks, and roadside motels that had been fixtures of that part of town since I was a kid.

The courthouse was a large gray cube, its façade inlaid with Greek idols and block letters telling all who entered that "impartial administration of justice is the foundation of liberty" and "this is a government of law, not men." In the great hall the paint peeled in long brown strips from the walls. The black marble floors and golden latticework over the elevator shaft were the last relics of the building's prime, which no one at P&P had been around long enough to remember.

We flashed our badges at the deputy standing beside the metal detector and locked our guns in the law enforcement vault just inside the entryway and rode the riptide of foot traffic up the big spiral staircase to the great hall on the second floor. Some people showed up to court in church clothes. Others came in their pajamas. There were old people in walkers and wheelchairs and babies, dozens of them, strapped to strollers or swinging from hips. Ministers in black coats shook pocket Bibles at congregations gathered along benches and windowsills.

The lawyers dragged heavy leather briefcases. The briefcases were trailed by file clerks hunched over fat white boxes. Pieces of paper escaped through unsecured flaps and vanished underfoot.

Many aspects of courtroom logistics were as presented on TV. The seating was church-style, long wooden pews and a few more ministers, who drew bigger and more enthusiastic crowds than the ones working the great hall. Families of victims and defendants hissed at each other. Deputies stationed at the door announced that people who couldn't conduct themselves civilly could take their issues outside. There was the court reporter and her curious device, with a face like a typewriter and keys like a tiny piano, and the clerk beside her, her nose pressed to the computer screen so that she could avoid eye contact with anyone seated in the pews. The inmates in their orange jumpsuits sat in the first row. A deputy in an olive-colored uniform sat beside them. Every minute or so the deputy glanced down the line to make sure he hadn't lost anybody.

All that a PO had to do to get a judge's attention was loiter alongside the prosecution table in the front left corner of the courtroom until a break in the action. The judge waved us up to the right side of the bench, where conversations were understood to be off the record. None of the four judges spent more than a minute looking over the warrant paperwork. The first three judges said nothing at all as they scribbled their signatures along the bottom of the form and handed it back.

I didn't know why I'd expected to have to explain myself. Our warrant paperwork could really say only one thing: we couldn't find the guy. It was hard to conceive of a rational follow-up question that a judge might ask.

The fourth judge, a middle-aged African American in glasses and three-day stubble, signed quickly but had a second look at the offender's name before he passed the warrant back. "I remember this guy," the judge said. "He was doing well, wasn't he?"

My predecessor had left behind very few case notes, but from what I could tell, the judge was remembering correctly.

"Even had a job or something?" the judge said. "A good one, right? Construction?"

I'd been surprised to learn that when you were off the record, judges talked like ordinary people. The rest of us were expected to maintain the usual courtroom courtesies. "That's right, Your Honor," I said.

"What happened? Crack?"

"Heroin."

"Christ. That shit's everywhere. They get started on the pain pills, end up on the needle."

That, I'd been told, was the trend. Pills, most of them legally prescribed, were the new gateway to heroin addiction. Once marketed as a miracle painkiller, the timed-release opioid OxyContin had become a corporate-greed cautionary tale. The first waves of doctors who prescribed it remembered receiving ironclad assurances from the manufacturer that the risks of addiction were negligible.

The judge, a New Orleans District favorite, wanted us to know that he knew what was going on in the city and what those of us trying to help were up against. He reached down from the bench and offered his hand. "Always good to see new faces in here. You guys have a tough fucking job. If I can help, you know where to find me."

I shook his hand and thanked him for the offer.

"Let me know if our mutual friend turns up," the judge said.

Before I could reply, he gave the assistant district attorney a nod that let him know he was ready for the next matter on the docket, and I followed Charles out of the courtroom. Start to finish, getting four warrants signed took less than twenty minutes. We grabbed our guns and got in the Crown Vic and made our way back into the field.

I was still mostly Charles's responsibility, but a couple of other senior POs filled in here and there, and I tried to learn something from each of them. In terms of supervision style, Charles and Beth appeared to stand at opposite ends of the spectrum at the New Orleans District. I met no one who was more assertive than Beth and no one with a softer touch than Charles.

By the end of my third month out of the academy, I'd figured out that I was better suited to Charles's methodology, but I had seen no evidence that I would get better results if I tried talking to people a different way. Charles and Beth and everyone else I worked with had assured me that if data existed showing that an easygoing PO got better results than a hard-ass, or vice versa, the department would insist we heed it. The dream of reducing incarceration without spending money was behind every decision Baton Rouge made, and forcing POs to adjust their supervision style was the cheapest fix imaginable.

The data just didn't support it. Revocation rates decreased when caseloads were low and POs had ample resources to offer alternatives to criminal lifestyles. In other words, revocation rates were tied directly to spending. Federal probation was the shining example. His first day on the job, the federal PO was given a binder of service providers that could address an offender's every need. Only 16 percent of federal offenders were sent to prison before their terms expired, a statistic made all the more remarkable when you considered that the federal criminal justice system is set up to prosecute complex crimes committed by sophisticated offenders. Federal probation begins with a more challenging population but produces far better results.

Forty-three percent of parolees in Louisiana would be back in prison within five years. Nationally, the parole revocation rate was closer to 25 percent. Another 11 percent absconded, meaning they stopped showing up and were never heard from again. Those numbers didn't include people who died of drug overdoses and people who completed their community supervision sentences as poor and addicted as they were when they got out of jail.

Federal probation costs close to $4,000 per offender per year, compared to the roughly $1,000 per offender we spend in Louisiana. A fourfold increase is nothing to sneeze at, but compared with incarceration costs, an extra three grand per offender is a pittance. A Vera Institute of Justice study found that the average cost to incarcerate someone in the US is $33,000 per year. At about $17,000 per year, Louisiana is on the low end of per-inmate spending. In five states, the annual tab exceeds $50,000.

As Beth pointed out in her discussion with Travis's mother, when people thought in the abstract about P&P, they didn't compare it to putting people in jail. They compared it to doing nothing. In budgetary terms, this meant that the comparison wasn't between 4,000 and 33,000. It was between 4,000 and zero. The relationship between spending money on social services and reducing need, and in turn between reducing need and mitigating risk, wasn't part of the conversation.

As I worked my way through the medium-risk portion of my caseload, I was struck by just how fine the line was, at least in the assessment tool's eyes, between maximum risk and medium risk. The only factor keeping many of my mediums from rolling up to max was that a parent allowed the offender to live at home. If I changed Travis's housing stability rating from medium to low, his risk score jumped an entire bracket.

Eighteen- to twenty-three-year-old offenders were more likely to live with a parent. Youth, which in isolation was known to increase risk, was offset by stable housing, one of the most reliable risk reducers. Charles and Beth agreed that under-twenty-one offenders should be supervised at max no matter what the assessment had to say about it. If their underdeveloped prefrontal cortexes placed younger offenders at greater risk of life-altering lapses in judgment—or, as Charles put it, "crimes that only make sense to adolescent brains"—they also made young offenders more malleable. Under-twenty-one offenders represented a PO's best chance of having an impact by talking and listening.

At eighteen years and three months, Sheila was the youngest offender on my caseload. Because she, like Travis, lived with her mother, the assessment had her at medium risk. All other indicators pointed to maximum. Sheila had been a fixture in the juvenile justice system throughout high school, mainly due to shoplifting charges. She was good at shoplifting. She estimated that she got caught no more than 10 percent of the time. She'd shoplifted just about everything—shoes, sunglasses, food—but her favorite items to steal were cosmetics.

"Her whole life's a game of dress-up," Sheila's mother told me. They lived in a crumbling double in the Seventh Ward, one of the city's poorest neighborhoods. Sheila's mother smoked crack in the living room. When I spotted the pipe on the couch cushion during my first home inspection, she told me she was too old to go to jail. It was a credible claim. The skin around her throat hung as loose as a bloodhound's. She walked with a limp from a fall suffered when she was high. Most of her teeth were false.

I would learn later that she was only thirty-seven years old. Born a looker, bored and fidgety at school, she'd started sleeping around and doing drugs for the same reasons as most of her friends in the Seventh Ward. Her own mother was always working the graveyard shift. Her father was in jail. When her older brothers and sisters got money, they didn't bring it home. Sheila's mother had figured she had about a four-year window to get what kicks she could before she took her place in line. She couldn't fault Sheila for making the same choices, but a mother's job was to try to interfere. Risk-wise, Sheila's mother believed the best thing Sheila had going for her was that she didn't drink or do hard drugs. The only mind-altering substance she liked was weed.

"The problem is," Sheila's mother told me, "she's having it for breakfast, lunch, and dinner. They've got her convinced it's good for you. 'Mama, it's from the earth.' Well, so's the motherfucking Ebola virus."

The latest research on marijuana has come out firmly on the side of keeping it away from young people. Frequent use can exacerbate the feelings of aimlessness and isolation common among adolescents of all socioeconomic classes. THC, the active ingredient in cannabis, is believed to present especially serious risks to young people who have experienced trauma and those who are genetically predisposed to depression and mental illness. Heavy smoking is believed to amplify the most distressing symptoms of those diseases and may increase the probability of early onset.

Being the weed police didn't interest me, but most of my coworkers believed we should do what we could to discourage the drug's use. We shouldn't be locking people up over it, but we were within our rights to badger offenders every time THC showed up on a drug test. If nothing else, we should make sure they understood the risks.

Most offenders I'd tried to talk out of their weed habit had dismissed the latest findings as callbacks to the antidrug fearmongering of the late eighties and early nineties, when the mass incarceration movement was in full flower and many states instituted "three strikes" laws that sent people to prison for life upon conviction of a third felony offense, even if all three offenses only involved marijuana possession. Even in those days, such sentences were rare, but they'd been threatened loudly and frequently enough to convince black offenders that any drug research peddled by the government was a means to the end of filling prisons with minorities. White offenders didn't get mass-incarcerated at nearly the same rates as black offenders, but those who passed through my office were no more favorably disposed to PO insights on drug dangers than their African American counterparts. It was a white guy who told me he believed I got a finder's fee for every drug addict I put in jail.

Like a lot of people, I tried weed when I was young, but I've never liked smoke of any kind, and all the smokers I knew were so sanctimonious about the stuff that I never felt like I was missing out on anything by sticking to booze. As an adult I knew plenty of well-heeled working people who lit up a joint at least as often as I poured myself a bourbon, and their brains seemed to be in fine working condition.

By the time I spoke to Sheila about her weed habit, I'd learned to begin by acknowledging that there were plenty of exceptions to the rule, or at least plenty of people for whom the drug's risks didn't appear significant, at least compared with the other risks of concern to P&P. If nothing else, I could plagiarize Charles's point about weed's potential to get your vehicle searched or your pockets turned out by a cop searching for more serious offenses.

Sheila shrugged. "Cops see me smoking all the time. They don't really fuck with girls."

The P&P roster bore this out. Sheila was one of only fifteen female offenders on my caseload.

Like many families in New Orleans's poorest neighborhoods, Sheila and her mother lived in a shotgun double, so named because in place of hallways, the rooms were connected by parallel thresholds, and if the homeowner were so inclined, she could stand on the front porch and fire a slug clear through to the backyard. The shotgun style was developed to facilitate airflow in the days before AC, and it did the job well enough to became the home of choice for thousands of early New Orleanians. Shotgun homes were built squat and sturdy to withstand the elements. Many of them had yet to meet the hurricane that could shake them from their foundations.

Where probation and parole inspections were concerned, shotguns presented an obvious logistical problem. If the bedroom you needed to inspect was in the rear of the house, the only way to get there was to start at the front and work your way through room by room.

The first three rooms of Sheila's house teemed with roaches. Mouse shit crowded the corners as if someone had swept it up but forgotten to come back around with the dustpan. The rooms had a scalded smell that I was learning to associate with places where crack was smoked.

Sheila's room smelled like perfume, the candy-flavored kind I remembered girls wearing when I was a teenager. Sheila's floors looked like they'd been freshly waxed. Her windows were spotless, her curtains pulled open and lashed to little golden hooks. Her walls were papered with pictures of her wearing either elaborate floor-length gowns or almost nothing at all. According to her mother, she'd been built like a pinup model since she was fourteen and posing like one since she was twelve.

"My mom can't come in here," Sheila said. "I love her, but she's not allowed."

In about a third of the pictures on Sheila's wall she was wrapped around a guy about her age. She identified each one by name as if she were rattling off conquests. No one had ever been able to hold her attention for long.

"I've had asses kicked over me," she said. "Motherfuckers bled for a piece of this."

She did a little twirl and laughed to show me it was all a lark. The guys she'd been with were petty thugs anyway. What Sheila wanted was a "don"—a drug-dealer with clout. Respect on the streets was nice, but fear was what you wanted your man to inspire. You wanted other men to know that if they made a pass at his woman, they stood to get their bones broken.

Sheila wasn't the first young beauty to be attracted to danger and power, but in neighborhoods like hers, the attraction was rooted in rational thinking. Absent upward mobility in civilian jobs, men who moved their product through violence and intimidation were the safe futures bets. The don whom Sheila described sounded identical to the guy Kendrick's housemates had told me about, with the beautiful car and the beautiful women, and I wondered just how many young people in this town had ended up dead or in prison trying to become a figure who was probably more myth than man. Every hour on the job presented a new opportunity to reflect on my own privilege and the extent to which a person's place of birth dictates his aspirations. If I'd been born in the Seventh Ward and wanted to get the attention of a girl like Sheila, there would have been only one way to do it.

Many criminologists were coming to view drug dealing as an addiction unto itself. Drug dealers were said to be "addicted to the lifestyle," not only the money and the girls but the thrill of the chase, the rush of living outside the law and getting away with it.

"Guy with the most dope and the most bodies gets the most pussy," Sheila's mother told me. "Same as it ever was. So who do you think these young boys are gonna take after? The schoolteacher? The fucking workingman?"

Sheila was on probation because she'd dashed into the bathroom and flushed her boyfriend's drugs when the police showed up at his house to serve a search warrant. By the time the detectives got to the toilet, everything they'd come to seize was gone. The boyfriend didn't get arrested. Sheila went to jail on obstruction-of-justice charges.

Sheila didn't blame her boyfriend for letting her take the heat. A man in the drug trade was expected to have warrants served on his place from time to time. If a woman with a clean record was around, she was expected to do what Sheila had done. While the woman was in jail, the man got back to earning. A first-timer like Sheila was only going to sit in OPP for a couple of days before she got a court date.

Sheila felt she'd upheld a code. The relationship was finished a month later, but guys higher up in the neighborhood drug gangs had taken notice. "Now everybody knows I'm ride-or-die," Sheila told me.

Here was another "gate," one I'd tried walking through with other young offenders, who tended to be especially candid about codes like ride-or-die and lacked the sense to conceal their feelings on the matter from their POs. To these men and women, the allure of the drug trade was about more than power and money. It was about solidarity of race and class.

Sheila put it like this: The law had failed to protect African Americans, and it had failed to protect the very poor; therefore, anything forbidden by law—the drug trade, for one—was probably good. To Sheila, a don was a Robin Hood figure, a rebel living outside the law because the law was unjust. The moral costs of the drug business—addiction, overdose, violence in pursuit of territory—were billed not to the rebel but to the institutions that made rebellion necessary.

Not everyone in the Seventh Ward felt this way. A neighbor I'd met on my way up the street had complained to the police that one of Sheila's boyfriends was selling crack on the corner. She complained again when the boyfriend threatened to shoot up her house if she didn't keep her mouth shut. She wasn't angry at the young man. She felt sorry for him.

"It's a false promise, what these dope dealers are selling," the neighbor told me. "But I can't blame our kids for believing it. Nobody else promises them a goddamn thing."

Sheila's mother told me she fantasized about going back in time and putting a bullet through the nose of the first guy who offered to get her high. He'd framed the drug life the same way they were framing it now, as a rebuke to a rigged system. "You're laid out on the floor," she said through a laugh, "punching holes in your brain, and they've got you thinking you're sticking it to the Man." She reiterated her relief that Sheila had stayed away from the heavy-duty stuff and suggested I start weaning her off the weed.

I said I would do my best, but I wasn't really there to talk to Sheila about marijuana or to inspect her home. I'd been sent by Sheila's probation judge to remind her that she needed to be in court the next morning for a hearing. The hearing had originally been set for the month before. Sheila hadn't showed. Usually a failure-to-appear warrant would have been issued by now, but Sheila had caught the judge's eye during the initial court proceedings. The judge was determined to see Sheila thrive on probation. She reset the hearing date and asked me to go out to the house the day before and pass along a gentle reminder.

"A judge pulling for you is a good thing," I told Sheila.

"I hear she's a hard-ass," Sheila said.

Offenders and POs alike considered Sheila's judge among the toughest at Tulane and Broad. Granted, a tough judge in liberal New Orleans would look like a pushover in neighboring St. Tammany or Jefferson Parish, majority-white jurisdictions that New Orleans offenders—black and white alike—considered difficult places to be on probation.

While parole decisions were made by the one parole board—seated in Baton Rouge and widely regarded as lenient about misdemeanors, ruthless about felonies, but on the whole consistent in its rulings—probation decisions were made by individual judges. In Louisiana, 194 judges heard criminal cases. Even within a single jurisdiction, judges' ideas about how to motivate offenders tended to vary. What a probationer could get away with sometimes came down to luck-of-the-draw.

Sheila showed up early to court dressed in a white button-up collar and long sleeves. The assistant district attorney called Sheila's case first and announced that this was a status hearing. Most of the people in the courtroom had never seen a status hearing before. It was well known that New Orleans criminal court dockets were crowded. Judges usually didn't want to see probationers unless they got in trouble. Status hearings were scheduled only for offenders whom judges deemed extremely high-risk or, in rare cases like Sheila's, offenders in whom judges had taken a personal interest.

The judge was in her late forties, with chin-length hair and a voice as flat and cool as lake water. "Thank you for coming, Miss Walker," she said.

"Yes, ma'am," Sheila said. Her voice deepened when she took the mic. For an eighteen-year-old with her name on a criminal court docket, she was a model of poise. She told me later that she'd been going to Tulane and Broad since she was a kid. Aunts, uncles, and her mother had been visiting the building for as long as Sheila could remember. They considered New Orleans judges reasonable people as long as you called them "sir" and "ma'am" and "Your Honor" and found subtle ways of reminding them that you hadn't had all the advantages they'd had.

Seven of the twelve judges were African American, and if an offender blamed his mistakes entirely on racism, the judge was probably going to point out that plenty of black people in America hadn't found it necessary to become drug dealers or drug addicts. Yes, blackness made your path through this land a lot more challenging, but it didn't set your future in stone.

Judges complained about poor neighborhoods where all the upward mobility seemed to be in the drug business. They said that most of the people seated before them in handcuffs needed opportunity a lot more than they needed prison. But every day judges heard from family members who held the court accountable when a son or daughter overdosed, and they heard from law-abiding people, nearly all of them poor and black, who wanted the drug dealers off their stoops and street corners.

What criminal court judges really wanted was help from the American social safety net. They wanted a city with equal access to education and employment. Some of the African American judges shared their own experiences with discrimination at the hands of the schools and the job market and the police. They broke down economic changes since the early 1980s, when the oil crash demolished scores of high-paying jobs that never returned to New Orleans. By the time the next boom happened, most of the oil companies had figured out that it was cheaper to do business in Texas.

Judges who were old enough to remember the oil boom remembered a time when majority-black cities like Detroit and Atlanta and New Orleans had strong middle classes. They touched on the decline of union labor, especially in the South, and the death of manufacturing, which was probably more the fault of the times than the politicians, but the politicians around here never seemed to be much help.

Sheila's judge rarely went on the record with her political beliefs, and I had yet to see her live up to her reputation for heavy-handed sentencing. Like most judges in the building, and most POs for that matter, she seemed to recognize that OPP didn't have what most offenders needed, and neither did P&P. This hearing itself suggested that the judge felt the need to take the matter into her own hands.

She started off by asking Sheila whether she was getting along with her PO. Sheila said that she was. The judge asked Sheila if she understood what was expected of her. Sheila said that she did understand. And then the judge urged, but didn't demand, that Sheila go back to high school and get her degree.

"Sure thing, Your Honor," Sheila said.

Sheila's public defender offered to put Sheila in touch with one of her office's social workers. The social worker would get Sheila reenrolled. On our way out of the courthouse, Sheila appeared genuinely excited about the prospect of getting back in school. She'd clearly been thinking about it for a while but hadn't known whom to talk to. The social worker materialized on the courthouse steps inside of five minutes, and I handed Sheila off and told her I would see her again in a month.

Sheila's mother called me less than two weeks later to tell me Sheila had quit showing up to school after the fifth day. When I got to the house, Sheila was seated on the edge of her bed painting her toenails. "What it comes down to," she said, "is I want to be out here."

"It's gotta be tough being a year older than your classmates," I said.

She nodded, but I could see that age wasn't really the problem. Sheila's new school didn't seem much different from the one she'd gotten kicked out of the year before. Like most of New Orleans's public high schools, it underperformed on state tests, and almost all of the students were poor, some desperately so. In the 2014–15 school year, 84 percent of New Orleans public school students were economically disadvantaged enough to qualify for government-funded lunch.

Sheila didn't have anything bad to say about the new school in particular or about the teachers or the principal. She left because she couldn't think of a good reason to stay. She didn't want to take the SAT or go to college. She wanted to get back in the drug trade in New Orleans. "The action's out here," she said.

In other words, school was for getting you out of the Seventh Ward. The Seventh Ward was where Sheila's friends and family were and where she knew the game and had a knack for playing it. In anticipation of blowback from the judge about her quitting school, Sheila took a part-time job at a Subway about a mile from her house.

"I'm glad you're working," the judge said during the next status conference. She didn't give Sheila grief for dropping out. She told Sheila she would see her again in thirty days. She called a five-minute recess and asked me to come back to her chambers.

I followed the judge through the door behind the bench. She had a firm handshake and a kind smile that she must have learned to keep hidden when she held court. She pointed me to a leather chair across the desk from hers. Judges did this from time to time when they wanted a PO's off-the-record insights. The month before, one of the more lenient judges had called me to her chambers to let me know that even though he didn't like seeing drug addicts go to jail, he was absolutely convinced that the offender on the docket that day wouldn't survive another relapse. If I caught even a whiff of drug activity during a home inspection, I should handcuff first and ask questions later.

Sheila's judge offered me coffee, which I knew to decline, and she transitioned immediately to the topic at hand. "She's so young," the judge told me. "There's gotta be something else we can do."

I wasn't here to be helped. I was here to be helpful. My observations of the offender's behavior and environment were supposed to inform the judge's decision about what to do with the offender.

"Her mom says she's just enamored with the drug thing," I said. "It's what she knows."

"It's what she knows." The judge repeated this as if it were a fresh insight, even though we both knew it explained just about every matter on the docket that day. "When I get young people in here, I just want to tell them that there's more to life than who's running the dope racket in New Orleans. But what am I to them?"

"She knows you're serious. She knows you cut warrants for people who don't show."

"I'm the lady in the robe who cuts warrants."

I could see that I was only going to get one more crack at this. "I think the only positive reinforcement she gets right now is from guys trying to date her. Maybe if she starts getting it at work instead—"

"So we're pinning our hopes on Subway?"

Subway had hired her despite her recent felony conviction. It paid her spending money—her mother's SSI covered most of the rent—and it kept her away from marijuana for eight hours at a time. Her manager was a former offender who was making a living wage there, with benefits. The work was hardly glamorous, and some of the customers were pricks, but when you worked at Subway, you didn't have to worry about the police finding your stash, and you didn't have to worry about getting shot in a turf war.

"If you stick it out here," Sheila's manager told me, "you can put all that other stuff behind you. But that's a big fucking *if*. Most of the girls I try to take under my wing don't hang around long enough to see their first check."

I relayed this to the judge. Like me, the judge had worked her share of boring, low-paying jobs when she was young, and she had always known that she would move on to better things. College was ahead of her, and law school, and then, with a little luck and a lot of sweat, the bench. It was easy to get tired of tall ladder/short ladder metaphors in this line of work, but we kept finding our way back to them. If a frontline job at a fast-food place looked like the top rung, it was a lot harder to bide your time there than if you knew you would keep climbing.

The second time I went out to the Subway, Sheila showed me her first pay stub. She liked her boss and her coworkers. Having money of her own, money that came from her own labor and not from a boyfriend or her mother's benefit check, was just as rewarding as everyone had promised it would be. Boredom was her main complaint. Freedom from fear of arrest or loss of life or limb—the very aspect of the civilian job that was supposed to be the source of its appeal—was, for now at least, the job's biggest drawback.

Sheila missed the action of the drug trade. She was having lifestyle withdrawal. She still went to parties and was still dating an up-and-comer in one of the neighborhood gangs, but she worried that her peers didn't look at her the same way anymore. Her boyfriend said that her holding down a day job reflected poorly on him. It made him look like he wasn't a good earner, like he couldn't provide for his girl.

You want to tell young people that the things they care about now won't matter in a couple of years. They'll make new friends, meet new people, see new places, gain and lose a half dozen jobs before they're settled, but this insight, like so many others I'd hoped to bring to the job, was tied to my own experience, to class if not race, and hopelessly inapplicable. Most people on probation and parole in the Seventh Ward didn't go away to college. They rarely left the city limits for any reason. When you don't go far from home, the local ecology is the only one you care about.

On my third visit to Sheila's Subway, she didn't notice I was there until I was standing right in front of her. Staring out the window, her gaze locked on some distant coordinate, she was the picture of a young person looking at her future. I couldn't guess what she saw her five-years-from-now self wearing or what the don on her arm looked like, but I knew what street she was on, and what corner. Sheila's dreams carried her only so far. When she looked to the future, she saw the past.

# FIVE

# addicted to the lifestyle

O f the 220 offenders on my caseload, I counted only about a dozen who could pass themselves off as the dons of Sheila's imagination. They had bombshell girlfriends and high-end cars that they tried to explain away by saying they made good tips or had a big night at the casino or inherited money from a wealthy relative. They tried to see me at third-party locations, aunts' and grandmothers' houses, but if I let them know that I saw no evidence that they actually lived on the premises, they gave me the addresses of their crash pads.

The dons had families and homes but didn't want to create a law enforcement record of them, and they certainly didn't want those places searched if the PO decided today was the day he was going to drum up some reasonable suspicion. Crash pads, purchased usually for facilitating trysts and meeting associates to plan business operations, were always located in rough neighborhoods, where the don's vehicle was the only nice one on the block.

Sometimes you knew a guy was a don from the first meeting. If he showed up to the New Orleans District wearing a Rolex and $300 sneakers, he wanted you to know. We couldn't arrest people for failing to provide a feasible explanation of their source of income, and I got the impression the dons got some sport out of flaunting their wealth before the underpaid government worker ostensibly in charge of their liberty. When we asked questions about a don's lifestyle, there was a Catch-me-if-you-can aspect to the answers. Evading law enforcement was one of the thrills Sheila had described in her glowing review of the drug life, and I tried not to give the dons too much of what they were seeking.

Damien played things differently than the rest of the dons, at least in the beginning. He paroled to his brother's house, a crowded double in Hollygrove, one of the city's poorest neighborhoods. He spent his first month on parole occupying a couch.

Damien was twenty-six and built like a grain silo. He was covered in tattoos, thickets of knives and skulls and crosses and fleurs-de-lis, and *Only God Can Judge Me* in old English across his collarbone, and on his forearm *Get Money Fuck Bitches. Get Money Fuck Bitches*, or *GMFB* for short, was one of the most common tattoos in our database, and for most offenders it was purely aspirational. During that first visit, I had no reason to believe Damien had been a don before he got locked up and did a year on a possession-with-intent-to-distribute charge. He said all of the things we wanted offenders to say after a stint upstate.

"Tired of this shit," he told me. "Don't feel like running anymore."

The chase had lost its appeal. He was ready to be a civilian. He would take whatever job I could offer. Loads of criminology research have shown that a job that pays a living wage is the most effective anti-recidivism measure there is. This is one of the few points on which almost all people who study crime rates agree, but the New Orleans District had no formal mechanism in place for finding jobs for offenders who were interested in civilian work. Every few months Dan the Regional Manager got word of a temp agency that was willing to hire felons, and he printed out flyers and posted them in our lobby. Offenders who couldn't get on with a temp agency were referred to JOB1, the city's official workforce development program.

I gave Damien the name of my contact there and told him I would call ahead and get his name on the list. My contact was actually Charles's contact. Charles had brought me out to JOB1 to meet him, a fifty-something caseworker in a tattered vest who'd spent most of his adult life trying to create a more equitable job market for poor New Orleanians. Charles had warned me beforehand that the caseworker wouldn't ask my name or seek any biographical information from me. He would shake my hand and go right into material.

The civilian job market in New Orleans was tough on nearly everyone, but black workers struggled the most. Many New Orleans workers were employed in industries where promotions and pay increases were scarce. A study by the Data Center, a nonprofit that gathers economic and demographic data throughout Southeast Louisiana, found that the local tourism and hospitality industry, one of the city's largest employers, with a workforce that was about half African American, paid an average of $34,220 a year, including tipped wages.

Nearly half of black children in New Orleans live in poverty, compared to 9 percent of white children. In the metro area, income for white households has held steady since 1979 after adjusting for inflation, while African American household income has fallen 7 percent, even as it has grown elsewhere, by 5 percent nationwide. Many well-paying jobs in the oil industry, at one time a key player in the Louisiana economy, left New Orleans after oil prices plummeted in the late seventies and early eighties. In 1980, black male employment in New Orleans was at 63 percent. By 2016 it had dropped to 52 percent.

Given market conditions like these, you could understand why a poor kid in New Orleans, especially a poor black kid, would be susceptible to the allure of quick money and quick power—the allure of the drug trade. The money became an addiction unto itself, and the skills that a person acquired as he rose in the drug world weren't transferrable to most other professions. In time, many drug dealers who tried to go straight came to see themselves as uniquely unsuited to lawful employment. Chest thumping, shit talking—all the Don't-cross-me-or-else measures essential to survival in illegal enterprises like drug distribution and robbery—were deal-breakers in the civilian workforce.

"Take the instincts that have gotten you this far," the JOB1 caseworker said, and shook his fist in demonstration of how impractical he knew this guidance to be, "and do the opposite."

I took his point. "But what else can you say?"

"Nothing. It's good advice. It's the only advice I can give to someone who grew up robbing and drug dealing. But I can't be surprised when they don't know how to follow it."

Damien had nine arrests and two convictions, one for unauthorized use of a movable—auto theft—and one for possession with the intent to distribute cocaine. He kept his appointment with the caseworker, and the caseworker told him what he already knew. "With that record, it's gonna be minimum wage."

He told Damien stories of offenders with worse records who had sucked it up, started in the dish pit or the deep fryer, and worked their way out of poverty. It wasn't impossible, provided your brother would feed you and let you live rent-free. In other words, people hoping to last long enough at a minimum-wage job to get promoted to a living wage would need help. If their families couldn't provide it, the government was unlikely to fill the gap. Offenders couldn't receive housing assistance at any point during the supervision period. Offenders on supervision for drug charges couldn't collect food stamps for their first year. Damien would have to lean on family. He should be grateful that he had family to lean on. Many offenders came out of prison with all their bridges burned.

Damien was welcome to his brother's couch for as long as he needed it, but the brother couldn't afford to feed him for more than a month or so. Damien came to the New Orleans District after his stop at JOB1 to report all of this. As far as I could tell, he was as candid with me about his past as any offender I'd met.

He'd grown up in the St. Bernard neighborhood, named for the housing project that stood there before Katrina. He'd saddled up with the neighborhood gang in high school because the gang was where the money and the girls were. I was still trying to get oriented to the gang landscape and learn all the names. I'd never heard of Damien's former gang but was able to confirm its existence in the master list provided to us by the NOPD narcotics unit.

New Orleans gangs were mostly local outfits. The 3NG gang took its name from Third and Galvez Streets, where most members lived. The Young Melph Mafia was named after the defunct Melpomene housing project. The project was gone but the gang lived on.

New Orleans gang territory usually added up to no more than a couple of streets. A single neighborhood could contain three or four gangs, and when the gangs were at war, neighborhoods felt vast and important, like little empires. Many local criminologists believed gang turf wars were key contributors to New Orleans's legendary provincialism and partly explained why offenders rarely strayed far from home. If Sheila's whole world was the Seventh Ward, there were gang members who'd spent their entire lives fighting for supremacy over a few city blocks.

Whereas Bloods and Crips saw themselves as foot soldiers in armies that spanned the continent, neighborhood gang members answered to no outside rank. The lack of a clear hierarchical structure made neighborhood gangs rasher in their decision-making, and consequently more violent. In international gangs, "OGs" ("original gangsters") could be counted on to remind youngsters that the main goal was to make money and stay out of prison. Some neighborhood gangs had no members older than twenty-five. If there are fewer decision-makers between the top guy and the foot soldier, and if most of the decision-makers are teenagers, getting the needed approvals to pull a trigger doesn't take as long. Hot blood has less time to cool.

Like drug dealing, which funds most gangs' operations, gang membership flourishes in neighborhoods where other opportunities for upward mobility are scarce. Gang membership offers immediate relief from poverty, loneliness, and harassment—as useful a recruiting tool as any. If you join a gang, you can start living the good life now.

Many gangs ask prospective members to prove their worth by committing acts of violence. Usually these acts further the gang's business interests. A prospective member can be sent out to shoot or maim a rival who encroaches on the gang's drug turf.

Damien didn't tell me what he'd had to do to earn his membership, but he talked a lot about his time in jail. Parish jails like OPP were designed for pretrial detention and for holding people with sentences for misdemeanors like battery and drunk driving. Parish jails weren't meant to hold people serving felony sentences or sentences longer than six months. That job belonged to the state prisons, which were generally cleaner and safer and offered more opportunities than parish jails for offenders to get a GED, attend substance abuse counseling, and learn a trade. Louisiana had far too many people serving felony sentences for the state prisons to handle them all. More than half of felony inmates served their prison sentences in parish jails.

The only lockups that offenders disliked more than parish jails were private prisons. Two of Louisiana's eight major prisons were run by private companies, and while they were relatively small facilities compared to a giant like the Louisiana State Penitentiary—Angola— private prisons were universally regarded as dismal places to do time. No matter where an offender served his sentence or how miserable the experience, many of Damien's peers saw them the same way the middle class saw college: as a necessary proving ground.

"If you don't do any time," he said, "people look at you like you're not committed to the life. Or they figure you're diming people out. Either way, you're a bitch. People won't work with you."

Every day of your sentence, you were showing the people running the drug game back home that you were trustworthy, you didn't fear a cop or a prosecutor or a judge. When you got out, the work would be waiting. There might even be a promotion in it for you.

"What did your old bosses say when you told them you weren't coming back?" I asked.

"They don't know I'm out."

The implication was obvious. He hadn't actually decided yet whether he was returning to drug work. I asked if any of the jobs on offer at JOB1 interested him, and he told me he would think on it and let me know. I wanted to make another play to sway the contest, but I'd already done everything I knew how to do. I'd listened with interest as Damien spelled out the challenges faced by a parolee trying to work up the nerve to try civilian life. I'd sent him to JOB1. I'd shaken his hand and wished him luck, and in parting gently reminded him that if he got caught with drugs again, there wasn't going to be anything his PO could do to keep him out of prison.

Two weeks later he called from a new cell phone number and told me he'd gotten his own place in the East. The apartment was in a two-story complex on Chef Menteur Highway—commonly known as "Chef Highway"—the six-lane thoroughfare that Broad Street merged into as it made its way out to the parish line. The complex stood less than a mile from the infamous Million Dollar Corner, where, if the drug dealers of the East could be believed, more crack and heroin was moved per day than anywhere else in the city.

When I pulled in, about a quarter of the complex's residents were either smoking on the second-floor walkway or drinking in the parking lot. By the time I found a spot and got out of the Crown Vic, most of the residents had hurried inside. Three people stopped me on my way up the stairs and asked me to tell their PO that they were doing okay and living where they were supposed to be living. I wrote their names in a notepad I'd learned to carry around in my back pocket. I would document these contacts in our case management system and save three coworkers a trip.

I wasn't surprised that the place was full of offenders. There was broken glass throughout the parking lot, cars on cinder blocks, railings hanging by a single rusty nail. The complex looked like it had been set up to accommodate people who couldn't get a lease anywhere else.

At the door Damien told me the landlord have given him a good deal. The interior was clean and nicely appointed. He showed me the new bed, the new TV, the four pairs of new Jordans, the closet full of Polo.

"Where's the money coming from?" I said.

He reached into his back pocket and unfolded a pay stub from a valet service in the French Quarter. "They're good tippers down there," Damien said. "Schedule's crazy. I'm working all hours."

He was checking two boxes at once. Cash tips gave him cover for spending that could not be explained by a minimum-wage job parking cars in the French Quarter. An unpredictable work schedule would explain why Damien might not be home if I decided to show up early in the morning or late at night. I knew he was back in the drug game, but I didn't know how well he was doing or how prominent his associates must have been before he went to prison until the next time I dropped by, about four weeks after the first visit. I called when I didn't get an answer at the door, and he told me he was around the corner and would be home in a minute.

He pulled up in a silver Range Rover with a fresh coat of wax. Charles was with me that day. He wolf whistled at the car as Damien climbed out.

"Business must be good," he told Damien.

Damien laughed as he unlocked the door to the apartment. "It's used."

"Previous owner took good care of it," Charles said.

Damien offered him the keys. "Want to take it for a spin?"

Charles shook his head. "I'm liable to put a dent in it."

It wasn't exactly a confrontation. Charles was letting Damien know we knew the score, and Damien was letting Charles know he knew we knew, and he knew there wasn't anything we could do about any of it unless Damien was sloppy enough to leave dope and guns lying around his apartment, and Damien was not sloppy.

There were more high-end clothes in the closet than last time. He'd filled the place with black leather furniture and a long wooden dinner table. There was nothing incriminating in plain sight. He threw open his closets and yanked out the drawers and invited us to do our worst.

He told us the gold chain on his nightstand was fake, and the new stereo belonged to his cousin, who was crashing with him for a while. He was very slick about everything, as dons always were, but when we came to the end he couldn't resist needling us about the Range Rover. It was used, but not *that* used.

"Y'all in the market for one?" he asked, and dug around in his wallet for a business card. "I can connect you with my guy."

"What part of town do you work?" Charles said. "What's your territory?"

Damien closed the wallet and put it back in his pocket and crossed his arms slowly, but I could see in his eyes that Charles had made the right play. Damien wanted this conversation. *Sometimes they show you to the gate,* Charles had told me. *Sometimes you have to find it for yourself.*

"Y'all sent me out on some minimum-wage bullshit," Damien said with a grin. "I'm not really the burger-flipping kind."

"Drug thing hasn't been good for us," Charles said.

The *us* didn't include me, the white guy in the room.

"Speak for yourself, brother," Damien said, spreading his arms and inviting Charles to have a look at just how good the drug game could be.

"Try zooming out," Charles said. "Tell me what you see in the East."

Damien shrugged. "All I know is, it's fair. You hustle, you get paid. I don't see any of that at the fucking burger joint."

They went back and forth a few more times, neither of them raising his voice, and neither of them budging from his position. We all parted on friendly terms, and Damien promised to be at the office first thing next month with a fresh pay stub from the valet service.

In the CrownVic, Charles said that the racial solidarity angle sometimes got offenders thinking about the costs of the drug trade, not only
addiction and overdosing but the mass incarceration of the young men
whom dons like Damien were putting on street corners with pockets
full of dope. For the first time Charles told me that he, like many of the
young men he'd grown up with, had given the drug game more than
a passing glance when he was young. He'd wanted the money and the
girls that followed the dealers around. More than that, he wanted to
work in a meritocracy.

This, Charles believed, was the most underreported aspect of the
drug trade's allure. Race and upbringing didn't factor in. The people
who got ahead were the people who were the most ruthless, the most
ambitious. And the spoils spoke for themselves. As a young man Charles
had been won over by the example of the civil rights movement, in
particular the refusal to compromise for personal gain. It was no good
to get yourself rich if in the process you helped hundreds of other
young black men ruin their lives. Charles didn't want to be the first
person to get a teenager high. He wanted to be the first person to help
him get clean.

Like everyone else at the New Orleans District, he'd had to power
through his initial disappointment at how few resources the state gave
him to do his job, especially compared to the vast sums it spent on its
prisons. By now he was past all that. This was year fifteen for him. He
was fully dug in. He'd made his choice about life and legacy, and that
choice entitled him to look squarely at men like Damien and ask them
to consider the possibility that they were on the wrong side of history,
a drag on the progress of the race.

He got angry with the dons sometimes, but in the end he was always able to look back on the young person each of them must have
been when he made his choice, or the first in a series of choices. Charles
wondered whether a less energetic set of middle school teachers, who
weren't quite as committed to illustrating the heroics of the black lead-
ers of the fifties and sixties, might have left his ten-year-old self with
a different sensibility about race and a diminished sense of shared responsibility to make the nation freer and fairer for the next generation.
Charles wanted to live in a country where it was just as crazy for a

young black guy to become a drug dealer as a young white guy, and he hoped I could agree that we weren't there yet.

I'd been out of the academy about six months by then, and I considered my office mate a mentor and a friend, but even among friends, the first frank discussion of race is always touch-and-go. All I could think to say about my own record on the matter was that I'd always thought I wanted a more equal nation but had never wanted it badly enough to put anything on the line. Signing up to be a PO was supposed to be a step in the right direction, and Charles encouraged me to be as sentimental as I wanted about the work.

"I mean, why else do this?" he said with a laugh. "It sure as fuck isn't the money."

And as had so often been the case in my life, I was aware of having gotten off easy, and of wanting to do right by the privilege. I thought of Damien every time I looked back on that conversation over the next two weeks, and I was surprised when he failed to show as promised on the first office day of the month. I found myself down the road from his place on Chef Highway later in the week and decided to stop in on him.

He answered the door in boxer shorts. He looked like he'd gained fifteen pounds since I'd last seen him. Most of it was in his belly, folded over his waistband, and the rings of flesh beneath his eyes. He didn't get out of the doorway but I could see that his furniture and stereo were gone. He was sleeping on an air mattress just inside the front door, presumably to give him the easiest possible access to the peephole.

"What's going on?" I said.

He thought for a moment. There were any number of excuses, but he'd already been candid about his source of income. "Let's say I got overextended," he said.

"Do you need to get out of town?"

He shook his head and tried to find the easy smile that said that he was a don and dons always had a plan. "I'm not gonna pass a drug test," he said.

Here was another warning sign. Dons never, or almost never, used their own product.

"That's okay," I said. "You're not due for a test this month. Do you need detox?"

He shook his head. "Give me till next month. I'll be back on my feet."

Time was all that I could offer him, and I told him he could have as much as he needed.

"Sure it wouldn't be better to lie low for a little while?" I said.

"I know what I'm doing." He tried again to find the smile and failed again and took a step back inside, my cue to move on.

"You've got my number if you change your mind," I said.

He pulled the door shut before I could turn around. I checked the parking lot for the Range Rover but couldn't find it.

Beth had a contact at the police district in the East. The contact had several reliable sources who kept him apprised of the latest power shifts in the drug trade. They would try to let him know if they heard anything about Damien, but drug murders usually happened too quickly for a source to get a potential shooter's name to police.

The police were lucky if they got a name after the fact. Arrest rates for murders in New Orleans hovered at around 40 percent. The NOPD homicide unit was, like much of the criminal justice system in New Orleans, staffed at half the levels the Department of Justice recommended. Witnesses never seemed to want to come forward to report what they knew. Some witnesses feared retaliation from drug dealers. Some feared the police.

The cop in the East said he would make sure a squad car passed through Damien's parking lot at least once per shift. The police district deployed plenty of manpower in that area anyway, due to its proximity to the Million Dollar Corner. POs were always in and out of the complex, but I guessed that a killer determined to do his job wouldn't be deterred by the presence of a couple of Crown Vics.

In a month's time the drug trade had provided Damien with food, clothing, shelter, and transportation. If I'd run him through the department's risk assessment at the end of that first month, his "need" score would have been zero. Another month and the drug trade had placed him in circumstances almost too dire to imagine, alone behind a peephole, waiting for a gunman to appear.

# SIX

# homebody

A month after Damien bottomed out, I was able to confirm that he was still alive. I had no idea how he was paying his rent or keeping himself fed. He looked heavier and more exhausted than he'd looked four weeks prior, and he wouldn't tell me anything new about his situation except that he'd been here before and knew how to handle it. I didn't take very much comfort in that.

For my first six months on the job I'd tried my best to abide by Charles's rule about keeping work matters at work. Kristin's technique when I lapsed into complaining about what the people on my case-load were up against was to remind me that I'd resolved to work on the micro level and to leave the macro stuff to the people in the capitol in Baton Rouge. I was free to vent about living conditions at the jail if I liked, but there was absolutely nothing a PO could do to speed up construction of the new OPP, much less to find funding for a detox facility that would mean fewer OPP visits altogether.

"Remember disaster prevention?" she always said in conclusion, and I always said that I did remember, I never really forgot, but it was nice to hear the words from another person, and then a couple of weeks would go by and I would lose my perspective again and return to her for another reminder.

We were in bed on a Sunday, getting ready to turn off the TV for the night, when I turned to Kristin and told her I couldn't get the image of Damien and the peephole out of my head. "If we'd had something to offer this guy," I said, "I think he wouldn't have gone back to the drug thing. I think he thought about going straight."

Her eyes told me I was talking again about things I couldn't control, but her voice was patient. "Who sees your notes? Where does the record of all this go?"

"On a server, I guess."

"They must pull reports or something."

"They run the numbers. That only tells you who went back to jail and who didn't. They need to read the fucking case notes."

It was a ridiculous thing to say. There were 7,000 offenders in New Orleans alone, and nearly 70,000 statewide. If there wasn't money for detox in the most violent and addicted city in the state, there wasn't money for a roomful of headquarters people to sift through thousands of pages of case notes. I riffed some more on the absurdity of having no need-remediation services on hand when your official, department-generated assessment tool viewed risk as a function of need. Kristin had heard all of this before, and she nodded along as I found my own way to the advice I normally called on her to supply.

"Anyway," I said, "above my pay grade."

"It's good that it still pisses you off," she said. "Most people probably just go numb after a while."

It was true that most of the POs putting in the longest hours were in their first five to seven years on the job. There were exceptions. A guy who'd started a year before me was one of the biggest slouches in the office, while a twenty-three-year veteran conducted more home inspections per month than anyone else at the New Orleans District. Most POs reported ebbs and flows of faith, but on the whole, my coworkers were remarkable in their determination to prevent disasters. Time on the job seemed to improve a PO's capacity to bounce back from a failure-to-prevent incident, but bouncing back wasn't the same as going numb, a lesson I would learn a week later when I got my first overdose death. Beth said I was extremely fortunate to have lasted so long without one.

The offender was a medium-risk guy whom I'd drug tested and sent to JOB1. He'd been clean for two months and had taken a fast-food job and showed me his first pay stub. He lived with his father, a warm, gray-headed man with a Section 8 voucher and a job cutting lawns in Hollygrove. If asked to rank the offenders I considered at greatest risk of overdose, I wouldn't have put him on the list.

His father had always been friendly with me, but when he found his son's dead body in his backyard, he demanded accountability from the probation and parole department. He told me that keeping the people under my care alive was the very least I could do. Beth was with me that day, and she let me handle the encounter as I saw fit. I couldn't think of anything better to do than stand there and let the offender's father say what needed saying.

"I'm sorry" was my only reply. I just kept saying it, and the offender's father kept telling me where I could put my apologies. After the fifth or sixth cycle, Beth gave me a nudge, and I told the father we had to go.

Back in the Crown Vic, Beth told me I'd done well. "Played it the only way you can," she said.

When an offender overdosed, accepting blame from his friends and family was the best service we could render. If we couldn't prevent the disaster, we could give the survivors an institution to hold accountable. We, in turn, once we were clear of the place and free to vent to one another, could push the blame up the institutional ladder. The bosses couldn't say we weren't sounding the alarm. We did the office visits, inspected the homes, wrote up the case notes informing the powers that be of what we were seeing out here in the field.

We raised hell once a quarter when Dan the Regional Manager sat us down in the conference room for an all-hands meeting and gave what passed for a pep talk at the New Orleans District. Because his desk was located there in the district, Dan the Regional Manager was more *one of us* than *one of the bosses*, but he spoke to the bosses on a regular basis, and so we believed we were within our rights to let him have it. We had more people on our caseloads than ever, and fewer POs, and overdoses were on the rise, and offenders lacked the resources or the know-how to make any substantive changes.

We could see that he was doing for us what we did for the families of deceased offenders: taking the blame for a broken system. He said that, absent new funding and a new mind-set from our bosses, our wins would have to come through grit and energy alone. He looked out on the room and saw plenty of that. He'd given the speech dozens of times and was good at it, and most of us were appeased. A few people weren't. A couple of them had conspiracy theories to share. The most widely held conspiracy theory was that headquarters wasn't really interested in seeing the New Orleans District succeed. Headquarters believed that the thinner they spread us, the less we would see of offenders. And the less we saw of offenders, the fewer of them we would take to jail.

In other words, the bosses weren't trying to fix problems. They were looking the other way. Meanwhile, offenders were going back to old habits and ending up back in jail whether the bosses liked it or not, and costing five to ten times more taxpayer money than it would have cost to help them in the first place.

In addition to the deceased offender, I ticked off a few other milestones around that time. I got my first two revocations. Both offenders had committed armed robberies while on probation. Firearms-related offenses were almost always guaranteed revocations, and as far as I could see, my recommendations that the offenders be sent back to jail had no bearing on the judges' decisions. The judges' minds were made when they read the police reports.

Both offenders had low risk ratings. I'd seen them only once and knew little about them. They both lived in crowded homes with families who fed them and provided for their basic needs—hence the low risk scores—but they were young and grew up in Hollygrove and Central City, respectively, and I was left to assume that they were seeking through robbery what other young men in those neighborhoods sought through the drug trade: a way up if not out.

When I decided on a corrective action to recommend, I reminded myself that if they'd been born in another neighborhood, these men might not have felt compelled to commit armed robberies. But there came a point when my duty to the general public—to the friends and neighbors who were likely to come into contact with the offender and his firearm—exceeded my duty to understand the need that had brought a man to this, which is just to say that when I thought about armed robbery and, increasingly, about all serious crime, I didn't think about what was right or fair so much as what was practical. If we couldn't address the needs that drove the armed robbers to violence, then the only way to stop them from harming other people was to take them out of circulation for a while, at great cost to both the armed robbers and the taxpayers.

I was more convinced than ever that need was the source of the trouble in most offenders' lives, and the true enemy of change, and I was fascinated by the moral decision-making of the very needy. Some offenders told me they believed it was okay to steal from a store, which was insured against loss, but not from a person, who probably had no insurance. Some said it was okay to shoplift or steal but not to sell drugs. Others said it was okay to shoplift, steal, and sell drugs, but not to use or threaten violence in the pursuit of money. Poor people had to make these calculations every day. Most days, most poor people, even the ones on probation and parole, chose to uphold the law.

About once every two weeks I found myself at Tulane and Broad asking a judge to give a lawbreaker another chance. Most of the probationers whose side I took had been arrested for minor offenses like marijuana possession, shoplifting, driving while intoxicated, or low-grade assault and battery. All of the judges in Orleans Parish could be convinced to cut offenders loose on misdemeanors. Judges never asked why I wanted an offender released or what I hoped to do differently with him this time around.

I guessed they knew the answer. I didn't have a plan. I was asking for the offender's release because I didn't believe that the offense in question presented enough of a threat to justify the cost of incarceration.

Later that month, I appeared in court on behalf of Ronald Landry. As far as I knew, Ronald was the only offender on my caseload who had been let out of jail with a pending gun charge. My predecessor had failed to show for the hearing after Ronald got arrested, and the combination of a lenient judge, an aggressive public defender, and an assistant district attorney who considered Ronald a worthy use of his powers of discretion had come together to set Ronald free.

One of the conditions of Ronald's release was that he use his freedom wisely, first by getting a job. Because the previous PO hadn't shown up to the hearing and filled in the judge on Ronald's limitations, and because public defender caseloads were such that few public defenders knew anything about their clients apart from the nature of the offense they'd been charged with, there was no one on hand during the previous hearing to make the case that a job wasn't in the cards.

When I had an offender on the docket, I walked up to the prosecution table and told the assistant district attorney that I would like to be heard whenever the judge had an opening. Judges knew that POs had enormous workloads. Most of them tried to get us out of the building as quickly as possible. Tulane and Broad courtrooms, which had once struck me as among the most chaotic places I'd ever seen, had evolved certain efficiencies over time. Moving probation cases quickly was one of the things the courthouse did best.

POs submitted all their paperwork through the district attorney's office. Assistant district attorneys were judged by their ability to win convictions. Probation and parole were post-conviction matters, and ADAs had no incentive to pay much attention to them. Most of the time, ADAs adopted a blanket position of agreeing with whatever the PO recommended to the judge. Public defenders, for their part, always wanted to get their clients out of jail.

A PO arguing for a release rarely encountered any resistance. I told the ADA, I told the public defender, and when the judge called us up for a sidebar, we said we were in agreement about what needed to be done. Ronald had the most lenient judge in the building, but I could see in the judge's eyes as we made our way to the bench that Ronald's case made him uneasy. The judge wasn't sure he'd done the right thing by letting Ronald out on a gun charge. He tapped his fingers against the wooden bar and chewed at the side of his lip as he considered what I had to say.

"He's having seizures five and six times a week, Your Honor. I don't think he can hold down a job."

"He's not on meds?" the judge said.

"They don't help," I said. "Or they don't help enough."

The judge chewed some more and did some more tapping. "Crap. I didn't know that."

"Me neither," said the public defender.

"Me neither," said the ADA.

It was a point made every day in that building, but it always bore repeating. Overcrowded dockets ensured that the people deciding what to do about all these human lives didn't know very much about them.

For all its limitations, the probation and parole department was the only arm of the criminal justice system that developed a personal relationship with the offender. Ideally, the personal relationship allowed the PO to guide the decision-makers—judge, assistant district attorney, public defender—to fairer and more practical decisions. It made the system a little more just.

"Okay," the judge said. "He doesn't have to work. But he has to stay clean and he has to keep a curfew. I'm out on a limb on this gun thing. I want you at the house every week keeping tabs. And I want him back here once a month so I can look him in the eye."

I agreed to the judge's terms. The judge called Ronald up to the microphone at the front of the courtroom and told him what was expected of him. Ronald replied with the customary "Yes, Your Honor," and another thirty days of freedom were secure.

The gun charge was looking more and more likely to be resolved without a prison sentence. The district attorney, who normally sought the maximum penalty on all firearms offenses, had been won over by the testimony of the gun's lawful owner and Ronald's codefendant's willingness to plead to a misdemeanor and do community service. Taken together, the news at the courthouse was as good as we could have hoped. I gave the Landrys' mother the latest when I checked in on them at their home later in the week. She was dressed in scrubs when I showed up and getting ready to head off to the doctor's office where she answered phones.

She'd been working full-time since she got out of high school and had often held down two jobs at once to pay the rent and support her sons. "When they're young," she told me, "you either stay home and starve with them, or you go to work and make sure they're fed."

There was a downside to the path she'd chosen. The boys came home from school to an empty house. They spent their afternoons wandering the streets of Central City. They got to know drug dealers and gang members with nice cars and nice clothes and good-looking women.

"When I was at work," the Landrys' mother told me, "the streets were raising my boys."

The Landry brothers moved as a unit, to the extent they could, given Ronald's poor health. The seizures kept him indoors on many of the hot summer nights when Central City was at its most violent. According to the Landrys' mother, Ronald's disability may have been the only thing that prevented him from racking up as many arrests and convictions as his brother. Javaron was thirty years old, and he'd been thrown in OPP more than twenty-five times since he turned eighteen.

After a certain number of felony arrests, the state police added a row of asterisks to the top of an offender's rap sheet accompanied by the headline "POSSIBLE CAREER CRIMINAL." Javaron had earned his asterisks in his early twenties. The Landrys' mother wasn't sure which of the neighborhood crews the boys belonged to. There were so many in Central City, always battling each other for the right to serve the neighborhood's crack addicts.

Wedged between the Central Business District, home of the Superdome and the skyscrapers that held most of New Orleans's highest-paid jobs, and the Garden District, where many of the city's top earners made their homes, Central City was a socioeconomic island. New Orleans's neighborhood boundaries are subject to debate—technically the Garden District and the Lower Garden District are separate entities— but it's enough to know that throughout the city the line where the rich people end and the poor people begin is apparent to the naked eye. Central City had more offenders per square foot than any other neighborhood. The Garden District had the fewest.

New Orleanians were so inured to the proximity of the poor to the rich that few of them gave it much thought. "They don't give a fuck about us," the Landrys' mother told me, "and we don't give a fuck about them."

Like their counterparts in the Seventh and Ninth Wards, most Central City offenders had never left New Orleans and had very rarely ventured outside their own neighborhoods. That wealth was more evenly distributed in some other American cities probably would have come as a shock to them, although if recent trends were any indication, the New Orleans model of income inequality was more likely to be the future of the American city than the past. Anyone who watched the national news knew that the rich had seen most of the recent economic gains, while the poor were no better off.

Very few offenders watched the national news, even though most of them spent most of their days in front of the TV. By now I had a good sense of offenders' television habits. If they watched the news, they watched local only. If they talked to their POs about politics, they talked about the sheriff or the mayor or the city council or the sewerage and water board. No one cared about the U.S. Senate or the president. Offenders didn't believe national elections had any impact on their lives.

Of course, there were people who felt this way in every socio-economic bracket, but the dangers of a strictly local perspective were especially acute among people in America's poorest and most violent neighborhoods. The more local your perspective, the more neighborhood dynamics mattered. If the neighborhood was run by drug dealers and armed robbers, you were more likely to consider a career in drug dealing and armed robbery.

When they weren't watching the local news, most offenders watched cop shows. During one home inspection when I brought Beth along, we walked in on the Landrys glued to the last five minutes of *CSI*. "So," Beth asked, "who are you pulling for?"

Both brothers fell over laughing. The Landrys always got a kick out of Beth. When they caught their breath, they said they always rooted for the cops, and they explained why. In TV shows, the bad guys were motivated by obvious malice. They stole because they were greedy. They killed because they didn't value life. The people who broke the law in New Orleans—that is, people like the Landrys—didn't see themselves that way. They broke the law out of necessity. Gang violence was written off in much the same way mob violence was written off in the movies: a means of settling scores among people who couldn't appeal to the criminal justice system for relief.

The cops on most TV shows were depicted as consistently righteous. They never used excessive force. They always read the Miranda warning. If they couldn't make the case by the book, they didn't bother making it at all. On TV, anyone with any sense could separate the good guys from the bad.

The three pit bulls piled atop the brothers' laps seemed as taken with the storyline as Javaron and Ronald. The female had just had a litter. The puppies chirped softly from inside a big cardboard box on the other side of the room. When the credits rolled, Javaron got up and went over to the box and turned the puppies over one by one. "I've got thousand-dollar dogs in here," he said. "No runts in this litter."

Javaron claimed the dogs were his only source of income. He didn't receive any government benefits. I'd sent him to JOB1, but he hadn't pretended to be interested in any of the jobs the caseworker had put him in for. Given his extensive criminal record, cashiering and back-of-house restaurant work was all he could hope to get.

"Can't get hired to do anything good," Javaron said. "Not gonna break my back for slave wages. Rather sit here and starve."

"Your brother would kill to have that choice," Beth said.

She always smirked when she needled, so that her remarks played more like teasing than dressing down. In general, the longer the criminal record, the more the offender seemed to appreciate Beth's confrontational method of supervision. Javaron was no exception. He grinned and jerked his chin at Ronald, still seated on the couch beneath the mountain of dogs. "Him? That's the laziest motherfucker I've ever met in my life."

Ronald pulled a middle finger out from beneath a dog and waved it at Javaron. "It's called a disability, bitch."

"Laziness?" Javaron said. "I don't think so. Never heard of anybody getting a check for that."

Javaron and Ronald spent most of their waking hours together and must have grated on each other's nerves from time to time, but when I was around, they maintained a playful give-and-take. I didn't take Javaron's remark about starving literally. There was always food in the refrigerator, the floors were swept, and the beds were made. The Landrys' mother had always provided for her sons, and she always would. She told me so every time I saw her. Unlike many offenders' parents, she didn't ask me to get her boys out of the house or strong-arm them into the job market. She was happy to have them home, on her couch, in front of her TV, and it wasn't hard to see why.

Javaron had been involved in the drug trade in Central City since he was a teenager. Fourteen years carrying a gun and selling dope, and he wasn't dead and wasn't in prison. His mother felt he'd beaten the odds. If providing him with clothes and a roof and a hot meal every night kept him from tempting fate on the streets, she was happy to pay the price. She would work a third job if she had to—whatever it took to keep Javaron retired: a homebody.

Unlike Damien, Javaron denied his entire criminal record when I asked him about it. I would never know whether age alone or some more malign force had pushed him out of the drug business. If he wouldn't admit to having been a dealer or an enforcer, I couldn't ask whether he missed it—which was a shame, because it seemed to me that Javaron contained the answers to a number of important questions. Had he been "addicted to the lifestyle," and if so, how had he broken free of the addiction? What kind of residue did fourteen years of the drug life leave behind? Was basic subsistence of the sort his mother provided enough to get most dealers off the streets? Javaron's mother had always been willing to take care of Javaron's basic needs, but the current parole period was the first one in which he seemed to take her up on the offer.

Because the judge had me stopping by the Landry residence on a near-weekly basis, I felt I knew the brothers' habits as well as anyone's on my caseload. They spent most of every day in front of the TV. Now and then they went out in their little yard with the dogs. Sometimes when I showed up, Javaron was on the floor with the female, rubbing her belly or whispering praise into her ears. When she lay on her back her enormous mouth fell open in a smile.

Javaron had a neck as thick as a whiskey barrel and not a touch of flab about him, and when you compared his body to his brother's, those afternoons spent lying on the couch looked like a tremendous waste of talent. When you compared Javaron to Damien, to the vagaries of the drug trade, you saw what Javaron's mother saw. It was better to waste your talent than to lose your life. By providing her boys an incentive to stay indoors, Javaron's mother was practicing her own form of disaster prevention.

The only thing she asked of me was that I lend a hand in Ronald's ongoing fight for disability benefits. I called the SSI office, as I'd done for Kendrick and a half dozen other offenders, and I got the usual response. If Ronald wanted SSI, a doctor had to say he couldn't work. Unlike Kendrick, Ronald had managed to get on Medicaid and, with his mother's assistance, to stay in the program's good graces, but he hadn't been able to convince any of his doctors that his epilepsy was severe enough to keep him out of the job market. The doctors, for their part, saw a man in his twenties who, if they kept adjusting the medication until they got it right, could do more with his life than sit on the couch watching cop show reruns. "They think getting a check is like you're giving up," Ronald said.

Ronald was due at the office the following Monday for his court-ordered drug test. He had a seizure while he waited in the lobby for me to finish up with another offender. His head knocked against the side of one of the folding chairs, and he bit down so hard on his tongue that he was choking on his own blood when the PO in the fingerprint room rushed into the lobby to see what was going on. The second PO who came to help had been a field medic in the Navy. He rendered what aid he could while Dan the Regional Manager waited outside for the ambulance.

I went back to the Landry house two days later to check on Ronald. He had a thick knot where his forehead had hit the chair. He stuck out his tongue so that I could see the tooth marks. He'd nearly bitten the thing in half.

"Jesus," I said.

Both Landrys laughed.

"Tongues are tough," Ronald said. "They can take a fucking lick."

With that, the Landrys and the dogs took their places on the couch and told me they would see me next week. "You know where to find us," Javaron said.

Those first months checking in on the Landrys, I almost always walked out of the house convinced that, relative to the rest of my caseload, the brothers were doing all right, which is to say that their needs appeared to be met. The Landry home was one of hundreds that made the case for a city where able-bodied teenagers didn't look to the drug trade for sustenance, but the brothers had come out of the most statistically hazardous years of their lives alive and unincarcerated.

As Javaron said, I knew where to find them. They weren't crouching behind peepholes. They weren't looking longingly through windows at the action they were missing in the drug trade. *Inertia, wasted talent,* or whatever other terms I might apply to the scene of the two brothers on the couch were tragic in their own right, but I didn't think they compared to hunger or addiction.

# institutionalized

An elevated highway served as an informal border between Central City on the west and the Central Business District on the east—or, if you preferred, between one of the poorest and most dangerous parts of town and one of the most prosperous. The other key landmark on the Central City–CBD border was the New Orleans Mission. From the street the building looked like a warehouse. EVERYONE DESERVES A PLACE TO CALL HOME was printed in faded letters across the outside wall.

Homeless offenders were the hardest ones to keep track of. In the morning, most of the homeless left the mission and decamped with friends throughout the city. Some went to the shantytown under the overpass. Known as Under the Bridge, the shantytown comprised several colonies of homeless. The most populous colony pitched its tents at the intersection of Calliope Street and Oretha Castle Haley Boulevard, two blocks east of the mission.

According to Volunteers of America, at least 10 percent of parolees are homeless upon their release from prison. At the New Orleans District we considered this a low estimate. Many offenders paroled to a friend's or family member's address only to arrive at the door and discover that the place was boarded up or, worse, that they were no longer welcome with the people living there. Internal accounting puts the "true homeless" population—the people who lived on the streets or in the shelters—at closer to 15 percent. Another 20 percent couch-surfed and were willing to spend a night or two in a shelter if the couch's owner put them out.

The longest-tenured mission resident on my caseload had been called Hard Head since the eighth grade, and he preferred that his PO address him as such. He was a sixty-five-year-old white guy from a small town in Mississippi, but his childhood had followed the same course as most New Orleans offenders'. His father wasn't around. His mother worked double shifts. When stress got to her, she went to the bottle.

At school, Hard Head cut up for attention. Teachers saw potential but could never bring it out. He developed a taste for fighting— schoolyard stuff, mostly. By eleventh grade he was sneaking into bars, taking runs at older guys. Somebody suggested he turn his aggression on America's enemies overseas. He got out of the Army in four years on a less-than-favorable discharge.

"Not dishonorable," he told me. "The one right above that. Where you still get some benefits."

He showed up in New Orleans in the seventies looking to get high. He did so for forty years, pausing only for state-imposed intermissions upstate. He still had his fighter's build, forearms tapered like a couple of ham bones and a long, clean jaw. He had false teeth and long gray hair gathered in a rubber-banded knot. Hypodermic scars ran from the crease of his elbow to the base of his biceps. "Feet got the worst of the heroin days," he told me, in response to my questions about his substance-abuse history during our first office visit. He propped a muddy boot at the edge of my desk and offered to show me the needle marks.

"I'll take your word for it," I said.

Many over-fifty offenders thought that if they told a sob story I would leave them alone. They knew I knew that young guys sold most of the dope and did most of the shooting. Hard Head had six convictions and five parole revocations. Two days after our office visit, he got arrested in the French Quarter for being drunk, sleeping on the sidewalk, and, after a search incident to arrest, being in possession of a "nickel bag," a very small amount of marijuana.

I sent notice to the parole board that I was letting him out of jail, and I faxed the release forms to the clerical room at OPP. As soon as he got out, Hard Head borrowed another homeless guy's phone and called to thank me and tell me he was heading back to the mission. I met him outside on the sidewalk. I could see that he wasn't happy to be back, and as I'd done many times before, I stood there and let the offender air his grievances. Most of what he told me I'd heard before. The living quarters at the mission smelled of bodily fluids doused in bleach. Mental illness, mostly untreated, lay down alongside addiction, venereal disease, and people who just couldn't get along with anybody anywhere else.

In the daytime, the mission functioned mainly as a big slapdash church. Testimonials were shouted across a congregation hall. Residents promised that yesterday's relapse would be the last.

Nighttime at the mission was another matter. The rats came out first, then the thieves. It wasn't uncommon for a mission resident to wake in the morning and discover he'd been relieved of all but the shirt on his back.

New Orleans District POs could expect about 5 to 10 percent of their caseloads to list the mission as a permanent address—in other words, as the only housing they ever intended to get. There were two other shelters in town. Offenders who got "missioned out" drifted downtown to the Ozanam Inn or uptown to the Salvation Army. Both facilities were cleaner than the mission. Reports of assault and robbery were less common. Consequently, demand was high. Vouchers at "the Oz" were good for only a couple of weeks at a time. Vouchers at "the Army" lasted longer, but the Army expected a ten-dollar donation and ran by far the tightest ship of the bunch. Homeless probationers and parolees were experts at getting put out of the Army.

The main incentive to staying at the mission was increasing your chances of coming into contact with an organization called Unity of Greater New Orleans. Unity occasionally managed to get a homeless offender a yearlong rental voucher. The vouchers could be extended as long as the homeless offender made reasonable efforts to maintain his quarters. Like most social service providers in town, Unity was bound by its meager budget to offer its assistance to only the neediest of the needy. Unity couldn't be walked in and appealed to. The only way for an offender to get on the list was for a Unity caseworker to come across him in her daily canvass of the shelters and Under the Bridge.

Trying to look shabby enough to catch the eye of a Unity case-worker was a competitive business. Offenders had gone as far as pissing their pants and rending their garments. Only one offender on Charles's caseload—compared to zero of mine—had landed a Unity voucher. Every time I tried calling Unity to make a case for someone, the woman who answered the phone gave me the same explanation of the Unity standard. "I know it when I see it."

Hard Head believed that the people Under the Bridge had a better chance of catching Unity's eye than the people at the mission. The Unity people wouldn't cop to this, and I told Hard Head I believed he was better off at the mission, but I couldn't tell him where to live. When he said he'd agreed to "bunk" with another veteran he'd met at a Narcotics Anonymous meeting, I changed his address in our case management system from "New Orleans Mission" to "None."

The tents Under the Bridge changed locations frequently. The only way I could hope to keep track of Hard Head while he was living there was to call him on the complimentary cell phone that would be coming to him by the end of the week. "Government phones," as they were known, were distributed out of little white tents that showed up overnight at the city's busiest intersections. When the supply ran out, you waited for the next tent to show, sometimes a week later, sometimes not for a couple of months. The phones were supposed to last a year, but they were made of spare parts. The homeless at the shelters and Under the Bridge were always stealing them from each other or getting high and rolling over on them and shattering their screens in their sleep.

The phone came with only two hundred minutes per month, but Hard Head assured me that he had no real friends to speak of and would have no trouble rationing out his phone calls so that his PO could get hold of him in a pinch. Until Hard Head's phone arrived, I should feel free to call his tentmate's.

His tentmate was in his early twenties. He had a patchy beard speckled with premature gray and a permanent film like baking soda around the edges of his lips. Like many veterans living on the streets, he'd sustained an injury during his deployment, been prescribed opioids for pain, and graduated to heroin once the prescription ran out. Most of the homeless veterans had deployed to Iraq or Afghanistan.

Hard Head was one of the few who'd caught the last breaths of Vietnam. The younger veterans who still had their looks and hadn't lost any limbs could usually find a woman to shack up with after a while.

"All us vets Under the Bridge," Hard Head told me, "were fucked-up long before the Army."

"Well," Hard Head's tentmate said, "Army probably didn't help."

Hard Head couldn't disagree with that. He estimated there were another fifteen or twenty veterans within a hundred yards of his tent. Most of the people living Under the Bridge scattered or zipped up their tents when I passed through. Drugs moved freely up and down the narrow footpath between encampments. Trash cans overflowed with empty fifths of gas station vodka.

Hard Head passed his first drug test but didn't disguise his drinking. They were working on it at the VA. He liked his counselor there. The young veterans laughed when he told them that the VA used to be much worse. Since the Walter Reed scandal, there had been political pressure to render adequate care. Hard Head believed that the same government that let him down in Vietnam was committed now to finding him a cure.

"Like I said," he told me, "I was gonna be somebody's problem no matter what. Army took me. Army's stuck holding the bag."

Saying he'd been destined for squalor since birth was usually an offender's way of saying that the PO could save his breath, but Hard Head had unconventional ideas about fate. If he believed he was genetically predisposed to becoming an addict and a homeless person, he also believed that the turnaround could touch down at any time if he kept himself open to it.

"If my life's proof of anything," he said, "it's that you never know what's coming."

The risk/need assessment gave Hard Head its highest possible rating. He appeared to own only two shirts and one pair of pants. Apart from friendship, Hard Head had nothing to offer his tentmate. His drug conviction disqualified him from receiving food stamps for the next eleven months. The tentmate had no convictions but traded his food stamps for dope as soon as the first-of-the-month balance appeared on the card. He and Hard Head ate most of their meals at soup kitchens.

Their only source of income was "flying the sign" on street corners throughout the CBD.

The police department was so undermanned that very few cops could be bothered to enforce panhandling regulations. Other panhandlers were the biggest check on Hard Head's revenue stream. Prime real estate was fiercely defended. A panhandler who thought you were encroaching could whisper in your ear that he knew where you slept at night. If you slept in a tent or on a bedroll under an overpass, protecting yourself from retaliation wasn't as simple as bolting the door. You could carry a knife or gun, but other people would find out that you had one and try to steal it from you. Or, if you were especially unlucky, the day you carried would be the day a cop thought you looked like the suspect he'd been canvassing Central City for, and you would get patted down and taken to jail on a felon-in-possession-of-a-firearm charge.

It was better to cede the plum panhandling territory and move farther out to the unshaded corners where the stoplights were shorter and the people passing through had less middle- or upper-class guilt to offset with a handout. Even there, begging beat sitting all day in your tent. If you could stand the heat, you could walk away with anywhere from fifteen to twenty-five dollars in a twelve-hour shift, enough for a couple of fast-food dinners and a forty-ounce bottle of Olde English 800, Hard Head's beverage of choice.

The third time I called Hard Head to arrange a meeting, he was on the corner midway through a begging shift. He had a good spot and didn't want to give it up, so I told him I would meet him there. I pulled the Crown Vic onto the curb and rolled down the window. Hard Head was holding a scrap of cardboard with HOMELESS VET written in black marker. At his feet were an empty water bottle and a white paper bag from McDonald's. When he saw me, he set his sign on the ground and picked up the McDonald's bag and hurried over.

"Mind if I eat?" he said. "Paid a buddy to grab me lunch."

I got out of the Crown Vic and leaned on the bumper. Hard Head put the McDonald's bag on the hood and pulled a large soda and a couple of ninety-nine-cent hamburgers out of it. The hood was scalding but Hard Head didn't seem to notice. A patchwork of scars had turned his elbows as white as chalk.

"Haven't had a drink in three days," he told me. "Junk food's the only vice I've got left."

I reminded him he was due for a drug test.

He took another bite and chewed slowly as he counted back from his last drug use. "How about Friday?"

"What did you use?"

"Crack."

"Sure you don't need detox?"

"No way. It was one hit. Buddy from the tents offered. Weak sauce. Head was clear an hour later."

He finished the first hamburger and rolled the wrapper into a little ball and put it back inside the bag. He took a big sip of his soda and let out a satisfied belch and unfolded the second wrapper, and he looked down at the little hamburger as if it were a brick of gold. "Life is good sometimes," he said.

I'd seen offender resiliency and adaptability take many forms, but none of them rattled my nerve center quite like the sights and sounds of the old man delighting in his $3 lunch. I, too, had adapted. I was past standing around, wondering what to do. I knew exactly what relief I could offer Hard Head: an extension until Monday for his drug test.

He didn't show. On Tuesday I rapped at the threadbare nylon hood of his tent. I smelled the booze sweat before Hard Head unzipped the tent and stumbled out into daylight. Behind him his tentmate snored atop a pile of beach towels.

"Guess it's gonna have to be detox after all," he said.

On the ride to jail he told me what had happened. He got robbed of his panhandling money two nights before. His tentmate was supposed to be keeping an eye on it while Hard Head was out for a walk, but the tentmate got too high and lost track of who was coming and going through the tent. When another guy Under the Bridge heard what happened, he offered Hard Head a bump. Hard Head figured the high would take the edge off and keep him from getting too angry with his tentmate. The hit was good, and the next day Hard Head made forty bucks flying the sign. He gave ten of it to the guy who gave him the bump, five to cover the day before and another five for one more.

He said he wanted to go to the Odyssey House sober-living facility when he got out of jail, and if Odyssey House was full, then Bridge House, and if Bridge House was full, then the place on the West Bank where they'd converted a bunch of run-down condos into a rehab. Over the last five years he'd resided at all of these facilities and a few others, subsequently shuttered. He'd completed his stays at each of them. He'd never been dismissed for conduct reasons or for getting high on the grounds.

Hard Head liked almost everything about the dry-out process. He liked the redemption talk, everybody sitting in a circle, making plans and promises. In the places that worked Scripture into the curriculum, he felt close to the New Testament God and fearful of the Old Testament one. He always managed to feel just as they wanted you to when you were there. He never had to fake it, like many of the people he'd encountered in dry-out facilities over the years. They were saying the words as you might say a mantra or a spell, hoping that repetition would make them true. It wasn't like that for Hard Head. He always believed this dry-out would be the last.

As the opioid epidemic reached into the most prosperous neighborhoods in America, the cottage industry of high-end rehabs saw explosive growth. Some of those facilities were day spas by another name, but many imparted best practices for avoiding relapse, such as cultivating a sponsor and a support system you can turn to in times of stress. Perhaps more importantly, they emphasized avoiding putting yourself in situations where you were likely to give in to the temptation to get high. One of the most critical go-bys for staying clean was also one of the simplest: Don't hang around people who can sell you drugs.

Even for addicts of means, this isn't easy advice to follow. In many cases, before the addict gets clean, other drug users are his inner circle. If he can resist reaching out to them, and he can go home to a quiet neighborhood where opportunities to encounter a drug dealer are few, he improves his chances of avoiding relapse.

A poor person in a poor neighborhood is far more likely to run into people who can get him high. If he wants to buy groceries or put gas in his car, he's almost certain to come across someone along the way who can feed his habit. Getting clean in a poor neighborhood means facing temptation several times per week.

Getting clean while homeless means facing it every five minutes. The only places with more drugs than the shelters were the places homeless people went when the shelters put them out. Hard Head estimated that there was more dope per square foot Under the Bridge than anywhere else in the city. Twice in the last week Hard Head had been offered crack for free. Neither of the guys who offered was trying to trap him or sign him up as a future customer. The guys with the drugs were trying to help. Later, Hard Head would tell me that he'd gone through detox at Odyssey House with the second guy a couple of years before. The dry-out hadn't stuck, but the friendship had.

Odyssey House's sober-living facility was an entirely separate entity from its detox clinic—the free one, to which I'd yet to get a single offender admitted. The sober-living facility was run out of an old red-brick mansion donated by some mysterious benefactor uptown. The screener who took my call remembered Hard Head and said he was always welcome back. If she was surprised to hear he'd relapsed, she gave no indication of it over the phone.

When Hard Head's jail detox was complete, Beth joined me to pick him up and deliver him to the tents. He wanted to fly the sign for a few hours so that he wouldn't show up to Odyssey House that evening with nothing in his pockets. The post-detox transformation was especially stunning among older offenders, who never failed to look a decade younger after they got clean. Hard Head thanked us for the ride as he climbed into the back seat. He didn't have anything good to say about his time at OPP, but he didn't really complain about it either.

"Aren't you getting a little old for that place?" Beth asked.

"It's no fun in there," Hard Head said. "But it's not like it's Vietnam."

"They should put that on the bumper stickers," Beth said. "*City Jail—hey, at least it's not Vietnam!*"

We all laughed about that, and Hard Head thanked us again for getting him clean and giving him a ride back to the bridge. We dropped him at the mouth of the tent, where he embraced his tentmate and grabbed his cardboard sign and set off on foot for the best corner he could get at 11:00 a.m.

"That's one tough bastard," Beth said.

"Too tough, maybe," I said.

"Institutionalized," Beth said.

Usually when people used this term, they were talking about prisoners. Beth and I knew it applied to plenty of people living on the outside. Poverty was the institution that truly shaped the men and women under my supervision. Whether you were trying to find the right corner to fly your sign or seeking out a Section 8 holder willing to let you trade your food stamps for a piece of her floor, you were living the life of a survivalist. You didn't make long-term plans. You didn't think about upward mobility. All your energy was tied up in holding on to your bit of shelter or finding your way to your next meal. While other people were going to school or learning a trade, you were cultivating skills unique to your station, like knowing whether to fight back against a band of robbers pillaging your tent or recognizing you were outnumbered and had better let them take what they wanted.

The risk/need assessment recognized that Hard Head was especially needy, even by P&P standards, but I'd been around long enough to know that all of my offenders were needy. The only people on my caseload who had money were drug dealers, and they rarely had it for long. Even the dons were never more than one bad play away from destitution.

Numerous studies have found that the rich and the poor consume about the same number of drugs, but whereas the poor end up in the criminal justice system as a result, the rich are allowed to continue their drug habits unabated. The enforcement disparity is obviously a serious problem, but I was beginning to believe that the scholars and activists trying to reform this aspect of the system were missing an important point. Drug abuse really is more hazardous for poor people. While wealthy or even middle-class drug users have their own beds to sleep in when they're coming off a bender, and health care providers to go to for detox or methadone or behavior-modification counseling to help them shake the habit, poor people who use drugs sleep it off in homeless shelters and tents. They don't have access to any of the modern medical advances that can make the disease a little more tolerable.

The fact that some early architects of the drug war had racist and classist intentions was well established by this point, but by the time I met Hard Head, I was convinced that if the drug war were called off tomorrow, police would still be spending more time responding to drug-related incidents in poor neighborhoods than rich neighborhoods. Poor people in America didn't have the means to cope with the fallout from addiction, and American social services weren't filling the gap. The longer it went on that way, the more drug use among the poor begat other high-risk behavior, and the more indispensable a police response looked. Most of the people we were locking up for drug-related offenses were so accustomed to it by now that they didn't even think to complain.

When I thought of need, I usually thought of all the aspects of daily life that offenders found intolerable, but it was just as important to think about the things they could tolerate, so that when a person like Hard Head determined how much of a given hardship he could handle, he measured it against going to war. When that was your yardstick, you could put up with almost anything. It also meant that people in serious trouble could look like they were all right long after they weren't. Even when need was apparent, risk could stay hidden until it was too late.

# PART TWO

## risk

# EIGHT

# ninety-day turnaround

K endrick had been clean for five months when one of his closest friends was murdered. The friend was a young guy, about the same age as Kendrick's housemates at Tina's Place in the Lower Ninth Ward. He stopped by the house from time to time to smoke weed and talk shit. He and Kendrick had been romantically involved for a short time. Kendrick was in his late twenties when he embraced his bisexuality. Even in this day and age, a lot of people in the Lower Ninth Ward still had a problem with it, but when Kendrick's housemates ribbed him about his sexual orientation, they did so "with love," Kendrick said, and he never took it to heart.

Some of them took the young man's death as hard as Kendrick did. They and Kendrick got some guns and packed into an old car and set off to find the shooter. He was long gone by the time Kendrick's posse was assembled. Rumor had it he was hiding out somewhere in the East. No one had a clear idea of the nature of the dispute between him and the dead man. Everyone assumed it was drug related. Both of the young men were involved with neighborhood gangs that were always battling for territory.

By morning, Kendrick and the posse gave up the search. They ditched the guns and went back to Tina's Place. A couple of blunts got passed around, and then some crack and some pills. Kendrick abstained. He paced the living room where the young men slept, and then he paced the lawn. He was seated on the front steps when the detectives showed up. They'd heard that the victim hung around Tina's Place from time to time and wanted to know if anybody knew anything.

The young men still believed in the code that said that you never talked to the police, no matter how badly you wanted a shooter punished for what he'd done, but Kendrick had come around to a more practical view of law enforcement over the years. He believed the old stories about cops planting evidence and beating confessions out of people, but the police department these days was so threadbare and sullen that you almost had to feel sorry for the bastards. The way Kendrick saw it, cops planted evidence and beat confessions out of people when they were bored and had nothing better to do. When they were solving only a little better than one out of three murder cases, you worried more about them giving up than trying so hard they were willing to break the law to get a suspect. When the homicide detective told Kendrick that he wanted to arrest the guy who had killed his friend, Kendrick believed the detective was in earnest, and he told him the suspect's name and the rumor that he could be found in the East. It wasn't the greatest lead in the world, but the detective was appreciative.

Everything Kendrick knew about the killing he knew through hearsay. He wasn't going to be called to testify, but he told the detective he wasn't afraid of taking the stand. After the detective left, the young guys at Tina's Place tried to give Kendrick shit about "snitching," and he did his best to set them straight. "The way I see it," he said, "we shoot this motherfucker, he's out of his misery. The cops get him, he's gotta do life upstate. He's not getting a better deal with the cops."

Besides, they'd already tried it the other way. They'd sought street justice but hadn't found their man in time. Kendrick wanted the young men looking up to him to understand that just because the system didn't seem to care about them didn't mean they shouldn't use it to their advantage when they got the chance.

Kendrick subscribed to some of the wildest government conspiracy theories I'd heard, including the one about crack's being created in a US lab to be siphoned by undercover DEA agents into the black community for the purpose of destroying the family unit. If you got Kendrick talking about the federal government, you always ended up in Roswell, New Mexico. On the local government level, though, he was a strict pragmatist. Narcotics cops went after the people who sold the tainted product. Homicide cops arrested people who couldn't handle turf disputes like men. Why shouldn't people like Kendrick work with them when it suited the community's purpose?

Kendrick's policy toward law enforcement was very simple. When a cop was doing something helpful, Kendrick was happy to talk to him. When a cop was trying to stir shit or shake people down for no reason, Kendrick kept his distance. The police were a lever of power, to be pulled or not pulled. When you had no power yourself, refusing to use other people's power to your advantage made no sense.

"You try to talk to these kids," he told me, "but their head's as thick as yours was at their age."

Kendrick tapped at the image of the young man screen-printed onto the commemorative T-shirt he was wearing, known across the New Orleans District as a "murder T." They were a common fixture of our lobby, and this one was typical of the form. The departed was depicted with a pistol in one hand and the other making a gang sign. He was flanked by doves and scriptural passages and the dates of birth and departure. The young man was nineteen when he died. In the picture he looked closer to sixteen, less a true gangster than a kid playing one.

"Started striking that pose when he was ten years old. Fierce as a motherfucker." Kendrick tapped again at the young man's image. "Some guys ask for trouble. This one begged for it."

Kendrick was torn between admiration of the young man's spirit and fury at his recklessness. In an unfair world, the kid had tried to take no shit. He'd tried to be in control inasmuch as he was able. According to Kendrick, the kid who shot him was the same way.

"They weren't big-time players, neither one of them," Kendrick said. "Fighting over scraps."

Kendrick went on awhile longer, and I could see that he wasn't coming to me for my insights on any of this. If anything, my lack of firsthand experience was my biggest asset. Kendrick wanted to vent to someone who had no connection to the situation. When he was through, we shook hands, and I told him I was sorry for his loss.

"You're gonna let the cops handle it from here on out?" I asked.

"I'm done."

"And the guns?"

"I gave them back."

This was as good an answer as I would get about the guns' where-abouts, and I didn't press the issue further. I stopped by Tina's Place later in the week. As usual, the living room was packed with people and the air was thick with weed smoke. I asked Kendrick if we could talk out on the lawn.

He told me he was still struggling with the fallout from the murder, and he looked it. The funeral had been the night before, and the police still hadn't found the shooter. Some of the young guys were talking about going headhunting again. Kendrick tried to talk sense into them, but they didn't listen until he "clicked out." He'd been clicking out since he was a teenager. He didn't just lose his temper when he clicked out. He turned into a maniac. It took four of his housemates to pull him off the guy he was whaling on. The guy was bigger and stronger, and he didn't stand a chance.

Click-outs seemed to scald Kendrick's nerve endings, so that he felt no pain, and they flooded his memory core. He recalled only flashes of what he did during a click-out. This one wasn't the first click-out he'd experienced since he started living at Tina's Place, and some of his housemates wanted him out. He stayed up all night trying to set things right. In the morning, shaking with weariness and residual rage, he went down the block to the crack dealer and got high. His five-and-a-half months clean represented the longest stretch since he was teenager. He'd been proud of himself for not getting high directly after the mur-der. He thought he'd achieved a milestone of sorts.

"Death of a loved one is the biggest test there is," I said. "I think most people fail that one."

As usual, I offered detox, which Kendrick understood to mean jail. Kendrick said he'd used only the once and hadn't felt the urge since. "Managed to shut it off," he said.

When he talked about his addiction, I got the impression he was picturing a malfunctioning gland, or an extraneous one, installed only in addicts. I'd read that some substance-abuse scholars preferred this concept of addiction to the more common disease framework. They reasoned that if an addict saw his addiction as an inextricable piece of himself—an essential body part—he would have to dispense with the notion that he could ever cease treatment. Whereas diseases could be cured, faulty organs had to be managed, lived with.

I offered sober living as an alternative, and Kendrick promised to take me up on it if he relapsed again. For now, he felt as I did about the last relapse. It was a onetime thing, the result of trauma.

"Next time I'll know," Kendrick said.

I wanted to tell Kendrick that I hoped he would never be tested in quite the same way again, but the possibility of a "next time" was very real, given the company Kendrick kept, and I settled for reminding him that he could always get hold of me if he changed his mind about sober living. I planned to leave him alone for the rest of the month. He called me a little more than two weeks later. He'd clicked out again, on another housemate, over something too trivial to remember, and his housemates had gone to Tina and asked her to put him out. Kendrick had accepted Tina's decision only to get in an argument with her over the balance of his food stamps. If she was cutting him loose before the end of the month, he wanted some money back. Tina argued that when you got put out for cause, you weren't entitled to a refund.

He put his clothes in a black plastic garbage bag and slung it over his shoulder and left before he clicked out again or went back to the crack dealer. He had enough money for bus fare to the mission, but he hated it there and was hoping to crash with somebody Under the Bridge. He was willing to offer the same deal he gave Tina: half of his food stamps, beginning at the first of the month.

I met him at a place called the Rebuild Center where homeless people could take a shit and a shower. There was always a line, but you could get there by foot from the mission and trust that your possessions wouldn't be taken from you while you were indisposed. For a homeless person in New Orleans, this was as good as security got.

The Rebuild Center was run by the local Catholic church, but people who partook of its services didn't have to agree to get evangelized. There was a courtyard full of park benches and washbasins and wooden trellises covered in jasmine. Some homeless offenders called it the Oasis. When I showed up to meet Kendrick, he'd just had a shower and a shave and felt better, but it was no substitute for your own bit of floor space and your own bathroom with a lock on the door. Tina's Place may not have met many people's definition of stable housing, but it beat homelessness by a mile.

"Only time you go to the Oasis," Kendrick said, "is when you're living in the fucking desert."

He went on to tell me he thought he'd found a taker for his food-stamps-for-tent-space deal, and now he was on to other matters. "These click-outs," he said, "if I have one Under the Bridge, shit's liable to turn ugly."

Just as homelessness made addiction much more dangerous for both the addict and anyone nearby, it ensured that mental illness would assume its most hazardous possible form. I had no doubt that *mental illness* was the right term for a condition that made a person surrender control of his body and memory in almost equal measure.

There was only one mental health provider in town that didn't require insurance. It was called Metropolitan Human Services District—"Metropolitan" or "Metro" for short. Like the Rebuild Center, Metropolitan's office was located within walking distance of the mission and the tents, presumably by design. There was a time when a person like Kendrick could walk through the front doors and get an appointment the same way he would get one at the emergency room. According to Charles, those days were over, but he gave me the phone number to the screening line and told me I was welcome to try my luck. I took for granted that Kendrick hadn't seen the news stories chronicling the downsizing that the state's mental health services were enduring as we spoke.

In the late fifties and early sixties, more than 500,000 Americans suffering from mental health disorders were housed in state hospitals. The "deinstitutionalization" movement, driven by cost-cutting administrations as well as human rights activists concerned about the living conditions in many facilities, caused the number of state hospitals to plummet throughout the second half of the twentieth century. By 2016, fewer than 40,000 mental health beds remained.

The Bureau of Justice Statistics estimates that as many as 800,000 mentally ill Americans go to jail or prison each year. Different surveys of the American inmate population have defined *mental illness* different ways, with some including all diagnoses, including depression, and others counting only inmates medicated for acute disorders like schizophrenia. Every survey agrees that a significant number of mentally ill inmates go undiagnosed, and that a true accounting of the prevalence of mental illness in the corrections population would probably come out much higher than any current estimate. The mentally ill make up anywhere from a fifth to a third of the US jail population and are anywhere from two to four times more likely than the general population to end up on probation or parole. When I called Metropolitan, I tried to let the screener know that I understood that the problem was big and cash flow was limited, but in my opinion Kendrick was as worthy a use of her resources as anyone.

"Our services are reserved for the very neediest," she said.

"If you could just sit down with him—"

"A few years ago, maybe. This year, not a chance."

Metropolitan could treat only people who came to them with a diagnosis. In other words, to get an appointment, a mentally ill person needed to show up to Metropolitan with his paperwork in order and the name and contact information of a doctor who could confirm that the individual qualified for services. Getting told by a service provider that I had the sequence wrong was turning into a familiar experience. If I wanted to get help for an offender, I needed to start at the beginning.

"I can't get to the beginning," I told the screener. "I don't have time. This guy needs help now."

"Honey," the screener said, "your tone is wrong. I've got crazy people screaming in my face all day over here. I don't need it over the phone."

I apologized and tried to reset. "I'm just trying to figure out why, if you're the provider of last resort, you're not set up to take last-resort-type people, if that makes sense."

"That's a question for the governor. I do the best I can with what they give me."

That was the end of the conversation. I told Charles and Beth what had happened, and they both laughed and said that dealing with Metropolitan was its own form of spectator sport. When my friends caught their breath, Beth suggested I try the courthouse. There was a new mental health program for probationers there. Kendrick was on parole, but I might be able to talk somebody into sitting down with him and writing up a diagnosis.

I called the courthouse and eventually got transferred to a clinical social worker who agreed to meet with Kendrick during her lunch break and try to write something up that would get him through the doors at Metropolitan. "No promises, okay?" she said. "Technically, Metro's not supposed to see him if he's not diagnosed. And I'm not supposed to be screening people who aren't on probation."

She was anxious about working outside the lines, but she'd seen enough of the public services landscape to know that the lines were crudely drawn. If offenders presented a complex set of challenges to which they'd adapted all manner of coping mechanisms, some more healthful than others, we who were trying help them needed to adapt as well. "When you have a moving target," the social worker said, "what good's a mounted gun?"

Social workers were always good for a metaphor. I reached Kendrick on his "government phone" and arranged to pick him up outside the tent where he was crashing. It stood about two hundred yards from Hard Head's tent and was in roughly the same condition. Kendrick's tentmate was an old guy who muttered to himself and looked right through me when I told him what I was doing there. He'd been getting services from Metropolitan for years. Inside the tent I spotted the knotted trash bag containing Kendrick's clothes and shoes. He was wearing black jeans and an oversized black T-shirt and a red bandanna tied around his neck. Charles, who'd come along for the ride, told him he looked like he was getting ready to rob a train.

Kendrick agreed to lose the bandanna. We could see that he'd added it in the hope of dressing himself up for what he perceived to be an important appointment. Black T-shirt and red bandanna were the closest thing Kendrick had to Sunday best.

We dropped him off at an office building about a block from the courthouse called Tulane Tower. "The Tower" contained the public defender's office and the offices of the court's social workers. Most offenders knew the place well. By government-building standards it was pretty nice, a coffee shop on the first floor and windows in every office.

I told Kendrick I would pick him up afterward. He said that wouldn't be necessary. He'd scraped together bus fare for a ride out to the Lower Ninth Ward to catch up with the guys at Tina's Place, with whom he was in the process of making peace. One of them would front him his fare back to the tents later in the day.

We let him off at the curb and watched him go through the Tower lobby and disappear into the elevator bank. "This is good work," Charles said. "That's a hard case right there."

He knew what his approval meant to me, but I wanted to appear older, wiser, and hardened by experience, and I said I wasn't getting my hopes up. I was taking a flier, nothing more.

It wasn't true. We went back to the office and I tapped my foot and stared at my phone until the call came, about ninety minutes after we dropped Kendrick at the Tower.

"I'm faxing you my findings," the social worker said. "You won't be able to say you weren't warned."

She wouldn't go into any more detail than that. The report was about two pages long. Kendrick had told the social worker about the killings he'd seen and the violence he'd done. He told her he'd beaten a girlfriend with a baseball bat. In middle school he'd pulled a gun on a fellow student and attacked a guidance counselor. He told the social worker that his father was a deadbeat. His mother had never wanted him and had never tried to fake it. He wanted to make somebody pay for the kind of life he'd had. He admitted that most of the people he'd made pay so far had been women. He worried about what he might do if he clicked out again.

So did the social worker. In her professional opinion, Kendrick represented an urgent threat to public safety. We should get him off the streets first and worry about treatment later.

I read the report to Charles, who told me what I already knew. "You've gotta tell Dan."

I took the report down the hall to Dan the Regional Manager. By the middle of the first page his eyes were moons. He finished reading, folded the document down the center, and asked for my take.

"He was letting off steam," I said. "I told him to be as candid as he wanted. I'm sure the social worker said the same."

"That's my read, too. But I'm not a mental health professional. And neither are you."

Our situation was actually very simple. When a mental health professional sounded the alarm on one of our people, we had to take him into custody. Dan the Regional Manager rounded up a half dozen POs and every member of the US Marshals Service fugitive task force he could get his hands on.

We met beforehand at a fire station to plot our approach. I gave a brief rundown of Kendrick's supervision history, and we set out for Tina's Place. No guns were drawn. No one raised his voice. The only object left behind by the operation was the milk crate Kendrick had been sitting on when the Marshals rounded the corner. I told Kendrick I would fill him in once we got to jail. The Marshals had other bodies to collect. The other POs had other doors to knock on. Soon it was just Kendrick and me and the visitation room at OPP, a small, cramped cell with a glass partition so battered that you could barely make out the person on the other side.

"I thought the lady from the Tower was sending me somewhere," he said.

"She was. She did." Kendrick's mind worked slowly, but it was all I could do to stay a half second ahead of it. "She felt like you needed more help than she could give."

"That's why I'm locked up? Because of what I told her?"

"You're here because we're worried that if you don't get the right kind of help soon, you'll hurt somebody. Or yourself. We don't want another click-out."

He pressed his knuckles to his forehead and sunk low on the stool. "Me neither. That's why I spoke up."

I told Kendrick that Dan the Regional Manager had promised to talk to the top guy within the Department of Corrections' mental health services division. Professional help was on its way. It sucked that Kendrick had to be behind bars to get it. It was a sign of the times.

Kendrick shrugged and said he would roll with it. What else could he do? I told him I would be back in a day or two with more information.

Dan the Regional Manager made calls and pounded out email after email. It was the first time I saw his temperature rise. He paused between keystrokes to tell me what he was thinking.

"I really thought I was done being surprised by this place," he said. "Here we've got a guy who wants help, and we've got a chance to give it to him, and all I'm hearing from Baton Rouge is we don't normally do it like this. We don't have a procedure in place. We're doing all this research about getting smart on crime, we're trying to find answers for people who, if they got clean or they got their meds on time, might not be our problem anymore, but when we get a chance to do something for one of them on the fly, we say we'll table it, figure it out at the next meeting. Why don't we say to ourselves, 'We have a doctor. We have a parolee who wants help. Let's get these two in the same room and see what happens'? What's stopping us from doing that? If we can't get anybody a job, and we can't get anybody clean unless we put them in jail first, why are we gonna pass up the chance to get some mental health meds to a mental health case?"

"I don't know," I said.

"Thank you," he said. "That's the answer I was looking for."

Later that day, someone in the leadership committed to sending down a van to pick Kendrick up from OPP and transport him to a prison outside of Baton Rouge that was supposed to be home of the best mental health resources in the state. Kendrick would get a sit-down with a licensed psychiatrist. He would get a prescription and a diagnosis. Dan the Regional Manager was quick to remind me that getting the go-ahead from headquarters was only half the battle. We still had to find funding for the operation.

We were sending Kendrick to prison under the auspices of a "technical revocation," also known as a "ninety-day turnaround," a mechanism the parole board had installed as an alternative to full revocation. A ninety-day turnaround was supposed to give a parolee a taste of what was to come if he didn't clean up his act. Most POs used it on drug addicts who appeared to be at high risk of overdose. Ninety days in jail cost the department between $3,000 and $4,000, depending on which facility housed him. It was a lot less costly than full revocation, but it wasn't cheap. To qualify a parolee for a ninety-day turnaround, a PO had to document violations and get the parolee to admit to them in writing.

Apart from his concerns about the click-outs, Kendrick was as compliant as maximum-risk offenders got. He'd had one relapse in the last six months. He'd kept me apprised of his whereabouts and was willing to appear at the New Orleans District anytime I asked. When I went back to the jail and met Kendrick a second time, I told him we would have to tell a white lie or two to place him where he needed to be. He said he was game for whatever got him out of OPP.

By then he'd been moved to the region of the jail known as Tent City. The tents reminded me of the squat white domes you find on the covers of golden age science fiction novels. Erected as a temporary solution to post-Katrina overflow, and still in use a decade later, Tent City was the site of a recent OPP escape. It was also supposed to be the best place to score drugs in the jail. Inside, the tents were spacious and a little cleaner and more sanitary, at least by my eye, than the rest of the facility, and inmates seemed to enjoy greater freedom of movement there. If you had to be in OPP, Tent City wasn't a terrible draw.

I'd called ahead and told the sheriff's switchboard that I needed to hold a parole violation hearing. The Tent City deputies set up a folding table in the common area. Kendrick and I sat together and discussed the phony violations: an overdue fee balance and his admission that he'd smoked crack a couple of weeks before.

"And they're gonna bring me back when it's over?" Kendrick said. "I don't know anybody in Baton Rouge."

I assured him that DOC would return him to New Orleans. If the van wouldn't take him to his tent, he could call me from wherever he landed, and I would scoop him up. We shook on the deal, and I went back to the New Orleans District and spent the next hour scanning and emailing the paperwork required to set the gears in motion. Less than a week after Kendrick signed the papers documenting his violations, the Department of Corrections came down and picked him up and drove him to Baton Rouge. Beth and Charles were both in the office when I got the call that Kendrick was an inmate once more.

"Prison for mental health care," I said. "You can't make this up."

"Nope," Charles said. "Have to see it for yourself."

"Most rookies see shit this fucked-up and they head for the hills." Beth was sitting in the offender chair with her boots propped on the edge of Charles's desk, and she raised an invisible glass to Charles and me. "Here's to gutting it out."

On the surface, there wasn't very much to be proud of here. A guy had come to me for help, and I'd arrested him and put him in prison. But anyone could choose between good and bad, between health-ful and harmful. You got your coworkers' respect when, faced with potentially disastrous outcome, you could engineer a less disastrous alternative—a "medium-bad," as these were sometimes known. Ninety days of mental health care behind bars were better than a click-out Under the Bridge.

A combination of poverty, addiction, and untreated medical condi-tions had made Kendrick a risk to public safety—and to his own safety as well. If he kept going as he had been, someone would get hurt. He knew it. He had told the social worker as much, and he had very recent history as evidence. A traumatic event had come along and pushed Kendrick's risk as high as it could go. He picked up a gun with intent to use it. If he'd found the man he was looking for, the time-tested arc from deprivation to capital offense would have been complete, and he and I would have had a very different conversation when we met in Tent City.

Until I'd read the social worker's report, I hadn't known how often Kendrick had done violence in the past or how many of the people he'd hurt were women. Some offenders would reveal these things to me. Most wouldn't. I couldn't hope to know very much more about anyone on my caseload than I knew about Kendrick, but you didn't have to spend more than a half hour with him to know that his needs were immense, and the risk of failing to meet them potentially cata-strophic. If the only way to meet his needs and reduce his risk was to put him in prison for three months, I had to be willing to do it.

Kendrick, for his part, hadn't uttered a complaint at any point in the proceedings. He knew he needed mental health care, and not only did he tolerate the pain and confusion he had to put up with to get it, he expected them. Public assistance was scarce and came only by way of suffering. If I'd tried to convince him otherwise, I would have sounded like another well-meaning but ignorant member of the comfort classes.

In a couple of weeks I would make a year at the New Orleans District. I'd come to know back alleys and secret pathways through neighborhoods I'd never set foot in before I became a PO. I'd seen poverty and addiction up close and on a scale I couldn't have imagined, but over the course of the past year nothing had surprised me as much as the change I'd observed in myself. If I wanted to help the people on my caseload, I had to be as adaptable as they were.

I'd come to P&P to keep people out of prison. A year later, my proudest moment, the one that my coworkers agreed was proof I could actually do this job, began with handcuffs and US Marshals and ended with a bus ride to the Department of Corrections.

# NINE

# the whole person

My first year on the job had seen no substantive change in the makeup of my caseload. About sixty cases expired and another sixty new ones came aboard. The risk distribution fell roughly in line with the previous year's. I had twenty-eight maximum-risk cases and another eighteen mediums with whom I met monthly—that is, three times more frequently than I had to—because I believed I'd seen warning signs the assessment had missed. I saw my other thirty-one mediums four times per year. Our visits usually lasted three minutes. I mostly trusted the assessment, which is to say that I believed that time spent on a medium-risk home inspection was better spent double-checking on a maximum-risk offender without a home.

My eighty-three minimum-risk cases were essentially strangers to me. I saw them only twice a year, both times at the New Orleans District. I didn't go to their houses or meet their families or have any idea how they spent their time. My twenty-two wounded and/or terminally ill offenders remained in "administrative" status, where they would remain until their supervision timed out. My warrants were still missing. Now and then one of them would turn up on a traffic stop and get brought to jail. Sometimes the judge or parole board would make him sit in OPP for a week or so in the hope of convincing him to get back in touch with his PO. Most absconders vanished again as soon as they got their release, and I went back to Tulane and Broad and asked the judge to sign another warrant.

I knew that some of my warrant cases, many of whom had lived at homeless shelters before they disappeared, were probably as needy as my maxes, but trying to track them down would have been extremely time-consuming, and time was a scarce commodity. I had to use every working hour wisely. I rarely thought of any but the forty-five to fifty offenders at the top of the risk/need distribution. When I checked in on an offender more than twice a month, I usually had reason to believe he was in danger, but a few offenders got extra visits because they gave me hope.

When I visited Sheila at Subway she was always cheerful, reaching into her pocket and unfolding the latest pay stub for me. Her boss had explained FICA to her and told her that some of the withholdings were an investment in her federally subsidized retirement, and others were an investment in her country and community. She was a taxpayer, and the money she didn't put to the future and the common good she got to take home and spend as she pleased. She remembered the first time she paid cash for a tube of the mascara she used to steal every time she ran out. It was kind of a thrill to get that first receipt and track those rows of numbers back to wages she'd earned honestly, one hour at a time.

She felt pride in her labor, and she felt most of the other things your first job is supposed to make you feel, including restlessness and the hope for something better. I told her stories of my early work, including the long summer I'd spent cleaning kennels for a veterinarian when I was fifteen, but we both knew that the path from scrubbing dog shit off rubber to a college education and a chance at a living wage was laid out clearly for me from birth, whereas for Sheila there was no obvious next step from here. I floated a GED, but to Sheila it was school by another name. I didn't push it, and I didn't notice a change in Sheila until the manager pulled me aside and said that in the last two weeks she'd become listless and sullen, and she'd been smelling so strongly of weed that a couple of customers had complained.

During a break between customers I asked Sheila if we could talk outside. She followed me out into the strip mall parking lot and leaned against the glass wall of the Subway and took off her uniform ball cap and held it in both hands at her waist. As long as she thought she was about to get arrested, she wasn't going to be honest with me. "The weed thing," I said. "Nobody's going to jail over it. But you could go to treatment. If it's making you feel shitty, I can try to get you some help."

"I don't feel shitty," she said. "I mean, I do, but that's why I smoke."

"Smoking helps?"

She scratched her neck with the bill of the cap and shifted her weight from her right foot to her left. "It used to help more."

A Subway parking lot wasn't an ideal setting for a breakthrough, but I'd learned to seize any opportunities I got. In every prior conversation, Sheila had described her smoking as purely recreational. Now she was suggesting it was a form of self-medication. The treatment I'd told her about was a set of six counseling sessions with a social worker trained to help offenders work on habit-forming but not chemically addictive patterns of behavior. We sent overeaters there, as well as gambling addicts, people who couldn't control their anger, and people who appeared to be using weed to treat depression or to get back to baseline so that they could face the day.

The program's scope was limited, but it offered a flexible schedule and was paid for entirely by the state. Dan the Regional Manager was advertising it as the first sign of intelligent life at headquarters. The bosses were finally coming around to the idea that spending money on offender needs in the short term could save a fortune in incarceration costs over a lifetime. If someone like Sheila could tame her habit enough to hold on to her job, she could keep paying taxes and avoiding police interactions. If she slipped deeper into depression and substance use, she was more likely to lose the job and return to the lifestyle she'd been living before, the one that found her flushing a bag of crack down the toilet and pleading guilty to a felony offense. Another felony after that and the former taxpayer could get shipped upstate, costing her fellow Louisianans fifteen to twenty grand per year.

Sheila agreed to try the counseling program. The first session was the following Monday evening. She called me afterward. The social worker was nice, but the program didn't really have a one-on-one component. It was more like an AA or NA meeting, of which Sheila had attended many with her mother. And most of the people in the program were in their forties and fifties.

"These people, some of them are all kinds of fucked-up," Sheila told me, and she laughed. "I get through hearing their stories and I'm like, 'Goddamn, I need a smoke!'"

Sheila seemed to be cured of her fears that I would take her to jail over her weed habit, and I could see that referring her to services, even if they ended in a wash, made my job easier going forward. The equation was as simple as it was obvious: if Sheila believed I wanted to help, she was more likely to tell me the things I needed to know to meet her needs—assuming, of course, I had access to programming that was up to the task. She told me she would complete the other five counseling sessions if I wanted, but if given the choice she would prefer not to go back. I told her to focus on work for now and reminded her that we were due to check in with the judge the following week.

Sheila showed up to court in her uniform and brought her check stubs and invited the judge to have a look. She beamed as the judge examined each check stub and commended her work ethic. When the judge mentioned that Sheila was due for a drug test, she fidgeted with her ball cap as she'd done during our last visit, and her gaze met the floor. I was standing beside her and gave her a quick nudge of reassurance. She didn't look at me but nodded to say she understood. The judge had observed every kind of silent courtroom communication, and she told me to join her for a sidebar while Sheila went down the hall to take her test.

"What's she gonna be positive for?"

"Just weed, Your Honor."

"So what's she worried about?"

I told the judge that when I'd learned that Sheila was self-medicating, I'd referred her to a counseling service, but it wasn't the right fit. Sheila was probably worried that the judge would hold her accountable for my failure to supply appropriate treatment.

"If she's doing group therapy," the judge said, "it's gotta be with people her own age."

Another thing I'd learned about judges was that they didn't mind letting you know when you'd misplayed your hand. Once she'd made her point, she was quick to absolve me with a "Not like you guys are busting at the seams with options over there."

Sheila returned a moment later with her test results. She had so much THC in her system that it was a wonder she could formulate a sentence. The judge folded the test results in half and dropped them in the trash can beside the bench. She made no mention of them in open court. She told Sheila she wanted her to try out a new program called the Day Reporting Center.

"I'm not ordering you to do this," the judge said. "I'm asking. You're working full-time and you're keeping in touch with your PO. As far as I'm concerned, your probation is going very well. I think the Day Reporting Center can make it go even better. But if it doesn't, that's okay. Tell your PO, and we'll try something else. Is that all right?"

"Yes, Your Honor," Sheila said.

The judge told her to hurry up and go so that she didn't miss work. Sheila scampered out of there, and the judge called me up again and told me she had meant what she said. Sheila had a job and was keeping in touch. If the new program helped her with the stress and the self-medicating, great. If it added to her stress or interfered with her work schedule, I should pull her out.

What we'd put together there in the courtroom could hardly be called a comprehensive treatment plan, but the process by which we'd arrived at it was, as far as I could see, just about right. It was how the system was supposed to work. The person who was paid to observe the offender reported what he observed to the person who was paid for her judgment. The judge had figured out that offenders wouldn't take our treatment referrals seriously until we allayed their fear that we would resolve any noncompliance the old way, with a three-year bid at the Department of Corrections. In the incarceration capital of the world, this wasn't an easy argument to make, especially in cases where we believed the best way to avoid a long jail term was to impose a brief one. I doubt I could have gotten Kendrick to buy into going upstate for ninety days for treatment until I'd first convinced him that I didn't want to send him upstate for any reason if I could help it.

Sheila took the judge at her word and told me she was looking forward to meeting new people and changing up her routine. Because she worked most weekends, she could attend the program all day on Mondays and Tuesdays and in the evenings Wednesday through Friday. The Day Reporting Center opened when the sun came up and ran until late in the evening. It was all-consuming by design, following the model of some of the most successful of the latest wave of American charter schools, which held that the best way to provide opportunity to at-risk youth was to occupy nearly all of their free time. Most of the offenders in the Day Reporting Center—the DRC—were between eighteen and twenty-five. Few had graduated from high school or completed a GED.

The DRC was physically connected to OPP in an annex full of pictures of the sheriff and his badge, but the facility contained no cells and only one deputy, posted at the door. A small central auditorium and a block of partitioned rooms hosted guest speakers and breakout sessions. The staff were passionate about their "clients," a term that turned out to be a partition unto itself.

Offenders were given bus fare to and from the DRC every day they showed up. The DRC was supposed to be a place where offenders could feel like paying customers—like people who had the means to hire a professional to discuss their fathers, their childhoods, their hopes, their fears. The DRC offered classes on parenting and conflict resolution. The counselors hosted résumé-building sessions. They coached offenders for job interviews. They talked about developing *the whole person*.

They weren't afraid to address off-color remarks about race or gender or the big one, sexual orientation. Racially the counselors were a diverse group, but only a couple were from the city. Most were from the Northeast or the West Coast, part of a vast migration of indefatigable young liberals who'd started coming to New Orleans after Katrina in the hope of purging it of its Old Southern ills. Like most of the young men in the program, Sheila considered homosexuality an aberration and believed that men who slept with other men deserved all the ridicule they got. She said as much when her counselor asked her not to refer to anyone in the program as a "faggot."

Sheila replied, "If it walks like a duck . . ." and nearly fell out of her chair laughing.

The counselor soft-shoed her way through this: "What I perceive as a counselor arguing for tolerance, you perceive as a white person telling a black person how to feel." Her voice didn't break until the last syllable. She wasn't angry, just confused. How could a population of mostly African American men and women raised in Louisiana not feel instant solidarity with every victim of every prejudice? The counselor explained that when marginalized populations cope by marginalizing someone else, the result is a more discriminatory society, of the kind that developed when poor whites in the Reconstruction South were coaxed by their betters into remembering that they might have been broke and they might have been illiterate, but at least they weren't black.

Sheila was willing to go along with the logic of this but ultimately fell back on the Old Testament. "Bible says to kill a faggot," Sheila told her counselor.

"What about slavery?" the counselor said. "The Bible's good with that, too."

"Fuck off," Sheila said. She kicked her way out of her chair and stormed past the deputy at the door and got on the bus and went home for the day. The counselor was okay with that. Developing the whole person wasn't supposed to be easy or painless.

I called Sheila after I spoke with the counselor. I expected her to tell me to tell the judge she was done with the DRC. Instead she told me that she liked the program a lot. She especially liked getting talked to like a grown-up, and she planned on showing up the next day at the usual time.

The implication seemed to be that, whereas the judge and I worried about pushing offenders too hard, the counselors at the DRC dealt frankly and squarely with their charges. They pissed off more offenders than I did, but they were also far quicker to gain their trust. When I asked the counselors how they'd learned to walk the line between calling someone out and making allowances for troubles that simply weren't the offender's fault, they told me they had trained themselves not to think about it. Just because you called someone out didn't mean you weren't trying to understand where that person was coming from. People who were exposed to violence and extreme poverty at an early age were bound to struggle with human interactions. They were bound to have difficulty holding down jobs and to seek relief through drugs and alcohol. To the DRC counselors, every problem presented by an offender was predictable, and most of them could be mitigated by a more aggressive social welfare state. Well-funded social-safety-net countries like Denmark and Sweden—all of Scandinavia, really—had less violence and addiction and far less incarceration than we did. So did much of western Europe and Japan.

But this was New Orleans, a poor city with a meager social safety net and limited paths to upward mobility. The counselors learned to focus on problems they could solve without money. They taught addicts to rely on their support systems: friends, family, neighbors. They trained violent offenders to manage their anger. They urged offenders who were in toxic relationships to get out, and they offered compassion and understanding to offenders who couldn't leave because they relied on their abusers for food, shelter, or money.

From the counselors I learned about "the turn," a term that referred to the moment when the counselor had to stop offering acceptance and begin demanding change. For me, this remained the job's most challenging proposition. I knew well enough that I was hardly the only voice in offenders' ears, but I couldn't help seeing relapses and arrests as reflections of my performance as a PO. I knew that when I made excuses for an offender's behavior, I was, on some level, making excuses for my own.

As I was coming to terms with this, a favorite offender picked up his third domestic-violence charge in eleven months. In that same span he'd gotten clean, gotten his GED, and turned a temp job into a permanent position on a construction site. The third time I told the judge that I believed the offender's progress should buy him some leeway on his history of domestic violence, I got a phone call from his victim.

"Y'all motherfuckers are gonna get me killed," she told me.

I explained my position as plainly as I could. "I don't want him to hurt anybody," I said, "and I don't want him in jail."

She didn't answer, but I could hear her breaths coming quicker and heavier.

"It's fucked-up," I said. "I don't know what to tell you."

"Tell me that. Repeat what you just said to me."

I didn't seem to have much choice. I repeated what I'd just said to her.

"I appreciate that," she said. "I mean it." And she hung up.

I told one of the counselors about the conversation. The counselor said that when you were speaking to victims, "the turn" was the moment when you stopped apologizing for flaws in the system—the "jail or nothing" problem, for one—and acknowledged that you had made a choice. I could have chosen jail. I'd put my offender's freedom over his victim's safety, and for that I deserved the victim's disdain.

"You fucked up," the counselor said. "Own it. Do better next time."

The counselors made "the turn" with POs, too, and were rarely bashful about it. Many of the counselors lived in the city's toughest neighborhoods. They used their privilege to intervene with overzealous cops and okay-with-the-status-quo school administrators. One counselor argued that public service could not be done any other way. Those of us who put in our eight hours in Hollygrove or the Seventh Ward only to retreat in the evenings to safer, quieter neighborhoods weren't making the full commitment.

"I mean," Beth said, after her first trip to the DRC, "where the fuck did they find these people?"

"California," Charles said. "It's the only explanation."

As usual, we took our comic relief where we could find it, but we envied the counselors their resolve, never more than on days when we could see that they were fighting losing battles. The counselors all agreed that the most disturbing aspect of drug-game culture was the "snitch code," whose logic always seemed to benefit the worst person in the room.

"Let me get this straight," Sheila's counselor said. She was as pale and slender as a soda straw, and she shut her eyes and screwed her long thumbs into her temples as she made her case. "The cops arrest me for somebody else's crime, but if I tell the truth—if I won't fall on the sword—I'm the one who loses my honor. I'm the snitch. You did the crime, I do the time."

When offenders weren't busy using this mindfuck on each other, they used it on their wives, girlfriends, even their sisters and mothers, some of whom ended up in the DRC as a result. Like many of the other women in the program, Sheila told the counselors that a man "in the game" expected his significant other to "take the charge" for all firearms or narcotics located in the trunk of the vehicle when the cops pulled him over.

"A real man needs a woman to take the heat for him?" the counselor asked, in her lilting, I-know-you-know-better way.

"Ride or die," Sheila said, not with a shrug or a wink but with all the conviction of a soldier saluting a flag.

The counselor believed they were talking about patriarchy. Sheila believed they were talking about honor. The counselors understood that these codes were, like the drug trade itself, kept alive by lack of opportunity. They never forgot that every conversation between counselors and offenders at the DRC was related to the national conversation about educational and economic and racial equality. Even so, it sucked to care and have the facts on your side and still fail to convince.

Despite her resistance to her counselors' insights on the snitch code and homosexuality, Sheila responded remarkably well to talk therapy. I wasn't privy to the details of Sheila's and her counselor's conversation, but both told me that the sessions were productive. Sheila had a lot of childhood trauma to work through, much of it related to her mother's crack addiction. She'd never told me much about that. There were places offenders would go with counselors that they wouldn't go with a PO.

This was as it should have been. POs were trained to recognize needs and risks that other sets of eyes might miss. This was our major contribution to offender rehabilitation. A background in counseling or social work was an asset in a PO, but we weren't supposed to be treatment professionals. The distinction between our role and a counselor's was never more apparent than when we sat down with offenders after they'd spent an hour with a licensed treatment professional. Sheila emerged from therapy quoting the two most important tenets we could hope to impart:

1. Her circumstances weren't her fault.
2. She still had the power to change them.

Hopeful that the DRC counselors would succeed where I'd failed at improving offenders' job prospects, I sat in on some group therapy sessions. By the third hour I could see that the counselors didn't have any easy answers. By the time they got admitted to the DRC, most offenders were hopelessly behind in the job race. Most had at best a ninth-grade education. All had criminal records, some of them extensive. And they all carried around the lesser-known but equally pervasive disability I'd seen again and again: They didn't know anyone who'd had any success at conventional work. They couldn't believe that any employer would take them seriously. They believed they spoke the wrong language and wore the wrong skin.

The offenders who got jobs overreacted to minor workplace slights. In the drug game this was necessary, the most common and reliable way of showing you weren't willing to be taken advantage of. People expected it of you. It played differently at Sears and Chili's. Bosses who tried correction were accused of being disrespectful. Customers who complained were told to piss off. Offenders who weren't fired usually quit within a few weeks. Compared with drug running, working for minimum wage was boring, and the pay sucked, and it was hell on the body. In eight hours on the corner you could make twice what you made in two weeks at the dish pit.

Sometimes offender poverty took unexpected forms. When the Audubon Nature Institute, operator of New Orleans's world-class zoo and aquarium, donated a day of free passes to the DRC, I learned that almost none of the offenders at the DRC had ever visited the zoo or the aquarium, even though many offenders lived within a long walk or a short bicycle ride of each. The twelve bucks you needed to buy a ticket wasn't in offenders' families' budgets. Zoo and aquarium day felt like a field trip, but in its little way it contributed to the DRC's ongoing effort to get offenders to widen their points of view from the particular block of the particular neighborhood where they grew up. The more offenders knew of history, geography, and maybe even wildlife, the less consequential the neighborhood gang hierarchy looked.

Sheila went to the zoo and had a blast. Even there, she presented a unique set of challenges to the counselors. The guys in the program went crazy for her. By her third day she'd become the boss of the ride-or-die crowd, ostracizing other female offenders who weren't as committed to the code as she was.

"She's got potential," Sheila's counselor told me at the end of her first week at the DRC, "but she's enormously disruptive."

Sheila skipped work the following Wednesday to "ride with" a couple of guys who were in the DRC on gun charges. According to the two male offenders' counselors, both were making headway, passing their drug tests and studying for their GEDs and prepping for job interviews, until Sheila came along. On Sheila's twelfth day in the program, the two offenders got into a fistfight over her. She cackled from the sideline, urging them to show her what they were made of. Her counselor sent her home for the day and then regretted it.

"We should have talked it out right then and there," the counselor told me. She felt she understood Sheila, playing the game she'd been taught to play from a young age. "In a dangerous place, the guy the other guys are scared of is the guy who's a safe bet. I get it. How can I not get it? And then I see it in action and I act surprised. Like my rules ought to take precedence in here."

Sheila didn't show up the next day or the day after. I went to Subway and found her at the cash register, laughing with a customer as she rang him up. I waited until the place cleared out to approach her.

"The DRC'll take you back if you want," I said.

"Do I have to?"

"You're working. You're keeping in touch. You don't have to do anything you don't want to do."

She hugged the cash register and pressed her cheek to the screen and shut her eyes. Her smile was the sort you see on a nervous passenger when the plane finally touches down. "I thought you were gonna take me to jail."

I thanked Sheila for giving the program a try. I called the counselor at the DRC and told her Sheila wouldn't be back.

"That's a relief," the counselor said. "It's wrong to say it, but fuck. It's a relief."

She pointed out that in choosing the job over the DRC and the DRC crowd, Sheila was in fact choosing independence. She didn't want to make her way in this world by tagging along with some guy. "A good thing happened," the counselor said. "It took us doing a bad job, but a win's a win, right?"

was in the judge's courtroom on an unrelated matter when she called me up to the bench for an update about Sheila. Despite the judge's promise not to take Sheila's performance personally, I'd been dreading telling her that Sheila and the DRC hadn't been a match. The judge didn't ask for details, and I didn't volunteer any.

"She's working and she's not getting in trouble," the judge said. "Normally I have the sense to call that a win."

She tapped at her cheek as she worked through her remaining options. "I'd really like to get her to quit smoking if we can. But if we can't, we move on."

I thought it was a good plan. I intended to leave Sheila alone until the next status hearing. Her mother called me a week after I saw the judge.

"She doesn't know I'm calling you," Sheila's mother said. "She crashed hard last night. Won't go to work."

Over the next ten minutes she explained that there was something I needed to know, something she and Sheila had kept hidden from me for reasons she hoped I would understand. The Sheila I'd gotten to know, the bright-eyed girl who liked to laugh and talk shit and roughhouse with the guys, was only half the story. There were plenty of nights when the guys pulled up to the curb and Sheila didn't come out. She spent about a third of her waking hours holed up in her room, trying to smoke out the dread that overtook her without warning, and often without an obvious antecedent, although Sheila's mother spotted one this time.

Something had happened between her and the boyfriend. Sheila wouldn't tell her mother much. Maybe there was another girl, or maybe the boyfriend heard about Sheila's running around with the guys from the DRC. They were Central City guys, and the Seventh Ward was nearly three miles away. To Seventh Warders, Central City may as well have been the dark side of the moon. Sheila would never have expected word to get back to her usual crew.

The reasons didn't really matter. Sheila was high, she was alone in her room with the shades drawn, and she was missing work. Sheila's mother asked me to go over, and when I told her that I thought the best thing for Sheila right now was some time to herself, she let out a cry and shouted, "You're supposed to be helping her! Do your goddamn job!"

It was the first time she'd lost her temper with me, and I met her stride for stride. "How the hell am I supposed to know she's this bad off if nobody tells me?"

"You knew she was smoking like a goddamn fiend. Lock her ass up for a week, show her you mean business."

"That's the last place she needs to be if she's depressed. There's as much weed in there as there is out here."

Sheila's mother laughed long and hard and without bitterness, as if we were finally speaking the same language. She told me that she liked seeing me flustered about her daughter. It hadn't occurred to me that offenders' families wanted an emotional reaction from POs. Charles, who'd been in the room throughout the phone call, advised me to keep my cool whenever possible, but if acting like a jerk bought me credibility just this once, I shouldn't walk it back.

Sheila's mother went on to tell me that Sheila was deeply embarrassed about her depression. She considered it a weakness. If word got out, she could be blacklisted from all the neighborhood crews. She would never voluntarily seek medical care for her mental health, but if I could somehow squeeze the problem through the gears of the criminal justice system—in other words, make treatment a condition rather than an option, a threat rather than a promise—we just might trick Sheila into getting the help she needed.

I wasn't accustomed to having offenders' parents tell me to trade in the carrot for the stick. Anyone could see that Sheila's mother had been living in fear of where Sheila's depression might lead for some time. She had lived in the Seventh Ward long enough to see firsthand the consequences of allowing mental illness to go untreated. She'd seen "click-outs." She knew how they ended when guns and grudges got involved.

I agreed that we should stop at nothing to get Sheila treated, but I also felt, as I had when trying to find an answer for Kendrick, that mental health was far too complex and specialized a topic to be handled by an amateur like me. Despite how Kendrick's interactions with the court's mental health division had turned out, I decided to tell the judge about Sheila's depression and ask if she knew how we might help. As it turned out, the judge next door was overseeing a new treatment program unofficially referred to as "mental health court."

Sheila's judge sent me to pitch Sheila to the mental health court judge, who said Sheila sounded like an ideal candidate: young, needy, and, best of all, ready to accept help. I pressed my luck and made one more request. "Can we call it something other than mental health court?" I asked. "Her mom thinks she'll bolt if she thinks we're calling her crazy."

"I don't care what you have to call it to get her here. When she meets my staff, they'll win her over. They win *everybody* over."

Mental health court was small and new. Fewer than a hundred of the roughly 4,500 probationers in New Orleans were part of the program. At the moment, mental health court wasn't supposed to take on any new people, but the judge, being a judge, could do what she wanted. Probationers in mental health court had monthly status hearings with the judge, weekly meetings with a social worker, and on-call access to a psychiatrist. The social worker helped offenders apply for Medicaid to cover prescription medications and helped them stay in the program once the paperwork cleared. Unity of Greater New Orleans, the rental voucher provider with the mandate to spend its limited resources on the neediest of the needy, didn't accept referrals from P&P or, as far as I knew, from any other institution that cared for poor people. Unity conducted its own canvasses of the mission and Under the Bridge, and made its own decisions about who deserved a voucher—who was truly the neediest.

Mental health court appeared to be the lone exception to Unity's rule. Sometimes mental health court convinced a Unity caseworker to inspect the tent the offender was living in and deem it unsuitable for human occupation. Mental health court was clearly doing something right if it had won over the good people of Unity, but all I told Sheila beforehand about the program was that the judge wanted her to sit down with someone who might be able to help her shake her drug use. She showed up on time for her appointment at the Tower, and as the judge had promised, Sheila walked out an hour later convinced that she'd found her people.

We'd known from Sheila's brief stay at the DRC that she responded well to talk therapy. Instead of self-medicating with marijuana, she could get drugs through mental health court that would do the job better, with fewer side effects. The services provided by mental health court cost Sheila nothing. As far as I could tell, mental health court was a perfect application of the risk/need model of criminal justice. By spending a few thousand dollars this year to improve an offender's mental health and keep her drug use in check, we could save tens of thousands in incarceration costs down the road. Sheila was able to keep her job while she was in mental health court. She had spending money. She paid taxes.

And then one Monday she didn't show. The judge deployed me immediately to Sheila's front door. Plenty of other people wanted into the program. If Sheila was quitting, the judge was going to the next name on the list. Her mother met me there. "You already know what it's about," she told me. "And he's the worst one yet. He's on these corners every day waving that fucking gun around."

I went to Sheila's bedroom and found her watching TV with the new boyfriend. The room reeked of weed. "A lot of time and money's being spent trying to help you out," I told her. "You can't just no-show with these people."

Because the boyfriend was there, I didn't mention what the help was for. Sheila told me the appointment had slipped her mind. I knew it wasn't true, but there was no sense in arguing here. I told her to call her caseworker and get a new appointment, and I about-faced out of there. As soon as my back was turned, the boyfriend muttered something to Sheila. Sheila hushed him immediately, and I knew the remark was at my expense, or rather at the expense of the institution I represented.

I wanted to tell Sheila's boyfriend that he could call me whatever he wanted if he would just leave Sheila alone. Mental health court presented a clearer path to freedom and self-reliance than any boyfriend, but the boyfriend was of Sheila's world, and we were the government and carried the government's long history of false promises to neighborhoods like the Seventh Ward. Sheila's judge had placed her in the best public assistance program I'd yet seen within the justice system, but it was the third one we'd tried—the fourth if you counted Sheila's one-week return to high school—and our credibility had suffered for our missteps. There was also the fact that treatment of the sort the mental health court counselors believed Sheila needed didn't produce results overnight. We'd gotten her to cut back on weed but we were a long way from imparting a new perspective on the drug trade or the collateral damage it wrought. A don still looked like the smartest bet Sheila could make, and I could tell from the flutter in her eyes that she believed she'd found one.

At the front door on my way out of the house, Sheila's mother asked what I was going to do. "I can't control who she goes out with," I said.

"Boy," she said, "who she goes out with is ninety percent of it."

I got in my Crown Vic and drove away. Sheila was the third-youngest person on my caseload, and I had the sinking feeling that we'd gotten to her far too late. I spent the rest of the day wallowing in what Charles and Beth laughingly referred to as "the Better-World Lament." In a better world, girls like Sheila could make their own way without relying on a man. Men like her boyfriend would have their pick of professions that offered decent pay without the hazard of a bullet through the eye. Young people in the Seventh Ward wouldn't get "addicted to the lifestyle" because they would never be exposed to it in the first place.

The Better-World Lament was helpful up to a point. In your spare time it reminded you to keep track of what your politicians were up to. On the job, it was useless. The job needed you in the moment, in New Orleans in the second decade of the twenty-first century. If I could keep my focus there, I couldn't help noticing that Sheila was smoking less now than when we had met, and she had a job, and she had treatment professionals on hand to talk to about her hopes and fears. Some of her needs were being met, and her risk was a little lower than it might have been if we'd never made the effort. You didn't dare call it a win, but you would be just as bold and just as foolish to say that it wasn't worth doing.

# TEN

# the descendants
# of masters

I was the greenest PO in the District for about fourteen months, until Lamar arrived. He was about forty and had spent his first twenty working years in various administrative positions within the state government. The jobs were easy but unfulfilling, and finally he'd decided to make a change. He'd applied to be a PO for the same reasons I had. He believed that the criminal justice system in general, and the community supervision wing in particular, would be at the center of the major structural changes to come in American social services in the next decade. He wanted to play a part in shaping crucial public institutions for the better.

Lamar shaved his head and was built like a heavyweight prizefighter, but he'd never set foot in a gym. In his spare time, he was a voracious reader and news junkie, always up-to-date on the machinations of state and city government. He grew up poor in New Orleans. When he thought about the two messages we were supposed to impart to offenders—*Your circumstances aren't your fault* and *You have the power to change them*—he worried that a lot of us focused too much on the first message at the expense of the second. After riding along with me for a couple of days, he offered roughly the same critique of my performance as Sheila. "Give it to them straight. They can take it. They've been taking it all their lives."

He let me know I was making the same mistakes with white

offenders as African Americans, which I guessed was supposed to make me feel better. He was older than me and had firsthand experience of the world I was moving through. I valued his opinion, but I didn't want him to think I hadn't taken the time to look critically at my own work.

"It's just that I didn't have to deal with any of this stuff," I told him, "so it's hard to know what I would have done in their shoes."

"You would have done what I did. What most poor people do. The right thing."

Lamar understood that the probation and parole population were the people in whom need brought out the worst—the people whose need spurred them to criminal activity. They were the people on whom public investment stood the best chance of improving public safety. Spending money on offenders was practical, but to Lamar it was also unfair, at least as long as poor people who didn't break the law got next to nothing in the way of government assistance.

Lamar's supervision philosophy was founded on the premise that most poor people followed the law. Drug dealers and robbers were the minority. Lamar believed that poverty grew antisocial behavior and that the best way to decrease risk in a population was to attend first to need. He also believed that in trying to make allowances for the needy, we sometimes inadvertently inflicted fresh damage on the neighborhoods that had already seen far more than their share.

"You cut a drug dealer loose," he told me, "and it's not your neighborhood he's going back to. Not your corner he's defending with a .45. Ask the people living next door to him if they think you taking it easy on this guy is really advancing the cause."

Like everyone else at the New Orleans District, he was astonished when he learned how few tools the department provided. He was disgusted when he learned that we had to put offenders in jail to get them detoxed, but as he went through the familiar new-guy paces, he became more convinced than ever before that the worst thing a PO could do to an offender was fail to hold him accountable. Lamar believed the POs of the New Orleans District were all, or almost all, engaging in what the George W. Bush administration had once referred to as "the soft bigotry of low expectations."

Lamar's office mate was the New Orleans District's most strident and vocal liberal. They made a fascinating pair, in lockstep on what the future justice system should look like—less jail, more treatment, more public assistance—but they had drawn wildly different conclusions about what an individual PO should be doing here and now to keep his charges from getting killed, overdosing, or going back to prison. "You're infantilizing these people," Lamar told his office mate, and the office mate countered that Lamar was forgetting that most people who grew up in Hollygrove and the Lower Ninth Ward and Central City weren't like him. He was a freak, a million-dollar body with a million-dollar brain who didn't give a damn about money. The only kind of work he'd ever done was in the public sector.

Like most of the office, Lamar and his office mate had found camaraderie in disagreement and even in occasionally losing their tempers with each other. Wins may have been rare at the New Orleans District, and they may have assumed unexpected forms, such as sending a mentally ill offender to prison for ninety days so that he could get a doctor's appointment, but we never forgot that we worked at a place where almost everyone cared deeply about the mission. "Not all state jobs are like that," Lamar said. His deadpan was among the best I'd ever seen, somewhere between a smirk and a sneer.

I brought Lamar along with me to check on Damien. He'd moved out of the crash pad in the East. He was living with his aunt in the working-class Gentilly neighborhood. The aunt's block was full of old people in small, single-family homes. Most of the lawns got mowed every week. Damien's aunt's place had a green-and-white awning and a row of red daisies planted along the walkway. The aunt let it be known from the doorway that she didn't want Damien on her property, and she wanted Lamar and me there even less. "I've got neighbors," she told us, but ultimately decided letting the neighbors see us milling around the front lawn was preferable to allowing us into the living room.

She shouted down the hall for Damien. He came out in a big white T-shirt and oversized jeans. He looked healthier than he'd looked at the place in the East. He'd lost some of the extra weight and rediscovered the smile I'd come to associate with a don at the top of his game.

"Don't be long," the aunt said, and went inside and shut the door behind her.

"Sorry," Damien told us. "She's old-school."

"Meaning what?" Lamar said. He said it in a friendly way, as if the question were a matter of academic curiosity.

"Church," Damien said. "Study hard. In bed by nine."

"My aunts were the same way," Lamar said.

"Let me guess." Damien extended an index finger and drew a circle around Lamar's gun belt. "You listened."

"I did my share of dumb stuff," Lamar said.

"Never got caught, though."

"I never sold drugs."

"Good for you." Damien turned his back to Lamar and tried the smile on me. "I'll be back on my feet in a few weeks. I've got some shit in the hopper."

"Like what?" I said.

"You really want an answer to that?"

I reached into my pocket and pulled out a flyer and handed it to him. The flyers had shown up at the office on Monday. One of the biggest construction companies in town was looking for twenty able-bodied offenders. There were benefits, and the pay started at eighteen bucks an hour, more than double the minimum wage.

Damien gave it a quick look and chuckled to himself. "This shit's never for real. They run your rap sheet and that's that."

"Not this time," I said. "They're only taking people with criminal records. The guy who owns the company found Jesus or something. He wants to help people the job market's overlooking."

There were twenty spots for 7,000 offenders. The flyer wasn't going to change the game for everybody, but for the lucky twenty who made the cut, it promised to be a transformative experience. A living wage, access to health care, the capacity to get a place of your own, and you didn't have to worry about defending your territory with a gun or going to jail if the police came across some of your product. The flyer represented the clearest path to true freedom I'd been able to offer anyone on my caseload.

Naturally the fifty flyers that the construction company sent us had already been photocopied a hundred times over. Some of the people I'd delivered them to were unlikely to ace the interview. Damien was different. Damien knew how to talk to people. He knew how to shake hands and look you in the eye. He was a don. The foreman would know he was capable as soon as he set eyes on him.

Damien folded the flyer in half and offered it back to me. "I'm good. You'll find another taker."

"Hold on to it. You might change your mind."

"You're a fool if you don't take this opportunity," Lamar said.

Damien rolled his eyes at me as if he and I were both in on the same joke. He balled up the flyer and tossed it back to me, flashed a peace sign, and made for the door. "I'll give you a call when I get the new place," he told me. He pulled the door shut behind him, and I heard the bolt click. Lamar and I stood alone in the grass.

"Well," Lamar said, "at least you got your flyer back."

As we made our way to our next stop, Lamar told me that Damien reminded him of people he used to know, people from his old neighborhood. "We had that guy," Lamar said. "Every piece-of-shit neighborhood has that guy. Every kid wants what he's got."

You were lying if you said you'd never pictured yourself driving the don's car, going to bed with his girl. But most boys outgrew it. They figured out that the don wasn't really on the side of the poor and the addicted. He didn't really want the neighborhood to improve. His business interests were served by keeping things as they were. If everybody got clean and got a day job, the customer base would go away. To Lamar, it was critical that we acknowledge all the reasons a life of crime could look rational to a poor person, but if we made too many allowances for offenders' choices, we would be treating the people we were supposed to help like they lacked free will. And if they lacked free will, what was the point of going to work for the institution charged with showing them how to change their lives? We would do well to remember that most poor people made the moral decision to abstain from the violence and addiction that had plagued the city for more than a hundred years.

"A guy like that doesn't need to hear that he didn't have a choice," Lamar said. "He had one. It wasn't easy, but it was still a choice."

"You think I should have pushed harder," I said.

"With the flyer? Hell no. He was never gonna go for that."

"Okay. I'll bite. What's he gonna go for?"

"Jail."

I had to laugh.

He laughed, too, but I could see that he meant what he said. "Like I said, I know that guy. He likes the life. He even likes the down slope, probably."

I filled him in on the rest of Damien's story: the quick rise and the still-quicker fall. Lamar had never heard the term *addicted to the lifestyle*, and he found it both hilarious and apt. "An addiction is exactly what it is," Lamar said. "And they don't make methadone for that one."

A couple of weeks later, Lamar got his wish: Damien went to jail, and on a serious charge. The arrest happened in a neighboring parish known for its by-the-book DA. According to the police report, Damien and a friend had showed up in the parking lot of a club armed with a couple of AR-15s. Someone called the police before Damien and the friend found the guy they were looking for. No shots were fired. The guns were confiscated and Damien and his friend were charged with being felons in possession of firearms. Before I could file paperwork alerting the probation judge of the new arrest, Damien was out of jail. He called me from his aunt's house. He said it wasn't what it looked like. He gave me the name of the detective who was handling the case.

The detective took my call, and he told me that the DA's office was willing to let the gun charge slide.

"Since when are y'all letting gun charges slide?" I asked the detective.

"Your guy knows where a lot of bodies are buried. And he's willing to dime out a couple of shooters out here who don't play by the rules."

I thought of Kendrick's advice to his young friends about using the system to your advantage whenever possible. Whether Damien was motivated by principle—by the rules, whatever they might be—or he simply saw a chance to incapacitate a rival, I would never know. He would never tell me anything more than he told me on the phone about that night in the parking lot. The next time I saw him, he was back in the apartment complex in the East. He was in a different unit, six doors down from the one he had been living in when he bottomed out. He was driving a Honda Accord instead of a Range Rover, and he'd yet to replenish his closet, but otherwise he looked like his old self.

And then a few more weeks went by and Damien got arrested again. He'd been feuding with a cousin over an old debt, and he'd left a note at the cousin's house saying that if the cousin didn't repay him in full, he was going to trash the house. A week later he broke into the house when the cousin wasn't home and took a baseball bat to the TV and the stereo. After Damien got arrested, I went to see him in jail and told him I would have to set a hearing so that the judge could address the new arrest.

"Do your thing," he said. "I'm not sweating this piddly shit."

I set the hearing and brought the police report to the probation judge. I stood next to the bench while she read.

"Is this for real?" she said. "He really threatened, in writing, to trash his cousin's house? And then went through with it? Is this guy out of his mind?"

It was a rhetorical question, but I wanted to answer it. "I think there's something he likes about all this."

The judge told me to have a seat while she thought things over. She handled a couple of other matters before she told the assistant district attorney to call Damien's case.

Damien and his defense attorney came up from the pews and took their seats at the defense table. Damien wore a black suit and a bright purple tie. I recognized his attorney from a billboard. He was always at the courthouse, but I'd never seen him up close. No one on my caseload could afford him. He walked like a track star fresh off the finish line. When he saw a good-looking woman, he winked or pursed his lips.

Because most probation hearings began and ended with my requesting the offender's release, I hadn't dealt with defense attorneys very often. When offenders picked up new charges, the public defender's office usually represented them. Only the dons and the better-off drug dealers hired private defense attorneys. Most of them were worth every penny. A local newspaper story on New Orleans public defenders reported that attorney staffing was in steady decline, from seventy-eight positions in 2009 to forty-two in 2016. There was no shortage of applicants. Ivy League grads looking for courtroom experience and, in some cases, a chance to earn some social justice bona fides got turned away every year due to budget cuts. With as many as three hundred clients per attorney, New Orleans public defenders had double the workloads recommended by the American Bar Association.

There was another factor that favored private attorneys. Criminal court judges are elected officials. The top criminal defense attorneys tended to be well-placed in churches and community activist groups—in other words, organizations that got people to the polls—and they contributed money to reelection campaigns.

"They don't write those checks out of the goodness of their hearts," Beth told me, but even the biggest cynics in our ranks tended to agree that New Orleans judges weren't consciously favoring private defense attorneys. Usually private attorneys got better deals than public defenders because private attorneys had the time and resources to prepare a stronger defense. There was no denying, though, that judges viewed public defenders as civil servants—more like cops, ADAs, or POs—and private defense attorneys as peers. Judges saw defense attorneys at fundraisers and galas. They moved in the same circles. At Mardi Gras, they went to the same parties and rode on the same floats.

Public defenders lived in tiny apartments in rough neighborhoods. They didn't go to fundraisers. They were lucky if they had enough disposable income to cover the utility bill at the end of the month. When they showed up to court, they didn't tell the judge that it was nice running into her on Saturday night.

After he got the usual pleasantries out of the way, Damien's defense attorney bashed the schools, the shabby welfare state. He suggested that race may have played a factor in the police's fingering Damien for the break-in.

The judge pointed out that Damien's cousin, whom she understood to be of the same race as Damien, was the one who put him up for the job, but on the whole she was moved by what the defense attorney had to say. When the defense attorney recommended drug court as an alternative to incarceration, the judge didn't ask me whether Damien had a drug problem. She didn't ask me anything. She told Damien he would be screened that afternoon.

The assistant district attorney objected. "Your Honor," he said, "the facts of the case don't point to a drug problem. I really don't see the connection."

He was a white guy no older than twenty-seven, with a champagne-colored pompadour and an American flag pin on his lapel, and the defense attorney made short work of him. The ADA didn't see the connection because he didn't grow up in the inner city and he didn't understand what people of color were up against in this country and what desperate acts the American experience could induce them to do.

"The rules are different for you and me," the defense attorney told the ADA, who, though obviously a rookie, knew a losing battle when he saw one, and he told the judge that drug court would be fine.

In principle, the ADA was right to object to the drug-court referral. The state supreme court oversaw all of Louisiana's drug courts, and its bylaws said that Damien's crime couldn't be a pretext for a drug-court referral. A probation violation could. At the moment, a probation violation was all we had. Damien hadn't been convicted of anything. He'd merely been arrested and charged.

Damien's judge was one of the youngest in the building, but she'd learned quickly on the job. Before she ruled on a violation, she almost always called the PO up to the bench and asked his impression of the dynamic in the offender's home. She recognized that we saw things she was bound to miss. She believed hearing from us allowed her to make more informed judgments.

Then and now, I believed that all the judges at Tulane and Broad cared what happened to the people brought before them, but the judges who asked the most questions and kept the closest tabs on offenders naturally became our favorites. I didn't fault the young judge for putting Damien in drug court, though at the time I had only a vague idea of how drug court worked. I knew it was run out of the Tower, where the mental health court caseworkers and the public defenders were headquartered, and followed roughly the same model as mental health court. Weekly settings before the judge were paired with extensive counseling sessions. I assumed that the goal was to get the offender to shake his drug habit, but the screener assigned to interview Damien told me that while most of the drug courts at Tulane and Broad were tailored to the needs of addicts, new drug courts had been launched to try to deal with the lifestyle addiction—in other words, drug court for drug dealers.

"The judge wants him in drug-dealer drug court for sure," the screener told me. Technically the screener was supposed to decide for herself which version of drug court the offender got. She didn't have to interview Damien for very long before she agreed with the judge's assessment. Damien didn't have a drug addiction. Damien was addicted to money and power.

Like mental health court, drug court was supposed to serve as a supplement to ordinary supervision. It operated out of Tulane and Broad and everyone in the program was on probation, but drug court got its funding from the supreme court and wasn't subject to the annual budget crunches at the courthouse and the Department of Corrections. Offenders were supposed to kick in more than $1,000 in fees over the course of the program, but drug-court judges waived arrearages for offenders who completed the program. As far as I knew, drug-court collections were taken about as seriously as P&P supervision fees.

When I asked Damien about the break-in, he told me his cousin was crazy, and the jury would see for themselves if it came to that. When I asked him about drug court, he told me it was just another game, and he learned the rules inside of an hour. When you got in front of the judge, you were supposed to proclaim that you realized the drug trade had hurt your community and you were committed to finding another way to earn a living.

In individual counseling and group sessions you were free to say just how tedious you found the whole charade. You sold dope because you wanted the good life, and dope was the only way to get it in the ghetto. America called itself the land of opportunity, but really it was the land of opportunism. Opportunism explained slavery and the eradication of Native Americans. Drug dealers in New Orleans saw themselves not as the descendants of slaves but as the descendants of masters. They were people who knew what they wanted and had the balls to take it. In a group session one of the dons was supposed to have said, "Thomas Jefferson didn't give a fuck who got in his way. Why should I?"

I got all of this secondhand from Damien. The counselors were bound to confidentiality about what exactly was said at the Tower, but I got to be friendly with a couple of them over the next few months and came to know their grievances. In one-on-one sessions and, to an even greater extent, in group therapy, the counselors were always on the defensive about their capacity to offer useful advice. The drug dealers played the race card on the white women and the gender card on the black women. They called the black men who worked in the program faggots or, in kinder moods, told them that they must not be as interested in providing for their families as the drug dealers were. They said that they got more top-flight pussy in a single Friday night than a workingman could pull in a hundred lifetimes.

In court they renounced their former ways and furnished check stubs from landscaping companies and sandwich shops and valet services. They promised to work their way up from the bottom. They thanked the counselors for taking the time to show them just how misguided their former lifestyle really was. A few threw in some religion for good measure.

When Damien was called to the microphone and asked for an update, he stuck to the facts. He was doing some valeting in the Quarter at night and cutting lawns by day. He avoided eye contact as he passed his check stubs to the judge. Between the courtroom obligations and the counseling sessions, three of them per week during an offender's first two months in the program, drug court was a major time-suck, and when you added on twenty-five to thirty hours at a minimum-wage job to convince the judge you were a law-abiding citizen, you had to push hard in your downtime to move enough dope to maintain your lifestyle.

The judge who oversaw Damien's section of drug-dealer drug court had always been one of my favorites. Off the bench he was foul-mouthed and casual. He wore tennis shoes and beat-up blue jeans. He had a temper but didn't hold a grudge. Five minutes after he chewed you out, he asked with genuine interest if you had anything interesting planned for the weekend.

He was also one of the courthouse's most vocal critics of mass incarceration. He referred to the state penitentiary as the Plantation. In his pep talks to young black offenders I'd heard him imply that some police in New Orleans had long had an Any-black-guy-will-do approach to naming suspects.

Like all elected officials, he was keenly aware that he had a constituency to answer to. As he made his rulings, he struggled aloud with the tension at the heart of the current moment in criminal justice. He understood that most of the people in drug-dealer drug court had chosen their profession for lack of any lucrative alternatives, and he supposed that he might have done the same if faced with similar circumstances. Then again, most people in the neighborhoods where the dealers made their living did not do the same. They considered drugs and violence a scourge, one they'd been asking the government to address for decades.

Many drug dealers started out as victims, but the judge often wondered whether treating them as such produced unintended consequences. By giving drug dealers a pass for their behavior, were we inadvertently creating more victims? Would the current moment in American criminal justice eventually be regarded as just as misguided as its predecessor?

It was easy now to see the mass-incarceration era for the tragedy it was, but in its early days it was widely perceived as an investment in violent and addicted communities. Mass incarceration was once embraced as a progressive cause, a vast government expenditure aimed at curing social ills. Like many judges, the drug-court judge had been a prosecutor in that era. He'd believed that tough sentencing of robbers and drug dealers could give law-abiding poor citizens a safer community. Now, with drug court, he was trying to course correct. He was trying to go easy on people who, if somebody had gone easy on them ten or fifteen years before, might not have ended up at Tulane and Broad, but he twisted in his seat every time he made a ruling, as if he thought the ground beneath him might shift again and he would discover that the measures he'd taken to help his constituents were causing them more pain and more suffering and making it harder than ever before for them to live in peace and seek prosperity.

The counselors and the judge and I met in the judge's chambers before each drug-court setting, and the judge made no effort to hide his apprehensions about the responsibility he felt to the people before him. After all, they were drug dealers, the people in the city at greatest risk of doing harm and having harm done to them. Every decision mattered. When Damien told his counselor that he'd quit his valet job and was now working as a freelance tattoo artist, the counselor told the judge that she had serious concerns. The business would be cash in hand. There would be no log of hours worked. We would have no way of knowing what Damien was up to when he was, or claimed to be, on the job.

When the judge heard something he didn't like, he hunched over and tugged at the heels of his shoes as if he were getting ready to pull a pistol out of one of them. "So you want me to tell him he can't do tattoos?" he said.

"I think he was better off with a day job, Your Honor," the counselor said.

"He was parking cars in the French Quarter. At night."

"He had a boss. He had structure."

"People have been known to sell drugs in the Quarter. Out of cars, sometimes."

But he saw her point. By requiring Damien to work forty hours at an honest job and occupying most of his free time with treatment, the counselor was hoping to put enough distance between Damien and his former lifestyle—the one he was addicted to—that he considered the benefits of a more conventional life. It was lifestyle-addiction detox.

"I think if we sign off on this tattoo business," the counselor said, "we're basically telling him he doesn't have to account for his time. He's free to sell dope all day."

The judge did the shoe grab again, this time in my direction. "What do you see at the house?" he asked.

Damien was still driving the Accord, but he'd filled out his closet and bought new furniture. "He's definitely got another source of income," I said.

The judge nodded. "So he's still selling, but the valet job means he's got less time to do it in."

The judge asked the counselor what she'd been seeing in her one-on-one sessions. This was murky terrain. The counselors were tasked both with maintaining the offender's confidentiality and with keeping the judge apprised of the offender's progress. The informal compromise reached by the drug courts was for counselors to give the judges a general sense of the offender's mind-set without going into particulars. "He continues to present a very different outlook in treatment than in court," the counselor said.

"In other words, he tells me he's walking the line. He tells you he's gonna do whatever the fuck he feels like."

The counselor shrugged. She'd gone as far as she could go. The judge respected that.

"Okay," he said. "We're in agreement. Tattoo idea is no good. He's keeping his day job. Night job. Whatever."

An hour later in court, he called Damien up to the microphone and told him the same. Damien asked the judge if he could be heard. He reminded the judge that people with criminal records couldn't always hold out for above-board employment and that bosses often took advantage of probationers and parolees because they knew their services weren't in high demand. If a boss treated a probationer poorly, it wasn't like he could just go get another job.

The tattoo thing was a chance for Damien to be his own boss, an entrepreneur. He'd loved art as a child but he'd gotten no encouragement from his teachers. "Your Honor," Damien said, "you know what these schools are like. You could have fucking Picasso in there and they would call him a hack."

All the drug-court offenders seated in the pews laughed. The judge warned Damien about his language, but anyone could see that he, too, was won over. He told Damien he'd changed his mind about the tattoo idea. Damien could ditch the pay stub life and start his business. What was the justice system for if not to defend the right to the American dream?

Damien had played us, of course, but at the time I was as captivated by his performance as the judge. When I looked at the judge, I saw a man who, entering the back half of his career, probably felt that he'd been wrong more often than he'd been right. He wanted to help people, but he had limited tools, and too often he didn't know how to use them. And he believed in Damien's wit and nerve. He saw what I'd imagined the hiring agents at the construction company seeing when Damien walked through their doors with their flyer. If Damien had never gotten addicted to the drug life, he could have done anything.

The longer I studied successful drug dealers, the surer I became that the lifestyle addiction wasn't fed only by money and power and the thrill of the chase. Getting over on authority figures was a fix unto itself. Conning a cop or a PO was one thing. All the dealers had done that at one time or another. Not many could claim they'd gotten a judge soapboxing about the American dream.

The judge wrapped up soon enough and told Damien he was free to go. Damien gave a little bow and thanked the judge for his time and his compassion. On his way out of the courtroom he flashed a grin at the rest of the drug-court offenders. A few laughed. Most kept their cool. He'd won one for the team.

I brought Lamar with me the next time I went to Damien's house. A woman in her early twenties answered the door in a bra and underpants. She flirted with us at the door, pursing her lips and offering up her wrists. "Come take me away, law man," she said, and blew us a kiss.

Getting lightly heckled by offenders' girlfriends was a matter of course. We handled it in the usual way, standing there in the doorway until she'd had her fill. "I'll be in the shower if you need me," she said, then went into the bathroom and shut the door.

We found Damien in the bedroom. He was pulling a polo shirt over his head when we walked in. He shook hands and was as friendly as ever, and as eager to show us around and open closets and pull out drawers. Something was different, though. Sweat beaded across his brow, and his breaths were slightly labored, and he wasn't quite as quick with his return volleys as Lamar drubbed him with the latest iteration of his anti-drug-dealing routine. Lamar had begun asking drug dealers to consider third-world places where abject poverty were facts of life and yet people still managed to make moral decisions. People chose not to steal, not to hide from pain in a needle. "The poor," Lamar said, "deserve our admiration. Not our pity."

"In my experience," Damien said, "poverty is pretty fucking pitiful."

"What does that say about your experience?" Lamar said.

Under normal circumstances Damien would have relished an exchange like this. Today he gave Lamar the last word. As we made our way back across the parking lot, I spotted the Range Rover, and I supposed the reclamation project was complete. Like any addict, Damien had bottomed out only to climb back to where he had been before. While the girlfriend occupied us at the door, Damien had had plenty of time to hide whatever it was he didn't want us to find. The symptoms of his anxiety—the sweaty brow, the slightly less confident demeanor—were subtle enough that few judges would have deemed them sufficiently suspicious to justify a search. They were, however, exactly the sorts of tells that we were getting paid to notice. In the Crown Vic, I asked Lamar whether he'd picked up on them.

"Why do you think I was carrying on like that?" he said. "Wanted you to have time to figure out what to do."

"You think I should have searched?"

"I don't think ransacking the place is the right play just yet. I think you stick with talk for now. But if I'm betting my life, I stand by my original answer. He's not stopping until you put him behind bars."

When you were dealing with a drug dealer, you had to weigh the risk to the offender—the harm done to him by putting him in jail—against the risk the offender posed to other people. In Damien's case, the latter risk was hard to ignore. On his way to getting his Range Rover back, he'd taken a rifle to a nightclub and trashed a relative's apartment, and these were just the risky behaviors I knew about. There were others, I was sure. Like Lamar, I was starting to think that the risk Damien presented might be contained by only one institution, and it wasn't drug court.

The following week, ten drug-court offenders told the judge that they had gotten licensed to work as vehicle auctioneers. They, like Damien, wanted to be business owners. They wanted their piece of the American dream. The judge could see that he was trapped. He couldn't say yes to Damien and no to them. As the weeks went by, the ranks of entrepreneurs deepened. By the end of the month, most of the day jobs had been abandoned in favor of small-business opportunities.

The counselors and I could see that the judge felt foolish. We wanted him to know that we were on his side. We all wanted to believe that as long as we showed compassion for the people in our care, they would be honest with us.

A few weeks after Lamar and I checked in on Damien, I found myself in the apartment complex again, meeting up with a new offender who lived on the floor below. I finished up with the new guy and went up and knocked on Damien's door. He was surprised to see me back so soon, but he had no misgivings this time. I told him I didn't plan to come in. I'd stopped by because I was curious about his childhood desire to be an artist. I asked if he would show me some of his work.

He reached into the entertainment center beside the door and pulled out a big plastic box, of the sort drills are kept in, and showed me the tattoo kit and a couple of pages of sketches. He had skulls and pinup girls and knives and guns and balls of fire. I can't claim any kind of eye for the fine arts, but anyone could see the talent on those pages.

I knew he wasn't making his living doing tattoos. That was a lie that Damien told a judge so that he could sell more drugs than he could when he worked as a valet, but the remark about his teachers' failure to nurture his artistic talent rang true.

"I liked to draw as a kid," I told Damien. "I wasn't any good, but everybody told me to keep at it anyway."

Damien laughed and stood there for a minute holding the plastic box, and I let myself think we were on the cusp of something. He wasn't going to renounce his profession just because I'd acknowledged one of the very many ways that my upbringing differed from his, but I thought he might open up just a little and show me something I hadn't seen before.

"Anyway," he said, and he put the tattoo kit down and gripped the doorknob. "You know where to find me if you need ink."

The next time Lamar and I worked together, he told me he'd been thinking a lot about Damien. He had a couple of dons of his own, and he'd tried the racial-solidarity speech and the dignity-in-poverty speech. To one guy he'd simply said, "You have a good brain. You have guts. You don't have to be a fucking drug dealer."

He'd been out of the academy only three months and already he was feeling that he'd brought the wrong message, or he hadn't figured out the right way to deliver it. He'd thought that the demographic similarities he shared with most offenders would improve his chances of reaching them, but sometimes he got the impression that the young black offenders actually preferred to take correction from a white guy than a black guy. Lamar had tried to see a marker of black pride in this: African American offenders expected white people to represent institutions bearing false promises but expected black people to hold out for better. Lamar no longer thought any offenders believed that. They wanted a white PO because they were more comfortable taking orders from a white person. It felt more natural, the way things had always been and always would be. If stated loudly and often enough over time, certain bigotries—the low-expectation one in particular— seemed to bind themselves to the DNA.

Despite all of this, Lamar was glad he'd taken the job. When you broke it down to its components, it was just as beautiful as he'd hoped it would be: the one man in trouble, the other saying he could help. It was ancient, noble work, and Lamar couldn't imagine a group of people who needed it more than the probationers and parolees of New Orleans.

Lamar hadn't locked up any of his dons. He'd had as good a chance as he would ever get with one of them. The guy had taken forever to open the door, and he'd made a major racket getting all of his illegal stuff out of view of the home inspection. Lamar had reasonable suspicion to conduct a search, but the offender had just gotten out of jail on another misdemeanor, and Lamar didn't want to send him back. Lamar believed that, given time, the offender would complete his GED and try to earn an honest living. Lamar thought of the offender every morning when he checked the NOPD arrest logs for the names of offenders on his caseload. Passing up the home inspection was an act of hope, and now Lamar had to live with the consequences.

As for Damien, he continued to get new clothes and new stereo equipment and new girlfriends. He passed his drug tests and said the right things to the judge. When other members of his cohort got arrested selling drugs, he called them amateurs. One of them got arrested by a PO during a home inspection. He'd left dope and money out on the kitchen table, and the PO needed only five minutes to find the gun that went with them.

Damien was more careful lately about home inspections. He answered the door by the second knock. He never gave me reason to believe he had anything illegal hidden in his apartment. The opportunity I'd passed up that day with Lamar in the East wasn't going to come around again.

Damien had plastic cups to piss in and counselors to talk to and a judge and a PO to appease. We'd installed a number of mechanisms to steer him away from the drug trade, and of course we also hoped he would be dissuaded by "the idea" that Travis's mother had told me and Beth about, but as the weeks went by and he passed every test, I could see that the opposite was true. The more of our mechanisms he defeated, the stronger his convictions grew.

Even then, I couldn't know whether the thrill came from a conscious belief that drug dealing was an honest pursuit that should be permitted by the law—in other words, a belief that Damien was right and we were wrong. I was beginning to think it had its foundation in that older belief Lamar had talked about, the one that went back much further than the drug trade and assured you that convention of any sort should be bucked because convention had never been on the side of your people.

"Your people" could be defined by race or class. White drug dealers appeared to get the same release from fooling a cop or a PO as black drug dealers. No matter how Damien got addicted to the lifestyle, I saw that every measure we'd put in place to fight his addiction had fed it instead. The best thing I could do to reduce his risk was to deny him the satisfaction I'd been supplying—the fix, if you liked—when I gave him passing marks on his home inspections. I was in the complex on Chef Highway twice a week, and I bypassed Damien's door until the judge asked me to perform another inspection.

I told myself that staying away from Damien was the most productive thing I could do for him right now, but I can't deny that I stayed away in part because Damien made me feel like I was bad at my job. I wanted him to get out of the drug trade and put his talents to socially productive use, but I didn't know how to bring him over to my side. If pressed, I would admit that I didn't think he was going to stop selling dope until I locked him up, and locking him up felt like a waste of time, money, and above all talent. I wanted better for Damien, but I didn't know how to get it, so I just quit knocking at his door.

# ELEVEN

# a product of hazard

Sometimes in the summer months we did our fieldwork at night. The temperature dipped after sunset, greatly decreasing your chances of dying of heatstroke under your bulletproof vest. This wasn't to say that the nights were pleasant. Eighty-five with 100 percent humidity was the norm from May to August, and what you lost in heat by waiting till dusk you gained in mosquitoes. The best reason to go out at night was to see another side of offenders. People who stayed inside all day usually came out at night, and vice versa. The landscape changed. You saw different faces on the stoops as you dragged your Crown Vic from block to block.

Central City always buzzed after dark. The drug dealers worked the corners and the alleys. Ten-year-olds sped up the sidewalks on bicycles. Sixteen-year-olds slow-rolled down the streets hooting at girls or shouting insults at friends perched on the hoods of parked cars. The middle-aged people on the stoops drank beer. Little kids seated at their feet lapped at Push Pops and Tastee-Ice and bobbed their heads to the boom of house parties and car stereos and DJs set up on tailgates and truck beds. We always kept the windows down in the Crown Vic so that we didn't miss anything. When we heard a siren we played the guessing game Cop Car or Ambulance?—although where you had one you almost always had the other.

The city's most vocal critics, most of them local, often mention how rare it is to go to a New Orleans party and not hear a siren in the distance, as if our two specialties—fun and death—are doomed to share a wavelength, but Beth didn't go in for any of that. When she heard the night music, she heard the city at its best. When she heard a siren, she heard lives being saved.

When we got to the Landry house, the brothers were sitting on the steps with their dogs. Once in a while neighbors would stop on their lawn for a beer. Most of the time the Landrys drank alone or with their mother. She was home that night, seated on the steps between her sons. She asked me what I thought of Ronald's chances of beating the gun charge.

I'd already filled Beth in on this, and she took the liberty of answering for me. "He's damn lucky. They don't let gun stuff slide."

"He didn't know about the gun," the Landrys' mother said.

"If they let off all the people who say they didn't know about the gun—"

The mother laughed. "You've got me there. But he's my boy and I believe him."

"I believe him, too," Beth said. "And that's a very good sign for him. As a rule I don't believe anybody."

The Landrys' mother laughed again. Like her sons, she'd come to appreciate Beth's sense of humor. "Y'all want to come in and see the puppies?" she said.

I was hoping for a quick stop, but Beth said that only a crazy person refused to go in and see the puppies, so I kept my mouth shut and followed her into the living room. The puppies had graduated from the cardboard box to a sort of pen, with a chicken wire border and newspaper covering the floor. They had almost doubled in size in the month since I'd seen them.

"Got buyers lined up for all but one," Javaron said. He stepped over the chicken wire and picked up a small white dog. "Any interest?"

"My son would go ape shit," Beth said.

"A boy should have a dog," Javaron said.

"*A* dog is one thing," the Landrys' mother said. "Nine dogs is how you end up in the nut house."

Javaron rolled the puppy onto its back and cradled it against his chest. It looked like a toy in his enormous arms.

We went back outside and hung out on the steps for a few more minutes and got the latest. Ronald was switching doctors again and hoping the next prescription would bring the seizures to heel. His tongue was still recovering from the attack he'd had at the New Orleans District. He considered it only a matter of time before another big one hit.

Javaron had tested positive for cocaine the month before. I wanted to see if he felt like he needed to go into sober living, but I didn't want to discuss it in front of his mother, even though the brothers had always told me that there were no secrets between the three of them. Beth tried her usual ribbing on Javaron, something about his doing so many pushups each day—"What are you up to now? Five thousand? Ten?"—that he had no time to get a job and help his mom out with the bills. Javaron just laughed, and his mother said that she didn't need help with the bills. She was happy to have her boys home under her roof and would pay whatever it took to keep them there.

Javaron wasn't high that night, and if he came off as a little less chummy than usual, I don't remember thinking very much of it. When I thought of Javaron over the next few days I thought of the joy with which he and his mother and brother teased one another, and I thought of him holding the puppy. When the last image you have of a person has a puppy in the middle of it, it's almost impossible to convince yourself that anything could be seriously wrong with him.

I was in Central City again the following week, this time around midday, when the Landrys were always home. This time only Ronald was there. He mentioned that Javaron had been heading off on his own lately. Ronald didn't think he had a girlfriend, and he hadn't run with a crew since he got out of prison. "Think he's just bored," Ronald said.

I viewed boredom as an opportunity for change. The next time I saw Javaron, I would try again to get him to JOB1. Those jobs with the construction company had come and gone, and Javaron hadn't shown any more interest than Damien.

"Maybe he wasn't bored enough then," Charles said. He saw boredom the way I did, as a spur to action, far more likely to be an asset to our cause than a liability.

Ronald was bored, too, but he was resigned to it. He'd given up hope that his doctors would deliver a medication that would enable him to work. He would keep trying new treatments to reduce his seizures, and he would keep trying to get SSI so that he would have a little money of his own. His goals were strictly subsistence-level. "Mom's not gonna be able to keep these hours forever," he told me.

Like most offenders, Ronald had adapted to his situation long before I came along, and he wasn't surprised to find out that I didn't know how to help him. He did tell me more than once that he appreciated the home visits. He would take all the company he could get. He loved the Saints and the Pelicans. Some visits, we didn't talk about anything but sports. Those were the visits when the PO-offender relationship felt closest to what I'd hoped it would be in my early days on the job, certainly not a friendship but not all business, either. I guessed it made sense that the easiest topics to discuss were the impersonal ones. Suffering heartache at the hands of the local football team was a hardship that cut across demographics, and if it represented an especially low form of conversation, I was in no position to be picky.

And it could lead to unexpected places. A sports story could turn into a story about watching a game with a friend or parent or grandparent who'd had a particular influence that the offender hadn't thought to mention until now. I was always trying to learn more about the people under my care, but even as I got better at steering conversation, I understood that my judgments were based on glimpses. I had at most an hour per month with the riskiest offenders on my caseload. I missed way more than I saw.

———————

When the homicide detective called and asked me about the Landry house, I believed he wanted to talk about Ronald. The detective had never heard of Ronald Landry. He was calling me because Javaron had shot and killed a teenager in a dispute over a woman. Exactly what passed between Javaron and the boy was never completely clear. Over the next week I would hear dozens of versions of the preamble to the shooting.

One way or another, Javaron was made to remember just how much clout he'd given up when he retired from the drug game. He used to be someone to be feared. Now he was getting shit talked by a teenager. He'd been able to walk away from the money he made at his old job, and the rush, but he wasn't ready to be a nobody. Pressed, he returned to what he knew. When intimidation didn't sway the guy challenging his authority, he pulled out a gun and proved he wasn't afraid to use it.

The detective asked me for any information that might be helpful to the investigation, and I was forced to admit that while I knew Javaron's daily routine as well as I knew my own, I'd failed in my many attempts to engage him in conversation about his criminal history. I told the detective I'd tried my best, but it wasn't true. I couldn't think of a maximum-risk case I'd worried about less than Javaron. He had food, shelter, and his health. Even within the maximum-risk portion of my caseload, I was apparently making unconscious resource management decisions. Pecking away at an offender's defenses took time and energy. When I couldn't get through, I got angry with myself, and I couldn't always shake it off before I knocked on the next door and tried to engage in the next conversation.

I was embarrassed to tell the detective how little I knew about Javaron. "Lives at home with his mom and brother," I said. "Raises dogs. Watches TV. Seemed like he was keeping to himself."

"He was, for a while. Retirement's hard on these guys. They miss the life."

I told the detective that I guessed the need to feel feared again, or powerful at least, was the only reasonable explanation for what Javaron had done. "I thought he was in a better spot than most, to be honest with you," I said. "Food to eat, a roof over his head. Good health, no major drug issues."

"I'm sure you did all you could." He let that line sit for a minute. "How often do y'all win these guys over?"

It was a friendly question, with nothing accusatory in it, and I gave an honest answer. "Everything that works costs money. If we had more, we could do more. The bosses don't see the connection between what we do and the murder rate."

"They don't see it here, either, in the fucking homicide unit. They ask us what we need, we tell them more detectives so we can catch more murderers. They come back with 'It's not in the budget.'"

Nothing the detective told me came as a surprise, but I welcomed the chance to commiserate. I promised to call back if I thought of anything that would help the case. I never talked to him again, but I kept trying to decide how to feel about what Javaron had done for a long time. It felt like vanity to blame myself, and it felt like dereliction to deny responsibility.

I revisited the positive cocaine test, a possible clue that Javaron was restless and seeking an outlet. When he'd told me about it, I'd played it the prescribed way. A first positive was answered with a conversation and, if needed, an offer of a sober-living referral. Even in the heyday of mass incarceration, they weren't revoking probation and parole over a single drug test. The parole board never would have let me lock Javaron up unless I could name other violations, but I could have asked more of him while he enjoyed his freedom. If Beth or Lamar had been Javaron's PO, they might have pushed him harder to get to work. They might have forced him back to JOB1. He might have hated working for minimum wage, but he would have been out of the house. Of course, boredom could have found him just as easily at work as it found him at home, and he could have responded just as violently there to his need for respect.

As usual, I brought the loss to Charles, and patiently he walked me through the department's own data on the topic. If there was evidence that a certain supervision style reduced recidivism and thus incarceration costs, the bosses would have insisted we heed it.

For the first few days after Javaron's arrest, I felt more sorrow than fury, and then I saw a picture of the victim. He was fifteen years old. Many of the eyewitness accounts had him mouthing off to Javaron and the woman whose honor Javaron was allegedly defending. Mouthing off was what fifteen-year-olds did. The sorts of adolescent indiscretions that got suburban teenagers punched in the jaw could cost a Central City teenager his life.

I wasn't supposed to pass judgment on Javaron. I was supposed to remember that if Javaron was part of the reason Central City remained a hazardous place to grow up, he was also a product of that place—a product of hazard. Long before he left his mark on his neighborhood, his neighborhood left its mark on him. I was supposed to remember that I didn't know how I would have turned out if I'd been born in Central City.

I have to admit, though, that I struggled with the numbers. If living in Central City put your chances of committing a murder at one in a thousand and living in the Garden District put your chances at one in a million, that was a very good argument for trying to make Central City more like the Garden District. But what about the 99.9 percent of Central City residents who didn't murder their neighbors?

I went to see Javaron in OPP so that he could sign some paperwork the bureaucracy demanded every time an offender became an inmate again. I didn't plan on doing anything but slide the forms through the glass partition and wait for him to sign. Most of the partitions in the visitation room were so battered that all you could see of the person on the other side of the glass was a ghostly silhouette. A silhouette was all I needed. The sheer mass of Javaron compared with the half-formed body of the teenager made my knees shake.

I couldn't pity him. I deemed him more victimizer than victim, and decided that the freedom he'd been enjoying when he took a life represented a system failure, an inability to properly assess risk. I thought to myself, *They never should have let him out of jail.*

He signed the papers quickly and slid them back to me. He told me his mother was going to come up with the money for a "paid attorney." "She knows this is my whole life on the line," he said.

I wished him luck with the case and told him I would get his paperwork processed, and I got out of there, but Javaron was with me on every home inspection that week. Had I missed a warning sign? A chance to save a life?

Charles tried again to talk me down. "Every PO here has had murders on their watch. You're thinking, 'If only I'd stopped by a few more times. Pushed a little harder.' And then a guy you push will go shoot somebody, and you'll wish you'd gone easy, given him space. I've been there, believe me. You have to try not to overreact to this."

"I missed something. I must have."

"Maybe he never let you see it. Never wanted you to."

"I'm supposed to see it whether they like it or not. That's the fucking job."

He couldn't argue with that, and he didn't try.

Charles reminded me that we came in late, after a lot of damage had already been done. We were the final catch basin. The shit that passed through this place had been in the pipeline a long time. He said his mantra again: *disaster prevention.*

"What would you call a murder?" I said. "If that's not a disaster—"

"I call it one out of 220."

He insisted that I recount the successful disaster-prevention measures I'd put in place elsewhere, and when I said I wasn't in the mood, he did it for me. There was Sheila, to whom we'd managed to give something akin to ongoing treatment, if not as comprehensive a version of it as we might have liked. And we'd claimed Kendrick as a win, too, even though prison obviously wasn't the ideal place to get a mental health diagnosis.

The addicted-to-the-lifestyle crowd were by far the most challenging to be optimistic about. The drug-dealer drug court had a compassionate judge and an experienced staff and a new-show-in-town sensibility that made it more adaptable, more open to experimentation, than most social programs, and still the prevailing feeling was of having shown up too late, with too few resources to make a real difference. That Damien could turn out like Javaron was now my greatest fear, and I was at a loss as to how to prevent it. By far the worst part, I told Charles, was not knowing what you could have done differently. "How can you adapt," I asked, "if you don't know where you went wrong?"

"Who told you we get to know?" he said, his smile as gentle as ever. "Who said there's always a lesson in this shit? Wasn't me. Sure as hell wasn't Beth."

Beth had gone uncharacteristically easy on me about Javaron. "I've had killers," she said. "Played the blame game with myself. Lost every time. You always lose. You know that, right? By now you ought to know."

Eventually Charles prevailed on me to ride with him back to the Landry house and check on Ronald. We found him in the front yard watching over the dogs as they sniffed around in the grass and relieved themselves. We went up the steps and sat on the porch with Ronald and the dogs. I didn't know how to open conversation with someone whose brother has just committed a murder, and I left it to Charles.

"The cops came to talk to you?" he asked.

Ronald nodded. "I don't know anything."

"They have to ask."

"I know." Ronald pulled the nearest dog onto his lap and rubbed its ears. "He told me I'm in charge of them until he gets back."

We could do little to help Ronald except sit and listen as he explained that his mother was taking on double shifts to pay for a big-shot attorney to represent Javaron. She'd been distraught for a couple of days, but since then she'd been focused on the mission, the same one she'd had for thirty years. She would do what she could for her sons.

Ronald wanted to help out but didn't know how. Charles and I told him that the best thing he could do for the family was to keep his doctors' appointments and try to get himself well. It was the right advice, but for Ronald it was another reminder that, through no fault of his own, he would spend his life seeking aid rather than giving it. He had to watch his mother come home threadbare and exhausted from double shifts, and all he could offer in return was to sweep the floors and feed the dogs.

"She doesn't ask me for help," he said, "but you know she needs it."

When he wasn't worrying about his mother or his brother, there was the gun charge to think about. His public defender assured him that negotiations were proceeding well, and the district attorney had indicated that he was open either to dismissing the charges entirely or to offering Ronald a misdemeanor. His record already had felonies on it, and he would never pay the fines. A misdemeanor sounded like a good deal to Ronald. If the DA changed his mind and Ronald got a felony, he was almost certain to go to prison for at least two years. I agreed to put in a call to the assistant district attorney and let him know that Ronald was complying with all the conditions of probation. I also mentioned that he was the only family his mother had left. The assistant district attorney said he'd already cast his vote for a misdemeanor. It was all up to the boss.

Ronald appreciated the gesture but took little solace in it. His life's rhythms were the same as they ever were. He slept, he woke, he waited, but it was all lonelier now. Javaron was gone, and his mother came home only to sleep. The dogs were his only company.

The next Friday night I tried to put the workweek behind me when I got home. Kristin and I had a beer and put something in the oven, and she mentioned a disagreement she'd had with a partner at her law firm. Some of the partners hadn't broken the habit of referring to female attorneys as "young lady." Every few weeks Kristin got fashion tips from a seventy-three-year-old supervisor "just trying to help."

It was a perfectly valid thing to be sick of, and she wanted only a moment of sympathy and understanding from her partner, but I couldn't give her even that much. "I don't know what to tell you," I said.

"I'm not asking you to tell me anything."

She wanted me to listen, and I couldn't do it. I told her I just wanted to sit alone and drink my beer. She obliged me.

Charles and Beth had both mentioned "compassion fatigue," the industry term for what I was feeling, though I was reluctant to let that explanation get me off the hook. Kristin never complained about the hours I'd spent grousing about my job. She asked very little of me, and I still managed to fall below the mark. I spent the weekend getting back in her good graces.

Beth and Charles both had sons who were entering their teenage years. The boys were putting homework off until the last minute, leaving a mess everywhere they went, eating their parents out of house and home. They were doing what thirteen-year-old boys did, but Beth and Charles sometimes struggled to maintain this perspective.

"Poor little dude," Beth said. "The way I reamed him last night, you'd have thought he burned the house down."

"Patience," Charles told me, "is a zero-sum game. If you leave it all at the office at five o'clock, don't expect a re-up until tomorrow morning."

I'd bitched about the job plenty, but I'd never felt the fatigue my friends had warned me about until now. Even after I patched things up with Kristin, even the most ordinary end-of-day courtesies took all my willpower.

On Monday, I told Dan the Regional Manager that I planned on taking a three-day weekend that week. I expected him to ask why, but he just shrugged his assent. "I'm burned-out," I volunteered. "If I don't take a break, I'm gonna flip out on somebody."

"Knowing when to say when is the only way to survive here."

He said this as if he were reading it off a bumper sticker, another piece of bedrock P&P wisdom. I wanted my outrage to be special, an indicator of an advanced sensitivity, but no one I worked with saw it that way. Everybody took losses. Everybody got sick afterward. They took a breather and got back to work.

Lamar had his first overdose around that time. I had my fourth. We rode together to give the families their opportunity to hold us accountable. Lamar's offender's family came within an inch of taking a swing at us. My offender's family was still in shock. They didn't absolve us of blame so much as let us know that they weren't ready to start the blaming process just yet.

I made a point of avoiding the Landry house as I steered us out of Central City. I hadn't talked to Lamar about Javaron since the murder, but when the story made the rounds, everyone at the office found out within a couple of days that I was Javaron's PO. When Lamar brought it up with me, I got the impression he'd been saving this conversation for the right time.

"I remember him," Lamar said. "He wasn't gonna let you in. It was just too late."

"I'll never be sure."

"My overdose, I could have locked him up. It was his second positive in five weeks. He told me he didn't need detox. I believed him."

"My third OD was like that."

"You just want to put your hands around the throat of this crap. But I guess that's what they were saying thirty years ago when they started filling the jails."

I pitied the tough-on-crime generation as never before. I, too, wanted to put my hands around the throat of the thing. I didn't want to wait for the days when place of birth had no bearing on a person's propensity for addiction or murder.

# TWELVE

# removed from circulation

would find some relief from two new programs that made the case that providing a wider array of social services would allow us to deliver a safer, fairer, and less costly justice system. The first program was something our mayor was calling NOLA (a common shorthand for New Orleans) for Life. The structure and administration of NOLA for Life relied heavily on the research of renowned criminologist David Kennedy. In recent years Kennedy had migrated from Boston to Chicago to New Orleans, offering his expertise to any mayor with an open mind and a murder problem. He expressed sympathy not only for the poor communities that had come to see the drug war as a racist conspiracy but also for law enforcement, whose earnest desire to get drugs and guns off the streets was worn down over time by a seemingly endless cycle of new drugs and guns filling in for the departed.

The most effective solutions to violent crime were social services that made upward mobility attainable for everyone willing to work for it, but transformative social services were expensive. Kennedy reasoned that the best way for poor cities in poor states to reduce violent crime was to target those people who were most likely to be its perpetrators or victims: gang members and drug dealers. Kennedy's assessment considered need the most important indicator of risk, but it also looked at less obvious factors like zip code. The neighborhoods with the highest densities of drugs and murders were the neighborhoods where young men were most likely to turn to dealing and murder to survive.

Before you could make your pitch to the young men with the highest scores on the risk assessment, you had to get them in the room. This was where P&P came in. We went to the homes of the highest-risk offenders and served them with official notice to report to Tulane and Broad for an hour-long meeting. Warrants would be issued for anyone who failed to appear. We didn't know any more than the offenders about what the meeting would entail. We were as surprised as they were when they stepped into the courtroom and saw their mug shots and arrest records flashing across giant projector screens. The mayor himself sat them in the pews and told them that every eye in the room was on them. We knew where they slept, where they hung out, where they conducted their business.

If they kept at that business, they would be back in court soon, and they wouldn't be wearing street clothes. If they wanted to consider other options, NOLA for Life had a bunch of them to offer, free of charge. GED programs, trade schools, housing organizations, substance-abuse centers—all had sent representatives armed with pamphlets and sign-up sheets. It was another thin budget year for the city, but Kennedy assured the mayor that there was no smarter civic investment than providing public assistance to high-risk offenders. Despite better-than-expected turnout at the first courthouse meetings, which Kennedy referred to as "call-ins," few offenders followed up with the service providers who'd taken their names. According to Kennedy, this was all part of the process. The lifestyle addiction wasn't cured with a single pill. You worked at it over time, the way chemotherapy worked at cancer.

A federal grant administered in concert with NOLA for Life paid POs eight hours of overtime per week to conduct evening curfew checks on the targeted offenders. It wasn't enough to tell these people we were invested in them. We had to show it by spending time and resources. We went out from 6:00 p.m. to 10:00 p.m. twice a week in groups of four POs and two NOPD officers. We shook hands with offenders' friends and family and urged them to badger the offender to take advantage of NOLA for Life's services. The offenders, for their part, played it all as we might have expected, promising to take the mayor up on his offer and thanking us for our concern about their future.

During those first rounds of curfew checks, we were just making small talk, but it was a thrill to be reaching out with more than the usual options: jail or nothing. There were real jobs, real job-training programs, and real housing vouchers. Even with the infusion of federal cash, we could only afford to target the 150 offenders with the highest risk scores. We were working on a small scale, to be sure, but for the first time we could offer drug dealers a sustainable alternative to the drug trade.

By the second month and the third round of curfew checks, we could see that Kennedy was right to caution us not to expect too much too soon. We were asking offenders to give up a profession that got them laid and made them money. The new life we offered came with fewer thrills and far less cash. And we who made the offer represented organizations—NOPD and P&P—that many offenders found difficult to trust.

I loved the program anyway. Cops and POs could do disaster prevention when necessary, but most of their time was spent moving through the community, shaking hands, getting to know people, hearing their hopes and fears, and helping out as needed. The curfew checks made me feel like the future I'd dreamed of might arrive sooner than I thought.

---

The other program fueling my hope was drug court. Certain aspects of it continued to frustrate my colleagues and me—like the drug-dealer section that Damien had hoodwinked. But on the whole drug court was producing remarkable results, and not only in New Orleans. A National Institute of Justice study followed drug court offenders for ten years. Recidivism rates dropped from 40 percent to 12 percent. The study estimated that drug courts saved taxpayers about $6,000 per offender in incarceration costs.

They did this by overwhelming needy people with care. Addicts could get counseling every day at the Tower if they wanted it. The drug-court caseworkers could jump the line at the Odyssey House detox when the need arose, and very few drug-court offenders were made to dry out in OPP. This made them less reluctant to admit relapses and more inclined to offer candid assessments of the events that made them relapse. A more honest offender was easier to treat with talk therapy.

Best of all were the incentives. Offenders who completed drug court got their probation terminated early, usually a year or eighteen months into a five-year sentence, and their fee balances suspended. The drug-court judges instituted this policy because they believed that a year of intensive supervision was far more likely to change an offender's life than five years of glancing in on him every three to six months.

Drug court was the model for mental health court, the program I'd placed Sheila in. A new veterans' court was being launched to partner vets with counseling tailored not only to drug abuse but also to PTSD and other challenges that arise more frequently among servicemen and -women. I thought of Hard Head, but he was on parole as opposed to probation and therefore ineligible for courthouse programming. I was convinced that the drug-court approach should become the model for all forms of community supervision. By compressing five years of supervision into one or two, P&P departments could offer offenders more programming and POs much smaller caseloads.

If the arguments for adopting this model came down to simple math, so did the obstacles. To offer drug court to everyone who wanted it, the state would have to think radically differently about spending. If an offender who'd received no services got arrested after the third year and served the next two behind bars at a cost of $33,000 per year—the average per-year prison cost in the US—your tab over five years was $66,000. Providing for community supervision at the federal rate of $4,000 per year cost $20,000 over the same span, and there was a good chance that at the end of it you would have a taxpayer repaying the system's investment. If you took the five-year view, fully funded P&P agencies were a bargain, but if you looked at only the first year of the five, or even at the first three, you felt like you weren't getting anything for your money, and you were left to conclude that the best course of action was to do nothing.

Space in drug court was limited by a budget set by the state supreme court, and I couldn't get every qualifying probationer a spot. I selected the ten addicts I deemed at greatest risk of relapse and sold it to them as fervently as I could. I encountered the usual hurdles. More time at the courthouse sounded to offenders like more chances for a judge to throw you in jail. The promise of early dismissal from probation was tantalizing, but most offenders simply didn't believe I was telling them the truth. I had tried to do right by them, and they professed to like me as much as they could like a PO. I was still a guy with a badge. I was still attached to an institution with a long history of false promises. In the end I succeeded in getting half as many offenders admitted to drug court as I'd hoped. It took about two months of working with their counselors and judges before they accepted that the program wasn't a trap. By the third month they all wanted to know why I hadn't sent them there a year before.

Travis was on my original list of ten, and I kept chipping away at him. Since losing the high-paying job on the oil rig he'd been working part-time at Wal-Mart and cycling in and out of relapse. He would get clean for a month, get high over a weekend, then call me on Monday to tell me he wasn't going to pass his drug test. He never wanted detox, and he was always able to clean himself up again and pass the test a few days later, and then the cycle would start over. He had another go at Suboxone, thanks to his girlfriend's seemingly endless supply of family money, but after six weeks of dosing as prescribed, he double-dosed again. He called and told me about it even though he knew the P&P drug test couldn't tell the difference between Suboxone and heroin.

"I'm telling you because I'm sick of this," he said. "I want it to stop."

I made the drug-court pitch again. "These counselors are trained to help people beat their addiction. That's all they do."

"Sorry," he said. "You're not getting me back to the courthouse. I don't care what they're selling."

I couldn't force him. There were about 300 total drug-court spots for nearly 4,500 probationers. Everyone agreed that drug-court time and money should be spent only on people willing to work the program. "You don't want to be an addict," I said, "but you don't want treatment."

"I don't want drug court."

I believed he wanted to get clean, and I believed offenders had reason to be skeptical when we promised new initiatives, but leaving him to his own devices was no longer an option. "I'm responsible for you," I told Travis. "If you won't go to treatment and you can't keep clean on your own, you're going to jail."

"You said you wouldn't lock me up over dope."

"If you're making an effort to get clean."

"I'm taking Suboxone."

"I hope it works."

We left it at that, and I moved on to the next guy on the drug-court list. Travis passed his drug screen the following month and told me he'd saved up enough money at the Wal-Mart job to get a little apartment in Algiers, one of the neighborhoods across the Mississippi River known collectively as "the West Bank." The girlfriend's family helped with the security deposit, but Travis was covering the first month's rent. The baby he and his girlfriend were expecting was due any day now, and Travis told me for the second time that he viewed fatherhood as a bridge to sobriety. "My little girl's never gonna know her dad was a junkie," he said.

I warned him that there would be stress to go with the joy of fatherhood and reminded him that the last time he was overcome with joy, during his first weekend home from the oil rig job, he found his way back to the needle. I explained that treatment was good for keeping you level through highs and lows, but he refused me again. He came in and pissed clean again, and I congratulated him on thirty days clean and ninety days working.

I wanted to be wrong about Travis, but addiction was all too predictable. His baby was born, and balancing work and sleepless nights took their toll. To get a fix, Travis needed only send a text message and drive a half mile out of his way on his route to work. A "bump" turned into a bender, and he lost the job at Wal-Mart. His girlfriend moved back in with her parents and took the baby with her. I didn't find out any of this until Travis's landlord called and told me that Travis had stolen his guitar. The police had come and made a report and put out a warrant for misdemeanor theft.

A few days later Travis was in the French Quarter, drunk and high. Someone bumped into him on the street, spilling his drink. It was almost certainly an accident, but Travis took it personally and overreacted. A couple of cops broke up the fight before it escalated. They asked for names and IDs and ran Travis in the system, saw the warrant, and took him to OPP.

I called the landlord and let him know Travis was in custody. I'd met the landlord once, an elderly African American who lived in the other half of the double he was renting to Travis. He'd had only trouble renting to addicts, but Travis had had a job and a baby coming, and the landlord had hoped for the best.

"What happens now?" he asked me.

"It's up to the judge. Either he goes back to prison or he gets let out."

"Not prison," the landlord said. "Not in my name."

"He's heading for an overdose. Prison might save his life."

"There's gotta be another way."

I wanted the old man to know that we'd tried everything we could. I took him through the case notes. I even read off Travis's failed drug tests so that he understood that this was hardly strike one.

He still wanted Travis to get another shot. He would even have Travis back as a tenant if he agreed to reimburse him for the value of the guitar. "I'm not rich," the landlord said, "but I can float him for a month or two."

"I'll do my best," I said. "You realize his case is in St. Tammany."

The landlord knew what this meant. Travis was a New Orleans District offender because he lived in Orleans Parish, but all legal matters related to his probation would run through the courthouse that had sentenced him. The St. Tammany Parish courthouse was widely regarded as the toughest in the state. If Tulane and Broad was a laboratory for every new experiment in criminal justice, the St. Tammany Parish courthouse was one of the last bastions of the old drug war, and they were waging it mostly on white people.

St. Tammany was Louisiana's wealthiest parish. Situated north and east of Lake Pontchartrain and known locally as "the North Shore," St. Tammany was built in large part by white flight out of New Orleans. In the 2010 census, St. Tammany was nearly 90 percent white and had a poverty rate of about 9 percent, compared to a rate of 25.4 percent in New Orleans.

The courthouse was tan and spotless. Its deputies wore starched shirts and grinned like insurance salesmen as they reminded you to please silence your cellular device. As I'd done many times at Tulane and Broad, I sat in the front row of the courtroom and waited for my offender's name to be called. I asked the judge if I could speak with him briefly off the record.

Like most of his colleagues in St. Tammany, Travis's judge was known to hand down lengthy sentences. He was in his mid-forties, young for that line of work, with a square head and a prep-school haircut. He called me up for a sidebar and thanked me for the work I did and said that because I was the one going out to Travis's house every month and watching him piss in a cup, he would defer to my judgment on what to do with him.

"I'd like to keep working with him," I said.

"What would you say to giving him a couple of weeks in the back to get his mind right?"

I understood *in the back* to mean in jail, and I slowly shook my head. "I spoke to the victim, Your Honor. He wants to give him another chance."

"It's been a bad overdose year." The judge pursed his lips as he tried to decide whether to keep his promise to let me have the final say in what happened to Travis. "I'd rather see him behind bars than dead."

In the end the judge was as good as his word. He told Travis that today was his lucky day. His PO and, more importantly, the gentlemen whose guitar he stole believed he could get himself squared away without the assistance of the Department of Corrections. Travis would be released later that afternoon. He waved me over as I was getting ready to leave and thanked me and promised I wouldn't regret advocating for him.

"Don't thank me," I said, "thank your landlord."

He promised he would, and he promised to be in the office first thing on Monday.

He was waiting in the lobby when I showed up. In the offender chair he was overcome with relief. He told me of the joy he felt when he held his infant daughter, and the promise he'd made to her and her mother never to be parted from them again. I believed he meant it. He wanted to be a good parent and live a normal life. He was tired of losing jobs and going to jail.

But I knew all the tells now. I could spot the twitch of the lower lip when someone was overplaying his hand, hoping to come across so focused and determined and earnest that I wouldn't think to suggest a drug test. I told Travis I knew what was going on, and he took off his glasses and folded them inside his shirt pocket and put his face in his hands. His blond hair fell in tangled corkscrews across his forehead as he muttered a long string of *fucks*.

I didn't ask what had happened. I just gave him an ultimatum. If he failed another drug test, I would arrest him and bring him back before the judge and ask for revocation. "It'll be two years before you get parole," I said. "It'll cost the working people of Louisiana thirty-five grand."

I let this sit for a minute, and then I made one more pitch. "Or you could let me enroll you in drug court."

"It's not for me."

"Then every Monday you're in here pissing in a cup."

"Every Monday."

My dread of those Monday drug tests began to creep into my weekends. To that point I'd recommended revocation only for offenders who had been convicted of felony offenses while on supervision. If Travis relapsed and I kept my word, I would be asking for a revocation because of drug use alone. My paperwork would cite the guitar incident as a consequence of Travis's addiction, but the true purpose of the revocation would be to keep him from dying of a drug overdose. The Department of Corrections was offering more programming than ever before. In prison there would be AA and NA meetings three times per week if he wanted them and social workers to meet with, if not at the intervals drug court provided. Travis would probably be too bored to refuse treatment.

When I asked parolees about treatment in prison, they all agreed that the DOC had made enormous strides in helping inmates prepare for life outside of prison, with particular emphasis on staying away from drugs. But it almost never stuck. When you walked through those gates to freedom, all the resolutions you'd made inside stayed inside.

Inmates were in a controlled environment that offered few opportunities to acquire drugs and provided food, shelter, and health care, eliminating many of the needs that triggered drug use among the poor. Prison treatment provided offenders valuable gudance but couldn't provide opportunities for inmates to deploy it. "When you're getting treatment upstate," one parolee told me, "all you're really doing is making promises."

Drug court allowed addicts to weave treatment into their everyday lives. It gave addicts tools and invited them to go out and try to apply them and come back the next week and say how they fared. Adjustments could be made on the fly. The program was designed to be adaptable.

The best thing prison could do for an addict was keep him alive. A prison sentence could buy Travis two years. They wouldn't be happy years, and they would cost a lot of money. The alternative seemed to be letting him kill himself. The alternative seemed worse. It got so that either result on Monday morning felt like a loss, and I started thinking that the best solution wasn't trying to control the people who used drugs. Instead I would go to the source, to the drugs themselves. My overtime duty with the NOPD looked like a perfect opportunity to do it.

------

Twice a week we went out conducting curfew checks as part of the NOLA for Life initiative. We'd been at them long enough now that we were getting to know not only the friends and families of the offenders on the list but also their neighbors. I was astonished by the power of simply showing up, talking and listening and letting people learn your name and shake your hand. I believed that almost everyone we spoke with wanted to believe we were starting something new, a form of community supervision that derived its authority not from a badge or gun but from time spent breathing the air and learning the faces. It was invigorating, but it wasn't really what I wanted. I wanted the drugs. We were dealing with high-risk offenders who worked in the drug trade, and sometimes by sheer luck we showed up right after a new shipment had arrived.

One night we walked in on enough heroin to bring the district commander and get our faces on the evening news. Backlit like a movie star, the white-haired commander touted the joint effort between state and municipal agencies. I can't recall exactly what he said because my attention was fixed on the clear plastic bag of brownish matter that the NOPD narcotics officer appraised at $100,000.

From the curb, the house was indistinguishable from the other shotgun doubles stacked like ragged tomes along both sides of the street. The interior contained iPads and video game systems and new TVs and new shoes still in boxes and shopping bags piled so high and deep that the central room was nearly impenetrable. Shoving his way through, the offender had led us right past the stash, folded atop one of the bags.

In the hall closet were more shoes and more new clothes. In the pocket of one of the jackets I found a couple grand in wadded hundreds. In the backyard an aboveground swimming pool had been squeezed so precariously between the fenceposts that its contents threatened to spill over into the neighbor's alley. The narcotics officer guessed that the offender was mid-level and rising, his spoils outgrowing his environment—literally, in the case of the pool. He would cut the stuff and package it and kick it down to the "corner boys," who would turn it into cash.

The offender signed a statement declaring that the heroin was his and his alone. His girlfriend and children were free to go. The police commander recommended that they plan on being gone awhile. The inspection of the rest of the house could last well into the night.

The cops reminded each other that the bust was sure to grant them a couple weeks' leeway with the rank, who were always clamoring for six-figure arrests. That the drug was heroin as opposed to meth or cocaine greatly sweetened the deal. There had been talk in recent months of tainted packages making their way down the Eastern Seaboard, and bunk product masked with the fearsome opioid fentanyl, better known as "horse heroin."

Late in the evening, after the heroin was booked into evidence, one of the narcotics officers discovered a brass key attached to a blue plastic diamond about the size of a playing card. A number, faded almost to illegibility, had been scrawled on a piece of masking tape wrapped around the diamond's midsection. The NOPD sergeant identified the find immediately as the property of a motel, one of the few in town that still handed out conventional keys. He knew them all by name. We were wired from the bust and the roads were wide-open at that hour. If we put our minds to it, we just might find a match.

Old roadside motels were still used as stopping-off places in the drug trade. I'd driven past the old motels hundreds of times, never conceiving of their secret lives, never imagining that one day I would go to them in the hope of finding the big stash from which tonight's had derived or, better still, a scrap of paper or burner phone containing the numbers of the guys on the next tier who were never seen, who always got away with it. As we cruised from one motel to another, the police sergeant told stories of his years working the night shift, prowling the streets of New Orleans in the early nineties, when the drug markets flourished and the city settled into an age of violence that culminated in 1994's record-breaking 421-murder year. "Seemed like no matter what we did, we couldn't stop the bodies," the sergeant said. "Meanwhile pay is shit. Morale's terrible. Department can't hire anybody good, so they start taking everybody. And I mean *everybody*. You've got a pulse and can pull a trigger, here's your badge. Before you know it, there's cops taking dope money. Cops doing hits. It got to where if you were doing the job right, you had better watch your fucking back."

The sergeant was bronze and muscle-bound and a born raconteur. When we parked alongside railroad tracks, he had a story about a train. When we parked at a motel that had once advertised hourly rates, he had a story about a prostitute. Despite his many interludes, we made good time across town. By midnight we had a match. The Crystal Inn was everything you could want in a drug motel. Cigarette butts and hamburger wrappers skittered across the parking lot. A half-drunk and unshaven clerk muttered to himself behind a desk bristling with potted bamboo.

The clerk said we were free to have a look at the room. According to the ledger, it hadn't been rented in some time.

The sergeant turned the key while the rest of us waited in breathless formation outside.

The room was empty, but the shift still felt like a win. I was astonished to find that it was possible to be well versed in the consequences of the drug war—mass incarceration, to name the most obvious—and at the same time invigorated by the sight of the dope package getting wrapped up, catalogued, and removed from circulation. There was less heroin on the street now than before we'd knocked on the offender's door, and we were able to hold this fact in isolation, to forget for a moment that other shipments would fill the vacuum and that most of the addicts who'd bought from our offender would find another supplier soon enough. Still, that one package—*our* package—would never go up another nostril or down another vein.

For the first time it occurred to me that the cops who got paid to confiscate drugs had it so much better than my fellow POs and me. The cops had simple goals—so much product taken down each week, month, year—and straightforward means of assessing their performance. You could set the dope on the scale, test it in a lab. You could score your work by weight and chemical composition.

P&P was in the hearts-and-minds business, where success was much harder to measure. We were judging our progress in conversation, in the look and the feel of a home environment. Even the piss test, our most precise instrument, was hardly an accurate assessment of our charges' attitudes toward sobriety. "Solving a crime," one senior PO liked to quip, "is a lot easier than solving a person." Or, if you preferred: getting a couple of bags of heroin off the streets was a lot easier than reforming a drug addict.

And the rewards of the drug score were instantaneous. To know that the product you'd extracted from Central City or Hollygrove or the Million Dollar Corner would never touch another human life— Damien would never get a chance to sell it, and Travis would never get a chance to shoot it—was as intoxicating a feeling as I'd ever experienced on this job or any other. When a shift went by and we didn't get any dope, I felt sullen and irritable, and I couldn't think about anything except my next fix.

# THIRTEEN

# best of the worst

The tells we'd learned to spot during home inspections weren't always easy to articulate in a police report. Some judges didn't believe we'd met the "reasonable suspicion" threshold before we opened drawers and looked under beds. We had to abandon a couple of stolen-firearms cases because the judges felt we were "fishing" from the moment we stepped into the house.

Some POs got pissed off about this. Even at the height of my infatuation with drug arrests, I was never all that interested in the court proceedings. I hadn't wavered in my belief that prison wasn't the answer to America's drug problem. I didn't care whether the people I took to jail spent more than a night there. I just wanted their dope and their guns. They wouldn't get them back, even if we couldn't convict them. (They could apply to get the guns back if the guns weren't stolen, but the guns were always stolen.)

Because many of the drug dealers could afford private counsel, few of them went to prison as a result of felony convictions stemming from our arrests. Double probation became an increasingly common compromise between the campaign to get drugs and guns off the street and the campaign to get out of the mass-incarceration business. It seemed a silent agreement had been brokered. Cops and POs would keep going after drugs and guns, and judges would keep trying to deter drug dealing without the use of prison. The drug courts continued to grow. The DRC got funding to add five new social workers. NOLA for Life kept hounding gang members to sign up for services.

If my cravings for new drug arrests were constant, my opportunities to make them remained few. I spent most of my time as I always had, conducting home inspections, attending drug-court proceedings, passing through the DRC. I went to the mission and rapped at the hoods of tents Under the Bridge. Hard Head had done his thirty days at Odyssey House and stayed clean for another ninety. Now he wanted back into Odyssey House. I didn't even have to fill out the usual forms. The screener told me she had Hard Head's information on file. All I had to do was drive him over.

He hadn't used heroin. He didn't need detox. It was just booze and weed this time, or so he said. He didn't look as bad as he usually looked when he bottomed out. I got the impression that what he really wanted from Odyssey House was a break from life Under the Bridge. There had been a lot of brawls lately and a couple of stabbings. About two weeks before, Hard Head had tried to stand down a guy looking to pillage his tent, but the guy was tougher than he looked and half Hard Head's age. Hard Head woke up on the curb with a two-day headache and a busted lip.

"Wasn't anything worth a damn in the tent anyway," he told me. "It was pride telling me to boot up like that. Should have just told the prick to have at it."

Hard Head blamed most of the recent disturbances Under the Bridge on the influx of young addicts from out of town. Hard Head called them "rail riders" and "hobos" and "gutter punks." They were in their late teens and early twenties, and some were from affluent families. It was hard to know whether a trauma caused them to bow out of their former lives or whether dope was to blame—that is, whether dope started the problem or merely exacerbated it.

There were a few veterans in the young people's midst, but most of the newcomers didn't appear to have been disillusioned by a single experience of violence or disgust with government action or inaction. They seemed to Hard Head like people who just couldn't cope with the times. They hated Wall Street and the pharmaceutical industry, who made for straightforward enough villains, but they also hated social media and all the other trappings of vanity culture. They talked of "un-plugging" and getting back to the land. They imagined that doing a lot of drugs and being homeless was a rebuke to a fallen world, and if they stuck with it, someone important would acknowledge their gesture and insist that things had to change.

When they learned Hard Head had been in Vietnam and had taken part in the anti-war movement upon his return, they wanted to hear all his stories. A couple of them carried around guitars and sang folk songs and saw themselves as the descendants of a more principled generation. They reminded Hard Head of some of the people he'd come to know in those days, people whose outrage was pure but who hadn't figured out what to do with it except try to numb it with dope. Hard Head wanted to be a cautionary tale to these young people.

"I tell them if you want to know where this shit ends, you're look-ing at it," he told me. "Getting fucked up all the time isn't a political statement."

To the gutter punks, the "rail life" was still romantic. They spoke of casting off yokes, of achieving a freedom that few Americans dared to dream of. Hard Head warned them that "flying the sign" would get old eventually. Hangovers would get worse in time. So would withdrawal symptoms. Hard Head believed that an addict saw his situation clearly only when he reached "true bottom." Most people had to get there only the one time before they made drastic changes, but Hard Head was called Hard Head for a reason. He believed he'd bottomed out more often than anyone he'd met in his decades of street life.

"Some people's talent is throwing a fastball," he said. "Mine's taking a lick."

He had other talents. A few days after he got to Odyssey House, one of the counselors got him a part-time job floating drywall and running wire. When Hard Head was sober, he was an ace with a wrench. Some of it he'd picked up in the Army. Some of it he seemed to have been born knowing.

I visited him at a couple of job sites. His boss spoke highly of his skill set. Hard Head walked me over to a socket he'd installed and tried to help me understand how electricity moves from the power plant to the lightbulb. "It's simple," he said. "I could teach you all this stuff."

It would have been impossible for me to take an off-the-books lesson of any sort from someone on my caseload, but the prospect of spending an afternoon learning basic home repair from Hard Head was unexpectedly appealing, and I let myself wish I'd known him in some other capacity. From there it was a short leap to the original question of this work. With the right help at the right moment, what could this man have done with his life?

Despite Hard Head's insistence that addicts would get to "true bottom" in their own time, he'd begun doing for the young people at Odyssey House what he'd done, or tried to do, for the gutter punks. He wanted the young addicts to see that there was nothing romantic about this life. It was no act of resistance. It advanced no cause.

In gratitude for his attempts to mentor younger people in the program, Odyssey House extended him another month. Hard Head and I visited in the lobby of the old mansion, and for the first ten minutes he was his usual self, chuckling as he complained about the madness of trying to reason with a roomful of addicts. He walked me back to the Crown Vic and listened to the engine and told me I needed to replace some belt or other.

I knew he was stalling, but I was in no rush. Finally he stuffed his hands in his pockets and glanced back at Odyssey House. "They don't talk enough about loneliness in these places," he said. "They tell you all the great stuff that's gonna happen for you when you get clean, but they don't get you ready to be lonely. All the good you burn through on your way to the bottom, it's not coming back."

"That's not true." I said this reflexively, my intuition versus his lifetime of proof.

Hard Head had never looked older than when he smiled at me then. "Maybe some of it comes back. If you've got enough time left."

I knew from past conversations that he had no living family except a son on the West Coast. That relationship was broken beyond repair. Hard Head would have been the first to admit that he'd made his share of bad choices, but it was impossible for me to look at him and not think that if he'd never come into contact with heroin, he might have been able to put his talents to better use. He might have had a home of his own. He might have held on to his wife and his son.

I told myself that when I took a heroin foil out of circulation, I denied a promising young person one chance to end up an old wreck living Under the Bridge. Without meaning to, Hard Head confirmed the necessity of my campaign to decrease the supply of drugs in New Orleans.

---

Less than a week after that talk with Hard Head, I was checking in on a female offender a couple of years older than Sheila. She'd been working at McDonald's for about three months and was up for her first promotion. She had a daughter about two years old and was sharing a double with a friend who had a Section 8 voucher. The offender chipped in half the rent in exchange for the friend's watching her daughter while she was at work.

The offender's boyfriend was on parole for armed robbery. He bolted out the front door when I showed up to conduct my inspection. I spotted a couple of crack rocks wrapped in sandwich bags on the dresser. I rooted around in the bedroom until I found the gun.

I knew that the offender wasn't selling crack and carrying a gun. Why should she suffer the penalties for her boyfriend's crime? "He's not looking out for you," I said, and urged her to tell me that the drugs and the gun didn't belong to her.

She may not have said "Ride or die," but I could see that she wasn't going to abandon the codes she'd been taught by anything I could say. Her boyfriend wasn't a don but he was an earner, and she was duty-bound to protect him. And now I was stuck. I had crack and a gun and an offender. I couldn't walk away. I had to confiscate the crack and the gun, and I had to take the offender to jail.

The district attorney ended up letting the gun charge go, but only after the offender agreed to take double probation on the crack. She sat in jail for weeks while the deal was hashed out. McDonald's took her back but her housemate wouldn't. She and her baby moved in with an aunt who demanded a far larger portion of her paycheck in return for shelter and babysitting services. I'd gotten rid of a gun and a couple of crack rocks, and the offender hadn't been sent upstate, but even though the system had performed as rationally as it could, the collateral damage of the drug arrest in this case had clearly exceeded the public-safety gains. It was one data point among many suggesting that my efforts to reduce the drug supply weren't keeping young people like Travis from becoming old people like Hard Head.

I kept going out on the NOLA for Life curfew checks, and the busts always gave me a rush, but the comedown hit me quicker every week. On our way back to the New Orleans District one of those nights, I confessed my misgivings to Beth. "You really think we're getting anywhere with this shit?" I said.

"Don't start with that."

"You've thought about it," I pressed.

"Of course I've thought about it. Of course we can't stop the dope. But we can't stop murder either. Are we gonna stop going after the murderers?"

I'd done this thought experiment myself, and I'd found that it missed a key distinction. "It's a question," I said, "of what your options are. With murder, the only thing you can do is hunt the fucker down. With dope, there might be a better way."

"The Portugal thing?" Beth said.

"The Portugal thing" had been a hot topic at the New Orleans District for several months now. Portugal decriminalized drug possession in 2001. Decriminalization wasn't legalization. There was no lawful, regulated drug market in Portugal. Large-scale drug dealers could still be arrested and charged, but users didn't enter the criminal justice system. Money formerly marked for enforcement was now used to hire social workers and clinicians to canvass homeless shelters and housing projects. They offered counseling, clean needles, and treatment for those with a will to make a change. Over the following decade, drug overdoses had steadily decreased across the country. As US overdoses continued to soar, Portugal's drug-related death rate was the lowest in western Europe. The US drug-death rate was now nearly fifty times Portugal's.

The Portuguese system wasn't beloved by all. Addicts could be found shooting up on street corners and in restaurant bathrooms. They woke on strangers' lawns. Homelessness was a problem. It was possible—though far from proven—that while fewer people overdosed in a decriminalized system, more people tried drugs, and some of them became addicted. They lost their livelihoods if not their lives. Portugal wasn't claiming it had cured the disease. If anything, the Portuguese system appeared to be based on a fundamentally gloomy argument: making drug addiction less deadly was the best any government could hope to do.

There was another model, in some ways more drastic: legalization. The most widespread instance of legalization was marijuana, which was lawful to produce, sell, and use in several countries and an increasing number of US states. A legal drug trade can't be expected to fully extinguish the black market. Black markets remain in the US states that have legalized marijuana, and the people who run them sometimes use violence to protect their territory. But most studies of legal drug markets conclude that most people who want to use drugs will buy them from licensed vendors that comply with government regulations. The product will be safer than street product, and taxed, and the tax dollars will fund rehab services for the very people paying the taxes.

Taxes also fund government efforts to police production and distribution. Policing doesn't include incarcerating customers, but dealers who fail to comply with regulations can still be subject to government penalties up to and including prison. The legalization model doesn't imagine a free-for-all. It suggests a reallocation of resources in a different direction. We had debated all these issues in the lunchroom at the New Orleans District. Some POs insisted that legalization was the only way to go, while others argued that the latest iteration of the drug war, in which possession penalties rarely included incarceration but dealers could still get prison sentences, needed more time to get a foothold.

Most of us wanted this middle-of-the-road approach to work, which is to say that most of us felt hopelessly conflicted about what to do about overdoses and addiction. Charles leaned toward the decriminalization argument, and Beth and Lamar toward sticking with the drug war, but even the people who believed they'd chosen a side struggled to resolve their disgust with addiction and their fatigue with the shortcomings of the current system.

"Here's the thing," Beth told a group of us. "When you make a change, you're on the hook for every unintended consequence that comes with it. And bet your ass there'll be unintended consequences with this shit. You get them when you make a little change to a little thing. We're talking about big change to the biggest fucking killer there is."

The unintended consequences included the people who would become addicts under the revised system who might not have otherwise, and a bunch of other things that nobody had thought of yet. This, Beth believed, was why longstanding solutions to large, complex social problems were so hard to modify, much less reconfigure from the ground up.

I continued to oppose the Portuguese model. In 2016, overdoses killed nearly four times as many Americans as murder. It was impossible not to hate this enemy when you saw every day the destruction it wrought in the streets and the homes of those you had sworn to protect. It didn't escape me, though, that hate often gets in the way of rational thinking. The rational response to that statistic might be that an increase in overdoses was a strong argument for trying something new, even something desperate.

So I resigned myself to going without a grand vision of the solution to America's drug problem. When I encountered drug problems on the job, I went case by case. I used my discretion. I got to choose when to deploy reasonable suspicion. I got to decide whether finding the dope stash reduced the overall harm or increased it. I searched fewer houses now than ever before, and sometimes I felt good about my choice, and sometimes I didn't. Overdoses kept coming, and some of the dead people on my caseload might have lived if I'd put them in jail.

The mother of one overdose case, a young white guy who split his time between his mother's couch and a tent Under the Bridge, had lectured me during the past few home inspections about the foolishness of the drug war and the prison-industrial complex. Now that her son had passed, she wanted the drug war fought on all fronts. There was no reasoning with this horror, and there could be no surrender. She told me I would have her son's blood on my hands for the rest of my life. I could have saved him. I could have locked him up.

I let her have at me, and I went to drug court and shook the hands of the people who'd reached thirty days clean or sixty or ninety. There, I was always reminded that treatment worked, but it took a team, and it took time and patience and money, and even if we got all of these things, success wasn't guaranteed. Hard Head was an extreme case, to be sure, but many addicts believed that "true bottom" was the only place where they could make a change, and it seemed that POs couldn't force them there, even with prison. The Hard Heads of the world seemed to believe that they had to find their bottom on their own, and no amount of life-affirming drug-court data could convince them otherwise.

I thought about this every Monday when Travis showed up for his piss test. On the ninth Monday he told me in the lobby before I took him back for his test that he wanted to be placed in Odyssey House for sober living. Rather than subject him to the test, which he would fail and after which I would have to put him in jail, I called Odyssey House, spoke with the screener, filled out the forms, faxed them over, and gave Travis a ride.

Hard Head was standing outside having a smoke when we pulled up. He waved the cigarette at me as I led Travis inside. By the time we were done with the processing, Hard Head had gone back in, and I didn't get a chance to talk to him until later in the week. I reached him by phone and told him about a young guy I wanted him to look out for.

Hard Head knew exactly who I was talking about. "He *wants* to get clean," he said. "He doesn't *need* to get clean. Big difference."

When it was Travis's turn to speak in the group settings, he lapsed often into nostalgia. He hadn't forgotten all the hell that came with the needle, but the hell wasn't the first thing he thought of. He still missed the high and how far away it could take you from your despair. The old people in the room exchanged glances. They all knew the score. He was nowhere near his bottom.

Sometimes Hard Head got frustrated with people who sought treatment too early, before they were ready to give themselves over to it, but he guessed the young, unready people were equally frustrated by the old guys who'd kept coming to this place, kept making the same promises, for twenty or thirty years. "If I'm really older and wiser," Hard Head said, "why the fuck can't I practice what I preach?"

Young people like Travis couldn't see their future selves when they looked at old-timers like Hard Head. The young still believed that if they ever had to get clean—if the want turned into a need—they could flip the switch. "We try to tell them we all started off believing that," Hard Head told me. "We were all young once."

Hard Head didn't know what to do about the drug problem in America. He didn't know how to reach the young addicts at Odyssey House, but he kept trying. He offered to be an off-the-record sounding board for people who had trouble expressing themselves candidly in a group setting. At the counselors' behest, he pulled people aside who were still getting high while in treatment, and he told them that he'd done it himself, and there was no shame in admitting you weren't ready to get clean. Programming was limited, and the spots ought to go to the people who would make the most of their opportunities.

It was always heartbreaking to see someone walk away from treatment, but the addict who realized he wasn't ready, and who voluntarily surrendered his place to someone who needed it, got to feel like he was contributing to a greater good. "It's dumb to leave sober living," Hard Head told me, "but if you remind them they're making room for somebody else, they don't have to feel as shitty about it."

Hard Head was making the case for what sociologists called the "harm reduction" model of fighting addiction. To many sociologists, the term *harm reduction* is synonymous with legalizing or at least de-criminalizing drugs, as Portugal has done. At Odyssey House, harm reduction was applied in a strictly literal way, the practice of selecting the most appealing of a host of unappealing options—the "best of the worst."

If you could get past the admittedly unsettling thesis statement— addiction is here to stay—harm reduction was the most optimistic approach to the drug problem on the market. It offered addicts a way to mark their progress on the path to sobriety, and it invited social workers, judges, cops, and POs to credit themselves and their charges with modest victories and to view setbacks as unavoidable. If harm reduction asked us to settle for a world in which drugs probably couldn't be confiscated out of existence, it also made the case that intervention saved lives. Most studies found that intervention worked best in places where the social safety net was robust and alternatives to incarceration were plentiful, but it could be practiced anywhere addicts wanted to get clean and public servants wanted to help. As one of Hard Head's caseworkers at Odyssey House put it, "It's better with money, but in a pinch, you can do harm reduction for free."

Hard Head had never gotten control of his addiction, but he could look back on his own life and easily distinguish times when he had a home and food to eat and a counselor's advice from the times when he was homeless and starving and alone. He used drugs during both spans, but he used far less when the support systems were in place and the punishment for using wasn't as severe. For an addict, the difference between a onetime relapse and a monthlong bender could be the difference between life and death.

Whenever he got discouraged by the stubbornness of the young people at Odyssey House, Hard Head reminded himself that harm reduction was the goal. If his counsel or his example could keep one of his friends at Odyssey House from one relapse, or if it could prevent a relapse from turning into a bender, it was worth all the time and effort he put into it.

When his second month as an unofficial counselor was up, he was worn-out, and he told me he was looking forward to getting back to the tents. I picked him up from Odyssey House and dropped him at the familiar spot at the base of the underpass. It was a windy day and his long gray hair whipped like a pirate's flag across his shoulders. I watched him take about three steps, and then I called after him. "Maybe that was the last time," I said. "Maybe you're clean for good."

As he thought this over, he fished a rubber band out of his pocket, pulled his hair back, and snapped the band into place. "Feels like it. Really does. But it's felt like that before."

He waved good-bye, ducked into his tent, found his sign, and set off on foot to his usual spot. I was trying hard to feel like we weren't back where we started. I told myself he was carrying something new. The young people he'd tried to help had worn him out, but they'd also given him a sense of purpose. He'd mentioned on his way out of Odyssey House that he would try to get in the habit of reaching out to the young people in the tents. He'd seemed more hopeful and, maybe more importantly, less lonely.

The contractor Hard Head had done odd jobs for while he was at Odyssey House was planning to use him again next week. Hard Head had promised to call the VA and get enrolled in counseling again. He'd stopped showing up after his last relapse for fear of disappointing his counselor.

I told him she wouldn't be disappointed in him. She would talk to him, or listen if he preferred, and I would check in on him every couple of days in case he needed somebody else to vent to. These measures would bring his risk down a little, and if we could keep him clean for another six weeks, he would be eligible for food stamps, and then his risk would go down a little more.

A few days later I was back Under the Bridge, and Hard Head's tentmate told me Hard Head had wandered into the mission the other day and taken part in one of the religious services there. "It's like some speaking-in-tongues-level shit," the tentmate said. "He never went in for that before."

I feared the worst. "Did he relapse?"

The tentmate shrugged. "Hard to tell with him."

He was referring to Hard Head's legendary resiliency. He could do more dope than most people before the effects began to show.

I called Hard Head on his "government phone." He sounded sober and said he would be back from "Bible study" in a few minutes. I told him I would wait. The tentmate sat on his mound of beach towels and pulled a bottle of piss-yellow tequila from a brown paper bag and commenced drinking. Soon enough Hard Head came ambling up the street, his HOMELESS VET sign in one hand and a small gray book in the other.

When he saw me, he held up the book like a sun offering. A golden cross gleamed from the cover. "Well," he said, "I know what's been missing."

"You found religion."

"It found me. Think it's been hunting me for a long time."

If harm reduction had taught me to be wary of quick fixes, it also reminded me that every day Hard Head spent speaking in tongues and studying the Good Book was a day he wasn't boozing or drugging. Every day he passed in the company of the Almighty put him a day closer to getting his food stamps restored, his need and risk reduced.

He spent about ten minutes trying to evangelize me. I told him I was a secular creature and supposed I would always be, but I wasn't ruling anything out. Hard Head felt he was proof that higher powers took unexpected forms and showed up in unexpected places. "Even here," he said. "Even under the fucking bridge."

In spite of myself, I was moved by the sight of the old man awash in the spirit. He clutched the book to his chest as if it were an old friend returned from far away. Hard Head told me he was praying for his tentmate to find the willpower to get clean. He was praying for the city, that it would rid itself of the scourge of dope and violence, and for the nation, that it would turn its attention to the sick and the needy. It was a good prayer, and I hoped that in time we got everything Hard Head was asking for, but for now I would have settled for some food stamps.

# PART THREE

## harm reduction

# the wait

We were taking a quick lunch break between field stops in the East when I mustered the nerve to tell Charles he'd been right all along about the nature of this work. To me, *harm reduction* had a nicer ring than *disaster prevention*, but the practical applications were the same. He laughed, as I knew he would, and assured me that everyone worth a damn in the job had to learn this essential lesson the hard way. "We all show up thinking we're the secret sauce," he said. "We're what this place has been missing."

The best way to reduce harm was to get offenders to use whatever public services we could provide. The addicts I placed in drug court continued to get clean faster and stay clean longer. The program helped them with their Medicaid applications and got the offenders who couldn't work enrolled in SSI benefits and the able-bodied offenders in entry-level jobs. When offenders became eligible for food stamps, drug court helped sign them up.

Drug-court graduations were cap-and-gown affairs held at the courthouse. The judges gave opening remarks. The counselors got up and told personal stories about the graduates. Friends and family members showed up and cheered the graduates as their names were read off and the judges officially declared their obligations to the Department of Corrections satisfied.

Offenders in the last phases of the program usually sat in the audience and cheered on the other members of their cohort. They were meant to look forward to their day on the stage, but for some of them, completing the program was a source of dread.

Lately we'd had a rash of offenders relapsing in their last month in drug court. When their counselors asked what had happened, the offenders were honest. If they graduated, they were off probation and out of drug court. They lost their access to services. Medicaid and SSI carried over in theory, but there was no one along to help the offenders stay in those programs' good graces. Before enrolling in drug court, most offenders had extremely negative views of the criminal justice system. Eighteen months later, offenders were so attached to the support systems they'd found in drug court that they were failing drug tests on purpose and asking their POs to get their probations extended another year.

The administrators of the American social safety net seemed like straightforward enough villains. If their job was to minister to the neediest among us, why weren't they more adaptable? Shouldn't they be able to do at least as well for their people as a court-administered drug program? I laid a lot of blame at the door of the welfare state, but I knew that the fraud the safety-net programs were charged with rooting out wasn't a figment of the imagination of the pull-yourself-up-by-your-bootstraps crowd. I saw plenty of it. The least needy people on my caseload—the dons, the drug dealers—had almost all figured out how to get food stamps, Medicaid, and SSI. The neediest offenders seldom got any benefits at all.

One of my colleagues had come to P&P from the food stamp administration and another from Social Security. What they had to say wasn't surprising. The truly disabled found the anti-fraud measures placed throughout the application and renewal process insurmountable, while the people who got a rush from getting something over on the government scaled them with ease. Most studies have found that public benefit fraud is uncommon overall—the USDA believes that no more than 2 percent of food stamp recipients are ineligible for the benefit—but I could understand why even occasional instances of it would motivate program administrators to tighten regulations and make sure the money went where it was supposed to go.

Around the time I was squaring myself to harm reduction as my mission statement, I ran into a former graduate school classmate who was teaching in the public schools. We didn't know each other well, but we'd always been friendly enough. We had misspent twenties in common. We'd both viewed graduate school as a last-ditch refuge from adulthood. After graduation we both spent another two years killing time before we entered, or tried to enter, public service.

When my classmate asked about my job, I told her all about my gradual embrace of harm reduction after eighteen months of secretly hoping I could find a silver bullet. She'd gone through a similar process and supposed it was the way most people went about public service.

Like me, she'd found most of her coworkers to be earnest and indefatigable. Ultimately she held the institution and the people who funded it mostly to blame. Unlike me, she'd concluded that her institution could not be saved. By most statistical measures, the New Orleans public schools were improving. Graduation rates were up, but fully reforming one of the most troubled school systems in America, with one of the poorest populations, was looking like a decades-long endeavor.

My classmate believed she couldn't reduce harm from within the system—at least, not the way the system was functioning now. She felt she was party to the harm. She wanted to get clean. When the academic year ended, she was going to do something else. She understood that the system would go on without her. They weren't going to stop having public schools any more than they were going to stop having a Department of Corrections. She didn't blame me for standing by my institution. She hoped I wouldn't regret it, and she hoped I remembered that you get only the one life, only the one chance to commit your time and talent to a cause.

Toward the end of the conversation, she brought up the rash of recent police shootings that had given rise to the Black Lives Matter movement, and I admitted that my work as a PO was only as effective as offenders' belief that I had their best interests in mind. The shootings got the most coverage, but scores of true-crime documentaries and cold-case podcasts raised new questions about everything from eyewitness accounts to confessions of guilt. Of course, miscarriages of justice were nothing new, but they were reported now as never before. After the shooting of Walter Scott in South Carolina by Officer Michael Slager, POs throughout the New Orleans District had observed a chilling effect. Even our most affable charges seemed reluctant to engage. And then, a few weeks later, it all just blew over, and I thought I knew why. In a town where the jail and the police department were both under federal supervision, incidents that scandalized the nation probably felt to many New Orleanians like old news.

My classmate and I agreed that public mistrust of American law enforcement far outstripped public mistrust of the American education system, and I argued that this was actually the best thing to happen to law enforcement in recent memory. When an institution is viewed as merely low performing, you only get minor tweaks, maybe an occasional cash infusion. When an institution's reputation craters—fairly or not—it has no choice but to go for broke and bring in the freethinkers. Intense public scrutiny of American law enforcement had opened it up to hosts of new ideas, some of which had produced very strange bedfellows. Left-wing anti-incarceration activists suddenly found themselves allied with libertarian think tanks on the topic of reducing public spending on imprisoning drug addicts. So far, the sea change that the P&P academy director predicted at my graduation was more a matter of theory than practice, but the theory was worth getting excited about.

Shortly after my conversation with my former classmate, Dan the Regional Manager secured a grant of some sort that allowed those of us who were interested to attend a host of seminars about new developments in criminal justice reform. At a mental-health-in-corrections seminar we were told that Rikers Island, New York City's massive jail complex, was now the largest mental health hospital in the country. I had no idea whether the factual basis was number of beds or dollars spent or antipsychotic medications dispensed. I don't think I was supposed to. I think what I was supposed to take away from the Rikers Island remark was that the justice system had wandered so far afield of its original purpose that nothing short of a national movement could rein it back in. The expansion of the jail population from roughly half a million people in the late seventies to more than 2 million today, and of the community supervision population (i.e., parolees and probationers) from about 1 million to more than 4 million, had turned a government apparatus designed to stem property crimes and violence into a warehouse for all of America's sins and shortfalls. Jails weren't designed to house the nation's addicted and its mentally ill, but they'd been doing it for four decades now, and the wardens were telling the politicians that they'd had enough. They weren't cut out for this.

Even people who weren't crazy about the idea of public health care were beginning to acknowledge that treatment was cheaper than jail. People who got their treatment in the course of their daily lives—that is, out of the prison context—were more likely to learn to live with it than people who got treatment because they were locked up and had nothing better to do.

We were presented with findings from the East Coast and the Midwest, from the Rust Belt and the flyover states, from places where the afflicted were mostly black and places where they were mostly white and places where they were mostly Native American. Everywhere the seminar givers went, they found poverty and addiction, and poverty and addiction always had the same effects: "system bashing," "victim denial," "appeal to higher loyalties and codes," "a taste for risk." The more seminars I attended, the more clearly I understood that this was why I put on the name tag and drank the scalded coffee and ate the soggy muffins: confirmation that New Orleans wasn't alone. The trouble was everywhere in this country, and most of the people trying to do something about it were smarter and better trained than I was, and they, too, very often went home confounded.

The seminars always concluded by reminding us that under the best of circumstances—unlimited time, unlimited money, shelter and support systems in place—people struggled to push away from what they knew, to risk short-term discomfort in pursuit of a better life. Modifying human behavior wasn't easy and probably never would be, and it was good to be reminded of this. By my third seminar I'd quit taking notes, and I nodded my way through the pie charts and Power-Point presentations. I just wanted to be in the room with people who were as daunted as I was and kept doing the work anyway.

---

The most unnerving takeaway from the seminars could be distilled into the following correlation: Our national incarceration levels were historically high, and our national crime rate was historically low.

Murder rates were down more than 40 percent since the early 1980s, when mass incarceration began in earnest. The jail boom was founded at least in part by politicians looking to deny voting rights to black and brown people. On this the historical record was distressingly clear. But the law of unintended consequences had dictated other outcomes. Many modern criminologists gave much of the credit for the crime decline to the churches and community centers and outreach groups that banded together to refuse to accept violence in their own neighborhoods, but the relationship between increased incarceration and decreased violent crime couldn't be dismissed out of hand. Most seminars insisted that the criminal justice system of the future would have to find a way to maintain the recent gains in public safety while dispensing with the unconscionable collateral damage that the mass-incarceration era had inflicted.

One of the more popular alternatives to incarceration-as-usual was to make jail less miserable, or at least more productive. Louisiana, of all places, was at the forefront of this trend. A reentry program founded by two Tulane and Broad judges had become a statewide model for partnerships between the justice system and employers looking to change an offender's life. Offenders facing ten years in prison could be released after two if they learned a trade at the Louisiana State Penitentiary in Angola. Jobs in auto repair, welding, and HVAC would await them upon their release. These jobs paid better than minimum wage, with opportunities for advancement. Offenders got benefits, often for the first time in their lives. They got bosses who understood that there would probably be an adjustment period. One failed piss test wasn't going to blow the operation.

Even St. Tammany was giving the reentry model a try. Of the first thirty-three inmates sent through the Angola program in one St. Tammany courtroom, only one recidivated. The Angola reentry program had been deployed on a small scale, and the offenders selected for it were people in whom judges had seen promise. Even so, the results were compelling. The offenders spent less time in prison, which saved money, and they started paying taxes within two weeks of their release, which put money back into the system. The employers taking risks on people with criminal records got to feel like they were part of the solution, and they encouraged other small-business owners to consider giving a reentry offender a try.

Another promising development was the proliferation of Day Reporting Centers. These were showing up all over the country to help offenders pass the GED test, receive as much counseling as they wanted, and train to develop the "soft" skills needed to pass a job interview. While much of the counseling available at Day Reporting Centers was aimed at helping offenders fight addiction and prepare to land employment, new research suggested that offenders brought up in America's most violent neighborhoods—Central City, for one—couldn't properly prepare for a career until they met with treatment professionals trained to unpack trauma. Offenders exposed to violence during their formative years had probably never had a chance to talk to a licensed counselor about it.

Trauma therapy was extremely specialized, and counselors who knew how to do it told us that they saw grown men cry, lash out, even threaten revenge. I discussed Kendrick with one of the trauma specialists at one of the seminars. He speculated that the counselor who met with Kendrick at the Tower had probably received extensive training relative to her particular role: formulating treatment plans for people suffering from mental illness. She wasn't a trauma expert, and so she didn't know what to expect, and came up with what seemed to her the safest short-term solutions for Kendrick and anyone who got in his way.

Trauma therapy asked people to reopen old wounds. Even experienced trauma therapists sometimes perceived a public-safety threat too urgent to ignore. It was delicate work, not to be undertaken lightly. POs shouldn't be trying their hands at it. In fact, most of the seminars argued that the biggest mistake made by community supervision outfits was taking on duties they were unfit to perform. Trauma counseling, addiction counseling, and treating mental illness required years of training. Counselors got thousands of hours of practice in a lab, under the supervision of other licensed professionals, before they went live.

The ideal community supervision agency didn't try to sub in for other entities better outfitted and better trained to the task at hand. A PO's area of expertise was going into the neediest neighborhoods and observing the people living there. We learned to spot tells. We used the information gained from our observations of the offender in his environment to point him to the service that would address his need and reduce his risk. We shouldn't try to render those services ourselves.

If the seminars were unanimous in their belief that P&P needed to be more carrot and less stick, there was a widespread consensus that we shouldn't discard the stick altogether. Some offenders simply wouldn't give public assistance a chance if the treatment referral didn't have an "or else" attached. I'd taken for granted that carrying the stick, whether literally in the form of the gun at my hip or figuratively in the sense of "the idea" that Travis's mother had spoken about, prevented some offenders from being as candid with me as they might have been otherwise. The seminars argued that we shouldn't worry about candor. Our goal shouldn't be to get offenders to tell us everything. Our goal should be to get offenders to tell it to treatment professionals.

To take a treatment referral from a PO seriously, the offender didn't have to like his PO or even give up his belief that the whole P&P system was a trap designed to lure people back to jail. The offender just had to believe his PO listened when he spoke. The offender needed to believe his needs were being heard.

According to the seminars, the best way to convince offenders that you'd heard their needs was to role-play. A PO could tune out a venting session, but he couldn't act out the offender's struggles and fears unless he'd taken the time to listen to the offender and process what he had to say. The offender could practice saying no to his drug dealer or yes to the family member whose assistance he'd been too proud to take the first time she'd offered. The training video promised that POs who tried role-play saw 15 to 20 percent gains in the most critical measure of our success: the rate at which offenders showed up to receive the services we referred them to.

To the old-timers, even the liberals like Charles, this sounded like touchy-feely nonsense, but the data was impossible to ignore. Baton Rouge certainly didn't intend to ignore it. We POs were also alert to the irony that we were now expected to try yet another way to convince offenders to use social services—yet the services themselves remained out of reach or nonexistent. To his credit, Dan the Regional Manager needled his superiors in Baton Rouge endlessly about this. They in turn reminded him that they didn't set the budget, and he asked that they sound the alarm to the people above them, as he had done.

We all agreed to try the role-play thing anyhow. Travis was one of my first test subjects. He was eager to practice telling people at Odyssey House to fuck off.

"It's all these wrinkled old pricks who come around saying you need to learn from their mistakes. I'm like, 'Bitch, you got high until your fucking liver blew. You quit because you didn't have a choice.'"

Playing the role of the older and wiser drug addict hoping to minister to the young, I borrowed liberally from Hard Head's biography as I cited the various consequences of a life of addiction. "Do you want to end up broke?" I said. "Homeless? Begging on the corner?"

Travis pulled his glasses off and tossed them on the desk and twisted his index fingers into his eyes. "You don't know what I've been through."

"Let's compare. You first."

When the session was over, one thing was clear. Travis was poorly suited to the conventions of sober living. He was supposed to take comfort in the proximity of other people with whom he shared the affliction. Talking about his past was supposed to be therapeutic. Imagining a future without heroin was supposed to give him hope, but he never felt hopeful at Odyssey House. He hated the counselors and their scolding West Coast piety.

"They're not trying to scold you," I said. "They're trying to keep you alive."

I wasn't from the West Coast, but it was easy to see that he put me in the same camp as the counselors. We were members of the cult of sobriety, promising a Better Life that looked to Travis like pure fantasy. Getting clean sucked. Why couldn't we say so? Why couldn't we leave it at that? By this point I had dispensed with role play. I was trying, as bluntly as I could, to get Travis to tell me what he really wanted if he didn't want to go to jail and he didn't want to be at Odyssey House.

"I want to go back to work," he said. "I want to come home at the end of the day and be with my girl and my daughter, not a roomful of smelly old junkies."

"You have two more weeks until you make sixty days," I said. "You've stayed clean the whole time you've been there. You may not like Odyssey House, but that doesn't mean it isn't helping."

He shifted in the chair while he considered this. "I make it to sixty and I can roll out?"

"I can live with sixty."

I thought on that office visit for a long time after I cut Travis loose for the day. It was hard to say what part the role-play session played, but I seemed to have gotten a more forthcoming version of Travis than I'd ever seen before.

I knew I couldn't have kept Travis at Odyssey House forever. The goal of a treatment facility was to take the person in, equip him with tools to help him stay sober, and send him on his way. The goal was to get him where he told me he wanted to be, back at work and reunited with his family and on his way out of the criminal justice system.

Travis called me on day sixty and told me he was heading straight to Wal-Mart to see about getting his old job back. After that, I could find him at his girlfriend's apartment in the East. "The next time you see me," he said, "I'll be working. I'll be a dad."

———

He'd been back on the job about two weeks when I got a call from his girlfriend's uncle, the one with the oil money who'd given Travis a shot on the rig. "I just left that shithole they're living in," he told me. "They can see me in court if they want the baby back."

I grabbed Beth and Charles and Lamar and a few other POs and headed over there. We knocked at the door but there was no answer. Charles got the landlord on the phone. He showed up a couple of minutes later with the key and let us in. We found Travis and the girlfriend passed out in the kitchen. They were both breathing, but it took them a couple of minutes to come to. There were needles in the trash can. We shook the place down but didn't find any dope.

Pizza boxes and fast-food bags covered most of the floor. The trash can was overflowing with wadded diapers. Ketchup from an overturned bottle had leaked into the carpet and assumed a brownish hue like dried blood. Travis and the girlfriend sat cross-legged against the wall while we completed our search. The girlfriend was dark-haired and perilously thin. The needle marks in her arms looked like blackheads.

Lamar stood over them with his arms crossed. "This is no place for a child," he said. "This is no place for anybody."

"Fuck you," the girlfriend said.

"She doesn't mean it," Travis said. "She's not cut out for this."

"But you are, right?" Lamar said. "You brought her into it."

"Fuck you," the girlfriend said again.

Lamar could see that this wasn't the time or place to give anybody the straight talk. He asked the girlfriend if she was going to puke. She said that if she was, she would be sure to let him know so that he could hold her hair while she did it.

"Sorry," Travis said. "This isn't her. It's the dope talking."

Beth and Charles agreed to wait at the apartment until the girlfriend's mother showed up to take her to the hospital. Lamar took the ride with me to jail. In the Crown Vic he tried to have another go at Travis.

"I was never an addict," Lamar said. "But growing up, I knew a lot of people who were. The ones who finally got free told me something I think about a lot. They said the trick isn't to think about what your life'll look like when you're clean. The trick's thinking about what your life looked like when you bottomed out."

"I hope this is it," Travis said. "I hope this is what I look back on."

Lamar and I knew what he meant. He hoped there was nothing worse to come, but he didn't believe he would have much say in that. I waited until we were halfway to the jail to ask Travis what triggered the latest relapse.

He shrugged and said, "Just life, I guess."

I didn't ask again. No one spoke for the rest of the ride. Travis looked through the window at the passing landscape as if every inch of it were booby-trapped.

At the jail, Travis passed the usual inspections. He knew what would happen next. Deputies from St. Tammany would pick him up and drive him across the lake for his revocation hearing at the courthouse on the Northshore.

I knew what I had to do. The next week in the St. Tammany Parish courthouse, I walked up to the bench and told the judge that the treatment options on offer at the New Orleans District couldn't stop Travis from using heroin, and as such, I believed the judge should revoke his probation.

In St. Tammany, this was never a hard case to make. The judge offered drug court as a last-ditch alternative. Travis declined. He didn't say why, but by then I could make an educated guess. He didn't want another gang of bleeding hearts to sit him in a circle and demand that he profess his allegiance to sobriety. He believed in choosing jail he was choosing freedom of a sort. He may also have believed what I believed: he wouldn't stop using heroin unless we forced him.

The judge called Travis up to the microphone and told him his probation was revoked effective that day, and he would be remanded to the custody of the Department of Corrections. Travis's hair was in his eyes and he stared blankly ahead from behind his thick glasses.

A deputy led him out through the side door. Travis didn't look back at me as he went. I sat in the front pew trying to decide how to feel about what I'd done. Travis would serve about two years of the five-year sentence. Research had shown little or no correlation between sentence length and sobriety upon release. The only thing prison could do, and indeed the only thing I was asking of it, was to keep Travis from overdosing while he was locked up.

I thought again of the price tag. The form of harm reduction I'd settled upon would cost the state about $35,000, more than enough money to pay for two years of housing, health care, and food stamps. On the surface these seemed like far worthier investments. For most offenders, they would have been the clearest path to harm reduction, but I believed Travis wouldn't survive to the end of the month if I didn't put a brick wall between him and his drug of choice. I'd seen six people on my caseload die of overdoses. Travis would not be the seventh.

When I got home from the revocation hearing that evening, Kristin looked even more exhausted than I did. The senior attorney at her firm who'd complained about her clothes was now weighing in on her work ethic, though I couldn't remember a Sunday that Kristin hadn't spent hunched over her laptop, cranking out billable hours. She sat beside me on the couch and put her head on my shoulder and told me that all she wanted was the opportunity to work someplace fair, where labor was judged on its merits. "I thought by my thirties I wouldn't let it get to me," she said. "I thought that into my twenties. My *late* twenties."

She knew I couldn't do anything about her job or, more broadly, about the kinds of bosses a woman was likely to have to deal with if she wanted to practice law in New Orleans. I hadn't lost my cool at home since my outburst after Javaron killed the teenager. I'd been trying to become a better partner, but putting aside my own grief after Travis's revocation didn't represent a surge of personal growth on my part. I had no desire to talk about what happened to Travis. What could I say about him that I hadn't told Kristin a hundred times before? Once addiction lost its power to shock, it went to work on you with its awful consistency. There were twists along the way, but the endings were so often the same that talking about them could feel as tedious as talking about the weather.

I focused that night on my partner's needs and gave what little help I could—an assertion that she'd been treated unfairly and that neither of us knew how to fix the problem, at least in the short term. "Something better's coming," I said.

She nodded. She believed it, too. She was wired for hope. It was one of the things I loved about her. "You're right," she said. "But it's the fucking wait, man."

We had a laugh and a drink and got in bed and turned off the lights, but I couldn't sleep. I kept picturing the apartment Travis had shared with his mother, with the clogged drains and broken mirrors and the roaches and the flies. I knew better than to spend too much time comparing my life to offenders' lives. That was how you made bad decisions, decisions that were more about you and your survivor's guilt than the offender and his needs or, in this case, his chances of avoiding a drug overdose.

Still, safe and warm in bed, with a loved one beside me, I felt that guilt as acutely as ever before, a heartburn that washed through my gut and pooled in my kneecaps, and it took me a long time to remember that as much as I hated putting Travis in jail, I hated the alternatives more. I did the math a dozen times and kept getting the same result, which meant that given the options at my disposal, I'd chosen correctly.

Something better was coming, though. I still believed that. I just didn't know what to do about the wait.

# FIFTEEN

# adaptable

D rug court remained a great source of hope for me, but the drug-dealer sections were still trying to find their footing. One of the youngest offenders in Damien's section got murdered in a drug deal gone wrong. In the pre-court meeting in the judge's chambers, the judge was distraught. The offender was in his early twenties. He was from the Lower Ninth Ward and grew up with a grandmother who was raising several other grandchildren and a daughter who had been an addict since she was a teenager.

In many ways his story was the one we'd heard so many times before. He got precious little attention at home or in school. He looked around his neighborhood and saw that the people getting the attention were the people with power and money, and they got it by joining up with the neighborhood dope crew. He was small and soft-spoken. He was no don. Damien and the other dons joked that he must have lied on his drug-court application to get into the drug-dealer section.

"Are we gonna learn from this?" the judge asked the counselors and me during our pre-court meeting. "Is there a lesson here?"

He wasn't blaming us. Powerful people need room to vent, just like everyone else, and it was the least we could do to sit quietly while the judge arranged his thoughts. "Doing the same thing over and expecting a different result," the judge said. "Definition of fucking *insanity*."

He asked again for suggestions. One of the counselors suggested that we rethink the group treatment model. Putting a bunch of drug dealers in a room together was having the opposite of the intended effect. They were supposed to be finding common ground in acknowledging the hazards of the drug trade, and copping to guilt about spreading violence and addiction. Instead, they spent most of their group sessions assuring one another that the drug life was honorable and virtuous, and that none of them deserved any blame for the collateral damage.

Those offenders who did express remorse or ambivalence about their profession were mocked, and the young, eager-to-prove types were encouraged to show the dons they belonged. Whether this played a part in the deceased offender's getting out of his depth in the drug deal that killed him was impossible to say, but the counselors were sure that the group therapy sessions hadn't convinced him to try another line of work. "The treatment model that works for other stuff isn't working for this," one counselor said.

"So we do more one-on-one," the judge said.

Everyone nodded tentatively. Here was the downside to being on the new-idea frontier. What we were trying was unproven, and the stakes were life-and-death. Every error had potentially catastrophic consequences. We went round and round for a little while longer. I told the judge that I'd been laying off Damien and a few other offenders who'd given me the impression that they delighted in getting one over on my home inspections, but I could tack the other way and check in on them more often, or earlier in the morning or after curfew. I could try again to win them over with "the idea" that they were being watched.

The judge shook his head. "If they love fooling you at nine in the morning, they're not gonna love it at ten at night?"

I figured this was a rhetorical question and kept my mouth shut.

Eventually the judge decided that the only substantive move we would make right now would be to reinforce the rule that everybody had to get a day job. "No more of this small-business bullshit," the judge said.

He wasn't saying that his decision to allow drug dealers to quit their jobs had caused the young offender's death, but he was acknowledging that Damien and the other dealers had played us by claiming they were opening their own businesses. When the judge announced the new rule—that is, reinstated the old one—the drug dealers told their counselors that they weren't happy with the judge for requiring them to spend forty hours per week doing something other than drug dealing. At their day jobs they had to take shit off ordinary people and kowtow to bosses, many of whom didn't know what wide berths the dealers were given in the neighborhoods where they plied their true trade.

The main thing they disliked about working day jobs was the decline in their earning potential. Of course, they couldn't say this to the judge. In court, most of them held the line and spoke of the pleasures of making an honest buck. At the Tower they fumed and raged. Inside of a month, two offenders assaulted the elderly security guard who stood watch at the door. From the beginning, the first offender had done a poor job of hiding his contempt for the drug-court proceedings, and the judge looked quietly delighted when he revoked the offender's probation.

When Damien attacked the guard, the judge was more conflicted. He didn't think he had much of a choice about revoking Damien's supervision. Since Damien was placed on probation, he had been arrested with a gun and destroyed a relative's property to collect on a debt. The gun charge had been dismissed, and we got the impression that Damien or one of his associates had convinced Damien's cousin to recant his testimony on Damien's debt-collection efforts, but the pattern of behavior was hard to ignore.

Damien told the counselor after the fact that he had, in effect, attacked the guard deliberately so that he could get out of drug court. Another dope arrest and they might have talked themselves into going easy on him, but Damien had seen how the judge responded when the other guy attacked the guard. He would do about six months upstate before he came back out on parole. As a parolee, he would be ineligible for drug court. He would still have a PO to deal with, but that was nothing. That was just a matter of making sure you didn't keep any drugs or guns at your house. He wanted to work his true profession badly enough to do six months in prison. Damien's strategy was cruel, but it was also ingenious. Yet again, I was forced to imagine how different his life—and many others' lives—might be if he'd gotten the chance to put his talents toward anything other than drug dealing.

D amien was my second revocation in the last eight weeks. Like most drug dealers, he had always been careful not to show me too much, and so it was harder to know where I went wrong but easier to absolve myself of blame for the final outcome.

Kendrick was different. I had probably spent more time with him than anyone else on my caseload. I'd been practicing harm reduction on Kendrick since long before I heard that term. I'd been more reluctant to heed warning signs, too, which I guessed was further proof that the line between investing the proper amount of time and energy in an offender and feeling personally responsible for his success was still hard to find.

I'd been proud of the acrobatics I'd had to do earlier in the year to get Kendrick shipped to the Department of Corrections for ninety days of mental health care, and I was furious when he returned and told me that the only treatment he'd received during that time was a handful of sleeping pills. He'd met once with a psychiatrist, who'd found no paranoia, no schizophrenia, no bipolar disorder, no PTSD. According to the psychiatrist, Kendrick's IQ was low-normal, somewhere in the high eighties. The DOC had recorded a suicide attempt back in 1997 and a write-up for urinating on a correctional officer, but Kendrick wasn't mentally ill. He'd had a rough life exacerbated by extreme poverty. In Louisiana, this didn't make him an outlier.

As always, I found blaming the bosses at the Department of Corrections therapeutic but fruitless. I had sent Kendrick to prison because prison appeared to be the only place that could give him a diagnosis, but I couldn't blame the warden—or whoever decided what to do about Kendrick when he got there—for deciding that prisons weren't on-call mental health hospitals. The prisons were already taking on far more than their fair share of the mental health burden in America. They weren't about to start administering mental health services to people on parole.

The psychiatrist's write-up gave me no reason to believe I would be able to get Kendrick an appointment at Metropolitan Human Services District. I called Metropolitan only because I'd promised Kendrick I would.

I went back and forth with the screener. Her answer was the same as before. Without a diagnosis, Kendrick wasn't eligible for services. I was getting ready to hang up when Kendrick gestured for the phone. I can't say what I was thinking when I gave it to him. I must have figured we had nothing to lose.

He cleared his throat and gripped the receiver. "I'm seeing ghosts! They're telling me what to do!"

He caught his breath and offered up his Social Security number.

He gestured again, this time for pen and paper. When he handed the paper back to me, a date and hour were printed in giant characters, the kind you might find on a second-grade penmanship test.

Adaptation is a remarkable process to witness. Kendrick's time as a citizen of the state of Louisiana had taught him exactly what to say in circumstances like these. There was still the matter of giving him directions to the facility and sending out reminders in the interim. A few days after our office visit, Kendrick's "government phone" went dark. I couldn't find him at Tina's Place in the Lower Ninth Ward or any of the homeless shelters.

A week later he reappeared at the office. He'd slipped up, had a onetime relapse, but "walked myself clean," he said. He passed his drug screen but made no mention of the mental health appointment. I called Metropolitan and tried a guilt trip on the screener. Metropolitan, I reminded her, was a public mental health clinic. Kendrick couldn't be the first patient to miss an appointment.

"And he won't be the last," the screener said. "If they don't want help bad enough to show up, we move on to the next guy."

In the end I prevailed on her to grant Kendrick the next available appointment, nearly ten weeks away. He thought sober living might do him good in the meantime. I got him admitted to a new facility on the West Bank I'd been hearing good things about. Charles was thinking about sending a guy there and agreed to ride with us and check the place out. It was a long haul, about fifteen miles from the New Orleans District, but well worth the drive. The program's founders had donated two blocks of clean, well-kept town houses manned by counselors who provided life skills coaching and substance abuse treatment to addicts. There was an in-house GED program for anyone who wanted it and nightly AA and NA meetings. The program director was a balding white guy in cargo shorts and an oversized T-shirt, himself a recovering addict who'd gone back to school after he got clean and gotten licensed to practice social work. He told me that the program had a good relationship with a temp agency that provided part-time employment for the program's clients if they were sober and able-bodied enough to participate.

The program director gave Kendrick and Charles and me a tour of the town house where Kendrick could stay as long as he liked. There were three small bedrooms with cheap floral-print curtains and a little kitchen with a microwave and a hot plate. The floors were spit-shined and the windows spotless. Most of the residents were between thirty-five and fifty.

"Couple of them had legit careers before the dope took hold," the program director told Charles and me later. "But most of them, most of their lives have been this." He made a circular gesture that I took to represent the cycle of addiction, to include bouncing from one treatment center to another. "We didn't really go looking for an older crowd. Just kinda happened. I think it's because we're so far out. Only reason to come here is you really want to get clean."

People who bailed out of Odyssey House and Bridge House could get to a neighborhood drug dealer inside of five minutes. The French Quarter was within walking distance of both facilities. The place on the West Bank, which would wait so long to come up with a name that it would be forever known at the New Orleans District as the Place on the West Bank, was located in the rear corner of a middle-class suburban neighborhood that backed up to a canal. An addict determined to leave treatment and find a fix will get what he's looking for eventually, but I could see that physical distance from the usual drug-dealing turf decreased the addict's chances of relapsing.

Kendrick wanted a break from the young guys. They smoked all day and roamed the streets at night. They were more of a crew than a gang—"Gangs make money," Kendrick said, when I asked him to explain the difference—but they liked getting into fights with other guys and carrying pistols in their waistbands and stealing tires and hubcaps. "If there's some petty shit to get into," Kendrick said, "these boys'll get into it."

Like Hard Head, Kendrick wanted his own experience to serve as a cautionary tale to the young, but the young were as thickheaded as the addicted. "Just young or just a junkie is one thing," Kendrick said. "Young *and* a junkie, you might as well forget about it."

The program director introduced him to his new housemates, a trio of middle-aged guys in thrift store denim. He shook their hands and thanked them for having him. He described himself as "low-key" and shot me a warning glance just in case I were compelled to quibble with that description.

Charles and I made the trip out there once more, about three weeks later, and found Kendrick in high spirits. He showed me his bed, the sheets pulled as taut across the mattress as a naval cadet's. He showed me his journal, with a list of goals scribbled into the inside jacket: "90 days clean," "2 years out of jail," "don't run out of food before the end of the month."

When I asked the program director how Kendrick was doing, he was candid. "You ever get his head checked out?"

Charles fielded that one for me. "If you mean did we send him to prison to try to get him a diagnosis, then yes. If you mean do we have anything to show for it, then no."

The program director had been doing this work long enough to get the joke. "We don't have much luck here either. It's one thing to get them on Medicaid. Keeping them on—that's another story."

He went on to explain that Kendrick could go from chummy to furious like no one he'd ever seen. Mood swings were common among people in recovery, and the program didn't overreact to them, but Kendrick's housemates had expressed concerns. A dispute over whose turn it was to sweep the kitchen was resolved by Kendrick's telling a housemate that he could either pick up the broomstick and go to work on the floor or Kendrick could pick up the broomstick and go to work on his housemate.

"We smoothed it over," the program director said. "There was blame on both sides."

The four housemates were drinking Cokes and playing cards around a small kitchen table when we walked in. Kendrick wore jeans and a button-up oxford shirt that the program director had gotten from one of the Goodwill or St. Vincent de Paul centers that provided the Place on the West Bank with free wardrobes for every new guy who signed up. If there was residual tension among the housemates, I didn't pick up on it. At Tina's Place, Kendrick's smile had always been cautious, as if it knew that bad news was never more than a knock away. At the Place on the West Bank, he belly laughed when one of his housemates talked shit about his terrible poker game.

"If it was dominos," he said, "I'd wipe the floor with y'all mother-fuckers."

Charles and I took our leave before we could dampen the mood. Kendrick was with people his own age who had suffered much of what he had suffered and who believed they had a long fight ahead of them and could win it only by standing together. Kendrick was a dozen miles and a wide river away from where he'd grown up, but for the first time since I'd known him, he looked like he was home.

"You're doing good work here," I told the program director.

He turned red and waved me off, and it fell to Charles to insist.

"The state won't pay for this stuff," Charles said. "If you guys don't do it, it doesn't get done."

Bridge House got a number of private donations and made money from its in-house thrift shop and auto repair facility, and Odyssey House hosted fundraising galas full of rich people and was supposed to have a long list of benefactors. No one was sure how the Place on the West Bank was funded. There was federal money for some of the services provided by sober-living facilities, but as far as we knew, most of the funding came from private citizens, and most of the labor was provided by people who worked for free or very cheap. Saying thanks to the private citizens who gave their lives and their money to a public good was the least we government employees could do.

Eventually the program director accepted our gratitude and shooed us away. The guy Charles sent to the Place on the West Bank wasn't as impaired as Kendrick, but he had roughly the same history of addiction and had behaved so badly at Bridge House the last time he was there that the program had essentially banned him for life. He was an old addict who wanted to get clean. He couldn't stand all the young addicts who were only in treatment because their PO was forcing them. At the Place on the West Bank, just about everybody bought in. There were no distractions. If you wanted to get clean, you could do it there. Charles's offender completed the program and got off parole.

Two days after Charles's and my second visit to the facility, the housemates convinced the program manager to put Kendrick out. To hear them tell it, most of the time he was easy to get along with. He could spin a yarn like no one they'd known. He had a sense of humor about himself. He never minded being the butt of the joke. But then out of nowhere he just went off. He threatened violence, and each threat struck the housemates as more credible than the last. The program director told me he was willing to have another go at Kendrick in a month or two, after everybody'd had a breather.

"I guess he puts on a good face for me," I said, and I knew that this, like his ghost story, was in all likelihood an adaptation. Kendrick had learned who he couldn't "click out" on.

This included the program director. "He's always 'Yes, sir' with me. He wants to be here. He wants to get along. Even the guys who want him out will tell you that."

On our way back to the East Bank, Kendrick told me the same. "I don't want to be like this," he said.

The appointment at Metropolitan was still eight weeks away. I couldn't do anything right now but tell him I believed he was trying. Kendrick relocated to Tina's Place for a few days, but he got in another fight with a housemate and relapsed again. When he came to, he realized he'd lost his food stamp card, and Tina promptly evicted him. He moved into a tent Under the Bridge.

The only consistent operation in Kendrick's life was the walk he made every two weeks from the bridge to the New Orleans District. He submitted his urine sample, sat in the offender chair, and gave me the latest on the homeless life. He didn't feel safe or secure Under the Bridge, but he had the familiar satisfaction that came of knowing how to handle yourself in circumstances that would have been too much for most people. He found a corner and flew a sign and made just enough money to feed himself. He found a tentmate he could get along with.

When the second Metropolitan appointment came around, he got there on time. The doctor diagnosed him with bipolar disorder and provided him with a prescription that he could get filled for free at Metropolitan's pharmacy. He had a couple of click-outs Under the Bridge, but they never amounted to much. No one who saw him in a rage wanted any part of him. After about eight weeks on the meds, the click-outs subsided. One day he wandered into the mission and somehow convinced a social worker there to help him get his food stamps restored. Tina was considering taking him back down the road. For now he was welcome to hang around the house by day and ride the bus back to the tents at night.

Kendrick's former housemates looked relieved when he told them he was getting help. He told them that a few of them could stand to have their heads shrunk a little. "They answered like you knew they would," he told me. "'That psych shit's for faggots.'"

He began practicing his own version of harm reduction, trying to get the young guys doing heroin and crack to downshift to weed, and the ones selling dope to try flying the sign or, if they really needed money, shoplifting. I suggested the role-play thing to help him through his fury with one housemate who he was certain had a death wish. The housemate went around with a gun in his shorts and picked fights with everyone who looked at him funny. He reminded Kendrick of his young lover who got killed the year before.

"The way it works is you pretend I'm the guy you're worried about," I said. "Just tell me what you want to tell him."

It was rough going at first, both of us snickering to cover our embarrassment, but the third time around, he found the right way to say what he wanted his friend to know: "It's fucked up, what you've been through. But don't take it out on yourself."

"It's good to have a plan," I said.

Kendrick laughed. "Little shit's still not gonna listen."

"You never know."

"The fuck I don't. But I'm telling him anyway."

We left it at that.

At our next office visit Kendrick told me that the speech turned out about how he had expected, but he was determined to keep at the kid until he saw the light. There was other news. After years of tomcatting, he'd committed to the woman who'd seen him through his worst relapses and who had promised to hold him to his treatment schedule. She and Kendrick had grown up together in the Lower Ninth Ward. She had a record and had been on parole in another parish. She was bagging at Wal-Mart now but looking for something better. She took mental health medication and believed in it.

I went out into the lobby to meet her. Kendrick's taste in men skewed young, but his girlfriend was about his age. The flesh around her lips and eyes had a scalded quality that I'd observed in a number of longtime drug users, but she had a sly, in-on-the-joke smile and greeted me with a whack on the back that nearly sent me flying into the metal detector.

"He's starting to buy in on the meds," she told me. "It takes time. They fix your crazy but play hell with the rest of you."

She'd gained fifty pounds since she began taking antipsychotics. The other side effects typical of the medication—headache, sore joints, sleeplessness—didn't bother her as much as her waistline. "Vanity's all in your head," she said. "Good thing they have a pill for that."

She had a laugh like a thunder roll and a habit of poking Kendrick in the rib cage when she made a joke. "This one couldn't gain weight in a donut shop."

He did get the sleeplessness, though, and he didn't mind telling me that his bowels were on their own schedule these days. No two movements were quite alike, but he kept refilling his prescription. At thirty-five, Kendrick had accepted that treatment needed to be a permanent fixture of his life. He had love and friendship and the closest thing to a clear head and steady nerves as he'd ever experienced. He wasn't going to go to college or run a business, but if he could hold on to good friends and a healthy relationship and freedom from violence and addiction, then by any measure he'd come a long way.

He'd done the hard work of harm reduction himself, mustering the determination and grit without which his plight couldn't possibly improve, but it was also true that we had pitched in at a couple of key junctures. I began to think of P&P as a bumper on a bowling alley, absorbing the impact when the ball got off track and gently nudging it back toward its destination.

When I got the news that Kendrick was back in jail, I was calmer than I might have expected. I went through the usual motions, studying the weeks before, trying to find the sign I'd missed. When I met Kendrick in jail, he told me he didn't remember how he got his hands on a pair of scissors or how they ended up piercing his girlfriend's thigh. The ambulance had come first to take Kendrick's girlfriend to the ER. The police came next to take Kendrick to OPP. He was booked for aggravated battery. The parole board wouldn't let him out even if I asked.

I didn't ask. I couldn't make a sensible argument that if Kendrick were released from jail, he wouldn't hurt himself or someone else. Even so, I was crushed when I read the police report. According to the patrol officer, Kendrick was babbling and incoherent when the police arrived. It took a team to get him in handcuffs. Once he was seated in the squad car, he settled down and his memory flashed back on. He didn't understand why he had stabbed his girlfriend, but he understood what came next. He'd yet to figure out how to adapt to good fortune, but bad fortune he knew how to handle. By the time he got to OPP, his head was right. It had to be if he was going to survive in there.

Even in failure, the harm reduction approach asked you to recognize short-term gains. Kendrick's near-fatal click-out might have happened a year earlier if not for the intervention we'd tried. We might have bought him a stretch of quality time that he never would have experienced otherwise. In that span he had friends and a lover and food and a purpose, in the form of the young people he hoped to steer away from poverty and addiction and incarceration.

It was one thing to tell myself this in the ride to the jail. It was quite another to be seated across the partition from Kendrick at OPP for the last time. "Is your girlfriend gonna be okay?" I asked.

I could only half see him through the battered glass. His index fingers drew streaks across the metal table on his side of the partition. The pattern was inscrutable to me, but I sensed that he was crunching the numbers, summing up his culpability. "She's like me. Been through worse."

He told me the story, or as much of it as he knew. Things between him and his girlfriend had been really good overall, maybe as good as they'd ever been, but he'd been thinking a lot about his murdered lover. He'd been spending time with the young guys again and growing increasingly frustrated that they weren't heeding his advice or taking his warnings seriously. There was no single incident that put him over the edge, but life in the tents was a constant scratch and claw. He got some shoes at Goodwill and woke to find that someone had pilfered them from his tent. One night, seemingly out of nowhere, he felt like if he didn't escape right away, he was going to do something drastic. He asked his girlfriend to get high with him. She tried to talk him out of it, but in the end she believed doping was better than the other things Kendrick was threatening to do. They bought from somebody they didn't know. Kendrick hadn't done something like that in years. The batch was bad and took them to a dark place. The next thing Kendrick knew, he was covered in blood and sitting in the back of a cop car.

I told him about a new grant that Dan the Regional Manager had been touting for the last couple of weeks. He'd sold it as another nudge in the right direction from headquarters, a sign that the bosses were, however gradually, embracing the treatment model as the future of community supervision. The grant targeted inmates with "co-occurring" disorders—in other words, inmates who suffered from both addiction and mental illness.

"They start you on meds and counseling while you're upstate," I told Kendrick. "Set you up with appointments when you get out, so there's a seamless transition to parole. I'm gonna recommend you for it if you're game."

"Hell yeah, I'm game. I'm not gonna be gone for long."

He'd already met with a public defender. He expected to do a couple of years on the aggravated battery. His girlfriend had come to see him in jail and promised to testify on his behalf. She intended to wait for him. She believed they were destined to be together. She wished they'd found each other sooner, but there would be plenty of life left when Kendrick re-paroled. They would do the things that worked: treatment, sobriety. They wouldn't make the same mistakes again. Kendrick took most of the blame himself and left very little for me, but just before we parted, he did ask if there was any chance that I could get him out of this.

"After everything that's happened, this is the only way," I said. "We were too little, too late."

He nodded and thought on it. "It was me who bought the dope. Me who decided to get high after I spend all week telling these kids how great it is to get sober."

He was being gracious by owning his fate, but he knew there was plenty of fault to go around. Today he needed to feel agency. If he didn't believe he could engineer a different outcome next time, there was no sense in even asking for parole.

"You'll parole again," I said. "We'll try again."

"See you on the other side," he told me, and he rang for the deputy to take him back into the bowels of the jail.

I had other stops to make that afternoon, and I tried not to think of any of my recent losses, Kendrick or Travis or Damien. When I passed the jail again on my way up Broad Street, I felt my chest tighten and the Crown Vic veering into the middle lane. I righted the wheel and punched the gas and let the thought of the three men in jail fill me with fury, and then I let it fill me with relief.

# SIXTEEN

# off the dole

After so many trips back and forth to the jail, I was actually looking forward to resuming the fight to get the neediest offenders on my caseload approved for SSI benefits. I complained to a favorite DRC counselor about the never-ending hurdles, and she reminded me of what I already knew: if you wanted to get SSI, you needed someone who knew how to work the system.

"You need a drug dealer," she said. "Ask them who their disability lawyer is."

"My guy has tried all the lawyers," I said.

Ronald had rattled off the names of a half dozen disability lawyers who advertised on TV. Most lawyers who represented people seeking SSI benefits took a piece of the benefits check in return for payment, as few people seeking SSI had any income of their own. It seemed like a tough way to earn a living—a volume business, to be sure—but none of the TV lawyers had been able to help. I figured one more name couldn't hurt. I hit up the next drug dealer who came to the New Orleans District for an office visit.

"Oh, yeah," he said. "I've got a guy."

He reached into his wallet and extracted a stack of business cards. He shuffled through until he found the one he wanted. He held it up to the light as if he were checking it for watermarks, then slapped it on my desk and winked at me. "I'm not even looking for a finder's fee."

"What's his secret?"

"You look at him, you know."

"That good, huh?"

"He pushed me through like it was nothing."

In other words, if he could get able-bodied men into the system, he should have no trouble with a genuinely disabled person. Ronald had never heard of the lawyer but figured it couldn't hurt to call. I don't know what the lawyer said or did that the other lawyers didn't. The offender who gave me the business card wasn't wrong when he said that for some lawyers, the look is 80 percent of what you're paying for, but I had to think that lawyers who specialized in navigating and/or scamming bureaucracies probably had to have some technical know-how to go with the $1,000 suits.

Ronald's case seemed about as straightforward as they got. He suffered from an acute medical condition that made it impossible for him to hold down a conventional job. He was exactly the kind of American the SSI program was designed to serve. Ronald described the lawyer as "slick" and the doctor whose testimony the lawyer relied on as "shady." Another way to look at it was to say that they knew the system and could bend it to their clients' advantage. In truth, I was more comfortable with Ronald's description. I didn't feel great about giving the lawyer more business, but letting Ronald continue to go without benefits seemed worse.

The lawyer came through. SSI worked out to less than $700 per month. Ronald used most of the money to help his mother with groceries and rent. It didn't make much of a difference. She was still working as much overtime as ever.

The little bit of money Ronald received every month wasn't enough to cover rent and utilities at even a modest apartment in New Orleans's worst neighborhood. It wasn't meant to. The first *S* in *SSI* stood for *supplemental*. SSI wasn't supposed to pay all of a disabled person's expenses. If the disabled person didn't have a parent, as Ronald did, or the good fortune to be among the households that received rental assistance in the city, he was on his own for shelter. I guessed that the SSI administrators saw their situation about how I saw mine. If someone wanted to double their budget and assign them the task of making certain that no disabled person lived on the streets, they would be happy to take on the new responsibilities. Until then, they had their lane and they were staying in it.

For Ronald, SSI was about more than money. "When they give you a check," he said, "they're saying it's not all in your head. They're like 'Yeah, your shit's fucked up.'"

SSI was validation that you weren't a malingerer. In granting Ronald benefits, the SSI administration was providing him modest but essential relief from shame about his unemployment. Ronald knew he was more fortunate than many SSI recipients. He had his mother, and he was happy to be able to help her out with expenses. In addition to the usual bills, she was paying for Javaron's attorney, one of the big names from the billboards. She was rarely home when I stopped by. When I did see her, she was always rushing out to catch the bus. She'd put on weight since Javaron's arrest, and her eyes were bloodshot. She needed sleep, and she knew she wouldn't get it.

One morning when we crossed paths on the front lawn, she told me that the DA's office had offered Javaron life in prison. "The lawyer thinks he can bring them down to thirty-five or forty, for a price. I tell myself, 'Work another shift, buy my boy another month.'" She nodded to herself as she did the math. "He'll be old and I'll be gone. But he'll still have his brother."

She wasn't looking for any reassurances from me about Javaron, and I had none to offer. She thanked me for helping Ronald to get approved for SSI. Every little bit helped. I explained that I'd done nothing except pass along the lawyer's business card.

I did have one piece of good news to report. The DA's office had decided to dismiss Ronald's gun charge.

"You're kidding," she said. "What the fuck?"

She knew the system. On the surface, Ronald's case looked like the sort that the DA was happy to prosecute. When you had a felon in a car with a gun, there wasn't much a defense attorney could do. That the gun wasn't registered to Ronald didn't help his case. The guns used in shootings were rarely registered to the people who pulled their triggers. The presence in the vehicle of an individual without a felony record—an individual who could conceivably claim lawful possession of the gun—was almost never a reason for a DA to dismiss a gun case.

People with clean records were often brought along on drug deals or burglaries or shootings to absorb the blame for criminal acts committed by people with serious records. "Taking the charge" for a gang member was often one of the first steps to becoming a member.

Taking the charge for the trunk full of dope was as simple as raising your hand. Gun charges weren't quite as easy to volunteer for. Where guns were concerned, "possession" was defined more like "access." As a felon, Ronald wasn't supposed to be within arm's reach of a gun, even if someone else in the room or the vehicle claimed ownership of it. Ronald was clearly in violation of the letter of the law, but the DA had decided Ronald hadn't violated the spirit.

When a case was dismissed, the DA didn't have to provide a reason, but the assistant district attorney in charge of the case clued me in off the record. "We just really didn't think this guy was up to anything."

An ADA deciding what to do with a case was in the same fix as a PO trying to decide whether to seek revocation. He compared the harm done to the offender by locking him up to the potential harm to the public by setting him free. The decision was supposed to be based on the facts of the case and the extent of the defendant's criminal record. I assumed, as Ronald's mother did, that the DA liked the case a lot when he read the police report and noticed Ronald's prior convictions. And then he had a look at him and decided he believed his story. He didn't believe that Ronald knew about the gun or had any intention of using it.

It was guesswork at best. If you understood violence to be largely a product of need, disabled people had as much reason as anyone to be regarded as risks. Some disabled offenders carried the lifestyle addiction. Earlier in the year, a New Orleans District drug dealer had fired at someone from a wheelchair. He'd landed in the chair a year before as a result of another shooting, itself the result of another drug deal gone wrong. The DA's office knew that gun violence could come from anywhere and still felt that, in Ronald's case, the greater harm was incarceration.

For a long time after that, Ronald's mother asked me whether the charge was "really dead." I tried to assure her that Ronald was safe as long as he stayed away from guns. Ronald told both of us that he knew his mother couldn't handle losing both of her sons to prison. He planned to stay inside, tend to the dogs, keep a low profile. He said he was okay with it. He didn't crave action. Ronald had never been feared like Javaron used to be. He didn't have to worry about what people would say about him now that he'd quit the life. Whatever need Javaron had satisfied by gunning down a teenager wasn't in Ronald.

I stopped by once a month for a little while longer, but soon it became clear that I had nothing further to offer. Getting Ronald to the disability attorney was the best thing I'd ever done for him, and probably the best thing I would ever do. Once I added SSI benefits to Ronald's risk/need assessment, he dropped to medium, and I decided to supervise him accordingly.

When I told Ronald's mother that she wouldn't be seeing as much of me, she said she was sorry to hear it. It had been nice having some-body from the government coming around to check on the family. I didn't take this to mean that I'd purged myself entirely of the negative connotations of badge and gun in Central City. I'd merely exceeded her very modest expectations, but this, too, was harm reduction of a sort. The Landrys' mother understood harm reduction as well as anyone. She'd spend the last thirty years working to buy her boys a measure of freedom, and now she was trying to buy Javaron's freedom all over again, one month at a time.

In the end the defense attorney delivered on his promise. Javaron admitted guilt and got thirty-two years. Given what she was up against, Javaron's mother had bought Javaron a good outcome.

Javaron's victim's mother could not do the same for her son. I never talked to Ronald or his mother about the dead boy. It wasn't my place to ensure that they were balancing their compassion for Javaron with regret for the life he'd taken. Javaron's mother might have wanted to understand another mother's grief, but she had enough of her own. The Landry house was a haunted place now, and I can't say I was sorry to see less of it. Most of my reasons for avoiding Ronald were sentimental. There were practical ones, too.

One of the most compelling lessons the seminars taught me was to get out while the getting was good. In other words, reduce what harm you could and then close out the case and turn your attention to the next guy. Like most New Orleans District offenders, Ronald was supposed to stay on supervision for five years. Even at medium risk, he became a drain on resources once I ran out of cures to try on him. Continuing to stop by a few times a year kept "the idea" going, which could curtail or at least defer a small amount of drug use—and there was always a chance you would walk in on a gun and take it out of circulation—but the seminars made the case that if harm reduction was truly our goal, we should compress all those five-year periods of half-assed supervision into two years of the real deal.

If we spent the money allotted to five-year probations in two, we could offer everybody an intensive rehabilitation program like drug court or mental health court or the DRC. We could check in on every offender monthly and get to know him well enough to make informed referrals. We could offer more treatment and put ourselves in a better position to get the referral right. One of the seminar givers put it like this: "If a person isn't worth supervising all the way, he isn't worth supervising at all."

---

The two-year rule only worked if all of your cases were getting the resources they needed. Even then, I supposed some offenders would need more time. I'd been Hard Head's PO for more than a year now, and even if I'd been able to provide him with housing and counseling and a steady wage, I couldn't imagine cutting him loose anytime soon. He told me he liked being accountable to somebody, and I tried to oblige him. We usually met up once a week. When he called me two days after our most recent visit and said he wanted to see me again, I grabbed Charles, and the two of us rushed over, expecting the worst.

The tent was unzipped and Hard Head was seated with his heels on the pavement. The flesh between his toes was so knotted with scars that you would have thought he'd stuck his feet in a fire ants' nest. There was a welt on his forehead and dried blood around the corners of his lips.

Between flying the sign and doing odd jobs for the contractor, he'd managed to save up enough money for a security deposit for an apartment. It was going to be something shitty in Central City or the Seventh Ward, but putting away seven hundred bucks and defending it from the marauders patrolling the tents was a major accomplishment. Hard Head was proud of himself and felt that a celebration was in order. He believed that his newfound faith had tamed his disease. He thought he could go to the bar and have a couple of beers and be okay.

"Thought I had that demon licked." He paused and reconsidered his position. "I thought Jesus licked him for me."

"He helps those who help themselves," Charles pointed out.

Charles wasn't religious but he'd learned to offer this advice when offenders placed too much trust in providence or, worse, interpreted the Scriptures to mean that our fates were preordained and there was no sense in chafing against them. Hard Head went on to explain that he didn't know why he had picked the fight with the guy at the bar, but he had no doubt that he was the one who picked it. He didn't know why booze made him mean while other intoxicants turned him into a kitten. "Right now," he said, "I can't account for much."

The money he'd earned was gone, every dime of it. Hard Head's tentmate, away at the moment, told him that if he bloodied up the tent again, he was going to have to find another place to sleep. "He's a good kid," Hard Head said of his tentmate. "But we've all got our limits."

Hard Head said he didn't need detox and he didn't need a pep talk. He knew what he'd done and he knew why he'd thought he could get away with it. "I'll pray on this," he told us, and he tucked his little gray Bible under one arm and his cardboard sign under the other and set off to find a corner to stand on.

---

Charles and I had both given money to the sign flyers sometimes, and other times we'd declined to roll down the window. In the days before I knew any homeless people—the days before P&P—I gave even less frequently than I did now. When I didn't give, I told myself that handing a homeless person money was the equivalent of handing it to a drug dealer. When I did give, I gave so little that I couldn't imagine it made any difference, and I felt worse than I felt when I gave nothing. I knew now that my original reservations were correct, but I'd drawn the wrong conclusions from both of them. Hard Head used the money to feed himself, and he used the money to make bad decisions. In the aggregate, the money purchased far more meals than bad decisions. Giving did some harm, but it reduced more.

When friends asked me whether they should give a buck or two to a bum on the corner, I always said sure, if they could spare it. When they asked whether the homeless were going to buy dope with it, I said sure, sometimes. I said that it was better to give your money to a food bank or a homeless shelter. Most shelters and food banks could be trusted to put a donation to its intended purpose.

But most of us weren't donating to homeless shelters or food banks. Most of us paid our taxes and expected them to absolve us of our obligations to our fellow men. If we were trying to weigh the practical aspects of whether to give a few dollars to a bum on a corner, we shouldn't compare the act to making a donation to a food bank or a shelter. We should compare it to doing nothing. This was why I gave money to some of the bums who asked. The ones who looked especially strung out I usually passed by. I didn't want to supply the cash that bought the overdose.

With this as my standard, I was hopeful that my occasional donations bought more food than dope, but I couldn't know for sure, and I saw no reason to tell myself otherwise. When answering my friends' questions about handouts, I tried to make the case that fighting poverty and fighting crime go hand in hand. I admitted that not all anti-poverty measures hit their mark. There was waste and fraud in public assistance, but if the P&P population was any indication, the ill-gotten gains were vastly outweighed by the help given to the truly needy.

If I could make only one point, I settled for this: I'd yet to encounter any one-size-fits-all solutions to poverty and addiction. Unintended consequences flowed from every form of assistance we tried. Even the most effective treatments didn't work for everyone. Travis refused to try a treatment court and Damien made a mockery of his, but for Sheila treatment had worked wonders. We couldn't know whether someone was susceptible to change until we gave her a chance to try it. Usually, if I kept my head, I could make this case, even to skeptics.

I didn't always keep my head. One night at a party at the home of one of my oldest friends, a guy I'd grown up with and watched with admiration as he opened a business and made it prosper, I fell into conversation with another of my friend's guests, a big shot in the oil business. I'd never seen the man before and would never see him again. Upon learning what I did for a living, he said, "You want to help these people? Here's an idea. Get them off the fucking dole."

"Do nothing!" I roared. "That's it! The answer we've been looking for! I can't believe we never thought of it!"

Needless to say, he was not won over. If anything, he backed away from me more assured of his position than ever.

My friend, the party's host, observed the exchange with amusement, and he told me with his usual good cheer that the company of people like the oilman was one of the prices you paid for success. As for my friend's success, he had what struck me as a healthy perspective about the role his middle-class upbringing and Catholic-school education played in it. "All I've ever had to do to get ahead," he said, "was work hard and ask nicely."

My friend's nose for business was rivaled by his capacity to find the human being in every blowhard and bully. He told me that what the captains of industry are really saying when they tell you to get people off the dole is that they believe the formula's the same for all of us: Work hard, ask nicely, and you shall receive. They're optimists, in their way. "You'd be a lot better at my job than I am," I told my friend, and he let me off the hook by saying he wouldn't want to carry a gun.

Kristin ribbed me a little on the ride home. She'd been on the other side of the party when I went after the oilman, but word had apparently traveled quickly. "Wasn't so long ago," she reminded me, "that you hadn't spent any more time in Central City than anybody else at that party."

She was right, as usual. For most of my adult life, I hadn't known what was going on in the poorest and most dangerous parts of my hometown, and that hadn't stopped me from believing I knew how to improve them. My pre-P&P assumptions were just as far off the mark as the oilman's. For the next few weeks I replayed the conversation with the oilman during showers and long drives and idle moments at stoplights. I wished that, instead of acting like a crank, I'd been cool and rational. I wished I'd thought to tell the oilman about Hard Head, who would, in the end, make as convincing a case for a properly administered "dole" as anyone on my caseload.

A few days after the bar fight, Hard Head was at a bus stop plowing through a couple of McDonald's Quarter Pounders when a young woman walked up and introduced herself as a representative of Unity of Greater New Orleans. I'd told Hard Head and all my other homeless offenders to play it straight if they should be lucky enough to meet a Unity caseworker. Rumor had it that if Unity sensed you were malingering or exaggerating your need to improve your chances of getting on the list, the rep would move on to the next guy. Hard Head didn't have to exaggerate. He just sat there at the bus stop and let the Unity rep examine the knot on his head, which by then had assumed a purplish hue.

The rep got Hard Head's contact information, such as it was, and said she would be in touch. He'd been robbed of his last three "government phones," and he would have to take fresh precautions with the current one. For the next few weeks he walked around with the phone stashed inside his boxer shorts. If he missed the call from Unity, the voucher would go to someone else.

His food stamps came back online within a week of Unity's granting him a yearlong housing voucher. In two weeks' time he went from living Under the Bridge and subsisting on fast-food hamburgers to sleeping in a home of his own and taking the long walk to the downtown grocery store to buy fresh fruit, vegetables, and chicken to bake in the little electric stove that came with the apartment. It was a modest Central City double, outfitted with the cheapest faucets, toilet seats, and doorknobs you could buy at Lowe's. Hard Head called it "my paradise."

He bought a couple of ferns and a bed and kitchen table from a consignment shop with money he made working for the contractor. Unity made him promise not to take in any boarders, but he felt he was within his rights to allow his former tentmate to use his toilet and shower and to join him for dinner from time to time. The mayor was going around promising to get housing for every homeless veteran by the end of the year, and Hard Head urged his tentmate to bide his time, stay alive just a little while longer.

"He looks worse every time I see him," Hard Head told me. "If he doesn't get off the street soon, he's not gonna make it."

Later he let slip that he'd bent the rules and permitted his former tentmate to crash on the floor a couple of times when he looked especially bad off, and each time the tentmate was gone by morning, to fly the sign just long enough to pay for his midday fix. I promised not to tell Unity that Hard Head was using his apartment to help out a fellow veteran, though I sensed that everyone there would have understood. They'd seen this before.

Hard Head's need was mostly eradicated, and it had taken much of the risk with it, but he didn't believe he could ever get it down to zero. Some part of risk was clearly intrinsic. Hard Head guessed we would never know the formula by which addicts were made, and maybe we were better off not knowing.

The apartment belonged to Hard Head for the next twelve months as long as he didn't do anything to get himself evicted. Landlords who received the rent check on time tended to be understanding in Central City. The voucher could be renewed for another twelve months, but the hope was that the first year under Unity's wing would allow the formerly homeless individual to begin saving money to pay his own way. Hard Head was still able-bodied enough to believe he could cover the rent for the apartment if he started saving now. The contractor he'd been doing odd jobs for was happy with his work, and he was also happy that Hard Head was willing to do it for minimum wage.

The VA provided Hard Head with health care. The lines were long, but he didn't complain. At my insistence he'd resumed getting counseling services there once a month. Sometimes he felt undeserving of the help he was receiving. True, he'd paid for his VA benefits in blood, and he'd lived on the streets for a long time before Unity came calling. Still, it was hard to believe he'd come this far: health care and housing and food and a job that allowed him to make use of his talents. He took pride in the slope of a roof when he laid the shingles, and in watching a lightbulb flick on when he ran the wire that powered it. Eventually his boss put him "on the books" and starting contributing payroll taxes on his behalf. At an age when most people were getting ready to collect their retirement benefits, Hard Head was finally paying into the system. "And wouldn't you know," he said, "I've got the nerve to bitch and moan when I look at the fucking deductions?"

Hard Head reached into his nightstand, grabbed the little gray Bible, and waved it at me. "A man's a petty, foolish thing," he said, and thumped the cover of the Bible with his thumb, "even though he's been taught how not to be."

He admitted then that the Word wasn't working as well for him as it did when he first came upon it. At the mission he'd been struck by a *feeling*, a matter of the heart and loins. Now it was all in his head. He could read about Jesus and believe in the teachings, but the spirit had moved away from him.

"Maybe somebody else needed it more," I offered. "Could be there's only so much to go around."

He blushed, and I tried to convince him that I wasn't making fun. His time as a zealot had served the harm-reduction cause, albeit in a roundabout way. If Hard Head hadn't believed that a higher power had tamed his alcoholism, he wouldn't have wandered into a bar and gotten loaded. If he hadn't wandered into a bar and gotten loaded, he wouldn't have taken the ass-kicking that made him look desperate enough to qualify for a Unity voucher.

In the evenings Hard Head went back out into the tents with his Bible. Sometimes he evangelized. Sometimes he just sat and listened. He stopped by Odyssey House, too, from time to time, but it was a long walk, and eight hours per day of manual labor sometimes found him in bed by seven. The people he tried to help told him that they knew his intentions were good, but they couldn't possibly take him seriously. He had a home and food and health care. He was, relatively speaking, comfortable. He no longer had hunger or dire poverty or fear of violence to spur him to substance abuse. The chances that he would relapse or that the relapse would kill him were greatly diminished by the help he'd received. The street people could see that "the dole" had improved Hard Head's prospects to such an extent that he no longer appeared to be a street person.

His friends weren't trying to make him feel bad about his good fortune, but he regretted that he couldn't bring all the homeless along with him. He couldn't get anybody detox, housing, work, or SSI. What services he did manage to provide—reading Scripture, letting down-and-out people vent—felt meager by comparison, although he could

easily remember times in his own life when he'd been grateful to receive them.

Some nights, loneliness still gnawed at him. He wondered what
his son would say if he knew the old man had finally cleaned himself
up and gotten a place of his own and was serving a purpose, or trying.
*Why now?* would be the crucial question, and the honest answer was
probably too simple to believe. After more than sixty years, Hard Head
had found the help he needed and the will to accept it.

# SEVENTEEN

# constraints of time and place

Sheila didn't suffer from any of the usual side effects associated with mental health medication. Her counselor assured me that Sheila would have reported it. Sheila told her everything. Much of their conversation was off-limits to me, but the counselor was okay with telling me that after Sheila got over her initial misgivings, she was as well suited to therapy as anyone the counselor had ever worked with. It was as if she'd been waiting her whole life for someone to ask her how she felt.

Sheila could be cutting about the world around her. She understood that in other neighborhoods, the best boys weren't the scariest ones. She recognized that being attracted to violence and cruelty in a partner was a defect, and she knew that it was not of her making, and she forgave herself. She may not have had a knack for book learning, but her intuition was spot on. She would make a great therapist. Of course, to get that job she would have to go to college. The counselors had gradually warmed her to the prospect of trying again for her GED, but her experience of school had been so unpleasant that the counselors couldn't see their way to redeeming that institution. Then again, if they could make a poor person born in the Seventh Ward believe that the criminal justice system was here to help her out, maybe no institution was beyond repair.

The main takeaway from most of the counselors' conversations with

Sheila was that Sheila was in love. In one sitting, she could denounce the dons and all they stood for, and in another she could go absolutely breathless as she told her counselors that she'd finally found herself a real man, feared by all who knew him, and he drove a good car and always had cash in his pocket and insisted on nothing but the best for his girl. When Sheila told her counselors that she was pregnant, she clearly believed she was delivering good news. She could see that her counselors didn't feel the way she did about it, and she lost her cool a little with them, as she used to do in the days before she started on the meds.

The counselors explained that they were concerned that motherhood would get in the way of some of the other things Sheila wanted to accomplish. She was in line for a small promotion at the Subway. She would get a little more money and a little more responsibility. When she went to her next job interview, she would be able to say that she'd been moved up the ranks at her last place of employment. It was a key line on any résumé.

We knew that her boyfriend didn't like her working. Sheila didn't say he was forcing her to quit, but we gathered from context clues that she believed fatherhood gave her boyfriend the right to instruct her. We could all remember what it was like to be young and infatuated, and to believe that the person you loved wanted only the best for you. Where the value of holding on to the job was concerned, we had the facts on our side, but we weren't going to win the argument with the father of Sheila's child.

At the home inspection that month, Sheila's mother called me to account, as I knew she would. "I told you," she said, "this fucking boy was gonna lock her in. Now she'll never leave this place."

Even though I'd had the same reaction to the news, I thought I should try to play devil's advocate. "She's happy," I said. "Maybe it's not for us to judge."

"The fuck it's not. I'm her mom. You're her cop. If not us, then who?" She found a laugh in spite of herself. "You know there's nothing good in this. Don't you dare cheer me up."

"You know I couldn't have kept her from seeing him."

"She would have had a hard time getting knocked up in OPP."

"What was I supposed to put her in for?"

"Y'all always think of something."

"It's not like that anymore."

She laughed again, but kindly. She wanted to believe I was right: times were changing, however slowly. We sat in silence on the stoop for a minute, and she told me, as she'd done once before, that she liked seeing my feelings hurt and my dander up. Now that POs were taking the time to get to know the people on their caseloads, we couldn't help caring about what happened to them. We finally had skin in the game.

I admitted that I, too, had been disturbed by the news of Sheila's pregnancy. I'd wanted her to have time to focus on her own needs.

"All I could give her was her looks," Sheila's mother said. "And she used them for what?"

"You gave her attention. That's more than a lot of people get."

We'd been candid with each other that day, but I could see I'd embarrassed her with this last remark, and she got rid of me in the usual way. "She's in back," she said.

Sheila was lying in bed with her hands folded across her belly. The air was thick with teenager's perfume, and I felt another pang, as if with the birth of the child the very air Sheila breathed would change. Before I could get a word out, she said, "I'm not quitting mental health court."

"Good."

"They're gonna set me up with a doc for after I finish."

She had only a few more weeks to go. When she graduated from mental health court, her probation would be terminated early, and the felony offense would be removed from her record. I'd been so preoccupied with worst-case scenarios that I hadn't stopped to commend her on the good work she'd done at Tulane and Broad. "You took a big leap with this stuff," I said. "I'm proud of you."

She craned her neck just a little and took me in for the first time since I'd entered the room. "My mom says y'all used to be nothing but punks."

It wasn't quite a compliment, so I knew I could trust it. I thought Beth and Charles would get a laugh out of it. The three of us had plans to go out to lunch that day. I was supposed to meet them at the office first. I hurried back and stuck my head into Beth's office. She was slumped at her desk. Her eyes were red and she chewed at a pinkie nail.

"Lunch?" I said.

"OD." Her shoulders rose and fell and rose again. "I had him in jail. Let him out. Knew better. I fucking knew. If I'd left him where he needed to be, he'd still be breathing. He'd be eating green bologna and pissing in a can and running me down every minute of it, telling everybody what a travesty of a PO I am, but, goddamn it, he'd still be alive."

"You can't—"

"The fuck I can't."

I went over and took her by the elbow and tried to extract her from her chair. I ended up having to call Charles in from down the hall to assist. Eventually we got her out of there and put some food in her, and soon enough she was her old self, practical and clear-sighted about the overdose. She'd been faced with the usual choice—to do harm to the offender by locking him up or risk harm to him and his neighbors by cutting him loose—and now she had to live with the consequences. The offender's family had gone easy on her so far, but that was always subject to change.

"This fentanyl shit," she said, "it's taking down veteran dope fiends. These guys are not amateurs. These guys know what they're doing, and they're no match for it."

In tiny doses, fentanyl got you about as high as heroin. A double dose could stop your heart. The addicts knew, but fear of overdosing didn't stop them any more than fear of prison. We didn't need fresh evidence of the power of addiction, but fentanyl came along and gave us some anyway.

Eventually our conversation made its way to the topic of the moment at the New Orleans District. The week before, at Tulane and Broad, Lamar had nearly gotten himself held in contempt during a revocation hearing. One of his dons had gotten arrested with a fresh dope package. The don's neighbors had complained repeatedly to Lamar about him and asked him to please put this guy out of business. Lamar told the judge that the don wasn't receptive to community supervision. He wasn't interested in counseling or treatment or change. He was interested in being a drug dealer.

The defense attorney was a star, and he made short work of Lamar's argument. New Orleans needed more jobs, not more incarceration. The offender was a businessman beloved in the community. Lamar was a heavy-handed law enforcement officer with contempt for his own kind. The judge dialed him back some on the last part but ultimately gave him what he wanted. The offender was placed on double probation and encouraged to continue his good work in the community. The deal was hatched mostly in sidebars, but they went on the record to make it official. The judge put Lamar behind the microphone and asked whether he wanted to add any special conditions to the double probation.

Lamar knew the judge was offering him a concession. He could ask for a curfew or additional drug tests. Lamar liked the judge overall, but he spoke his mind anyway. "What's the point of adding conditions," Lamar said, "if he doesn't have to abide by them?"

The judge called him back up to the bench and dressed him down off the record but in full view of the entire courtroom. She thought he knew better. He wasn't some kid. He was a middle-aged man who'd spent his whole adult life in government service. He was supposed to understand chain of command. He was supposed to know how to get overruled like a grownup.

The defense attorney was a campaign contributor with connections in churches and community activist groups, but Lamar didn't really think the defense attorney's campaign contributions or political connections had anything to do with the judge's ruling. Lamar just thought the judge had been misled, and he wanted her to reconsider. He told her so again, and again she told him she'd made up her mind. After that, Lamar took his reprimand standing up and thanked the judge for not holding him in contempt. She warned him that the next outburst would earn him a night in OPP.

Word traveled fast through the New Orleans District, and Lamar was cheered up and down the halls. True to form, he said he didn't think he'd done anything heroic. The judge had asked a question, and Lamar had given an honest answer.

"She doesn't have to go back in the neighborhood," Lamar said. "She doesn't have to answer to the law-abiding families who are just trying to go about their lives without getting shot by a drug dealer."

At the staff meeting that quarter, Dan the Regional Manager painted a rosy picture. He told us that the numbers from curfew checks and the other NOLA for Life measures were in, and they had very good things to say. In addition to a 17 percent decrease in murder rate since NOLA for Life got started, the city had seen measurable declines in "group violence," broadly defined as violence committed by organizations in furtherance of criminal enterprises, as opposed to violence committed by individuals in the course of normal human emotions like anger and jealousy and greed. The sample size was too small for success to be declared, but the early returns were promising. If nothing else, the data suggested that needy people engage in less risky behavior when the people supervising them can offer something other than prison.

The news wasn't all good. Most of the gang members and the dons couldn't break from the lifestyle addiction, even after we applied the new forms of assistance made available by NOLA for Life. Overdoses weren't slowing down, and the supply of drugs in New Orleans appeared to be as plentiful as ever. We were still a poor city with failing schools and few opportunities for upward mobility in our most violent neighborhoods.

Dan the Regional Manager was getting ready to retire and seemed to be trying out material for a farewell speech. He admitted feeling some heartache about the work he was leaving behind and the work that was left to do. He made the joke Charles made in my early days about how nobody really set out to go into the disaster prevention business, but in time he had come to believe it was honorable work if you were suited to it. I would always remember him fondly for all the hell he'd raised to get Kendrick to DOC for mental health treatment. Otherwise I didn't know very much about him—not nearly enough to feel sentimental about his moving on.

Even so, a person looking at the end of his life's work is always an uneasy sight. People always wish they'd done more. In his time working in the criminal justice system, Dan the Regional Manager had seen the crest of the prison boom, but he'd also seen the beginning of the era we were in now, when even the wardens were looking for new ideas about what to do for people in trouble and people in need. Toward the end of the speech you could see that he wasn't sure how to wrap up. He said something about progress being a jagged line and something else about the arc of the moral universe, and he thanked us for our time and our service and staggered off the stage.

Later in the day Charles, who was a lot closer to retirement than I was, heard something I'd missed in the boss's remarks, particularly in the uncharacteristic rambling there at the end. "Dan and I came to do community supervision in the days when all anybody wanted to do was lock guys up," Charles said. "He sees things getting better and feels like the fates fucked him. He's walking out the door just as the job's starting to look like what he signed up for."

I shrugged. "You get what you get. You make the most of it."

I considered this the unofficial motto of the New Orleans District, a creed that applied to all of us, but Charles bristled. "Easy for you to say. You showed up right at the turn."

It was one of the few times he was genuinely gruff with me, and I took his correction to heart. That the work happened to be turning into what I wanted it to be just as I appeared in the doorway was another gift to be counted. Of course, the changes we'd seen so far were incremental at best. At another lunch later in the week I told Beth and Charles how Hard Head came by his rental voucher. Beth summed it up like this: "So he needed about five stints upstate, let's say twenty relapses, a decade in and out of the tents, a barroom ass kicking, and about forty gallons of heroin pumped through his veins before he could meet the mark for the free-housing people."

"Plus Jesus," Charles said.

"Right," Beth said. "Can't forget about that. He got divine intervention, too, and the poor son of a bitch still barely made it out alive."

These days were better than the days before, but we were a long way from where we wanted to be. Refusing to settle was as essential as recognizing progress. Given the constraints of the time and place in which the New Orleans District was compelled to operate, Hard Head had to be considered a winning outcome. I called Ronald a win, too.

Roughly a third of high-risk offenders on my caseload would join Damien and Travis and Kendrick in the Department of Corrections, bearing out the essential logic of the risk/need assessment again and again. The neediest people on my caseload were at the greatest risk of causing harm to themselves or someone else. When I couldn't get them a job or housing or food stamps or health care and couldn't fit them into drug court or mental health court or the DRC, the Department of Corrections was always willing to step in.

Sometimes after I sent someone upstate, I worried I'd been too hasty in my decision-making. Other times I could plainly see that I'd made my move too late. I'd waited until someone got hurt, and I heard about it from the offender's friends and family or the victim's. Even the worst losses sometimes contained bits of harm reduction, and I was getting better at finding them after the fact. Medication had slowed Kendrick's click-outs. Having a home or even a piece of floor space had greatly increased Kendrick's capacity to stay sober. There were spans during the parole period when Kendrick was as clean and healthy as he'd ever been, and posed less of a risk to himself or other people. His two major risk spikes were the result of a friend's murder and a bender that was itself the product of the accrued stress of homelessness. Kendrick's harm could be contained if we provided the right resources or even did a better job of supplying him with the ones we already had.

It was much harder to find anything redeeming to say about the work we'd done with Damien and Travis. Travis would never believe that our intentions were good or that we could help him. Even if he had believed it, his addiction remained the dominant presence in his life. It was nice to imagine that going upstate would get him to commit to treatment, but I'd seen no evidence of this in any other offender. Prison would prevent him from overdosing while he was in it, and it would cost the Louisiana taxpayer about thirty-five grand. That was all I could say for sure about Travis's two years in the Department of Corrections.

Damien's addiction was just as powerful as Travis's, and even harder to remedy. What sort of civilian work could offer the same combination of money and excitement that the dons got from the drug trade? Building cities with better schools, jobs, and housing for poor people was the only way to make the drug trade less appealing in neighborhoods like Central City. This was all, of course, beyond the purview of the New Orleans probation and parole office. Sometimes I took comfort in knowing we had more modest goals, but there were days when reducing harm or preventing disasters didn't feel like much of a contribution, and I struggled to see with my own eyes the bits of progress that I'd pointed out so often, and so forcefully, to other people.

The last time I spoke with Sheila, I was coming off a rough revocation first thing in the morning. The assistant district attorney, usually a friend, let everyone in the courtroom know that the probation department was responsible for the collateral damage that brought us to Tulane and Broad that day. Charles spent the rest of the morning making the rounds with me and trying to buck me up.

When we pulled up to the little house in the Seventh Ward, Sheila was seated on the top step of the stoop, scrolling through text messages. When she saw us coming up the lawn, she put down the phone, held out her wrists, and gave me a wink. "Last chance to lock me up," she said. "Friday's graduation."

"You're done getting locked up," I said.

Sheila shrugged and picked up the phone again. "I don't know what I'm gonna do."

She didn't look up again. I congratulated her on completing mental health court, and Charles and I walked back to the Crown Vic.

Charles started the engine but left the shifter in park. "If she doesn't know what she's gonna do," he said, "then she hasn't ruled anything out."

He was right. There was harm reduction here if I wanted to see it, but I couldn't help wishing for better. I imagined a parting in which Sheila reformed her don and went back to school and became a lifelong believer in the value of treatment. Charles had been doing harm reduction long enough to know that making your peace with it was a process, and the final and most challenging step was to quit looking for better tools and better resources—better times—and get back to looking for the better you, more patient and adaptable, perfectly suited to these times, this place. You could give this person less, and he could do more with it, and he never forgot that the people from the generation before were given less still, and managed to be useful anyway.

Through the windshield I searched Sheila once more for a tell, but she'd already told me everything. Charles knew it, but he gave me all the time I needed. I nodded to let him know I was ready, and he pulled the shifter into drive and we got back on the road.

# EPILOGUE

Two thousand and sixteen, my last year at the New Orleans District, felt like a tipping point. In a six-month period I attended three week-long seminars, all of them run by young, energetic sociologists convinced that probation and parole were the last undiscovered islands of the American criminal justice system.

The sociologists didn't believe, or at least they didn't profess to believing, that the problems at P&P stemmed from lazy or incompetent staffing. They believed our performance wouldn't improve until we got the tools we needed to do the job. Some of the sociologists asked the POs to chime in. What did we want to see happen in the near future? Our ideas had to be revenue neutral, meaning they could be enacted without raising taxes or moving money from one government agency to another. We would have to find funding within the Department of Corrections.

In the New Orleans District lunchroom, the POs who'd attended the seminars agreed that any idea we presented to the sociologists had to have a chance of appealing to both district attorneys and criminal justice reform advocates. It was no use pitching something that couldn't gain widespread support. With these restrictions in mind, we came up with an informal top-three list.

    **1.** Shorten the standard community supervision period from 5 years to 2. Offenders are most amenable to accepting services during the first 2 years of supervision. If, during that time, the PO can't make the right referral or the offender can't get in the right mind-set to take it, the game is effectively over. The first two years are also the best time to catch offenders committing serious violations. After a dozen home inspections and office visits, offenders know what POs are looking for. Offenders with something to hide figure out how to hide it. If, as year two draws to a close, the PO believes the offender would benefit from continuing programming or, conversely, if the offender is deemed a danger to himself or other people, the judge can extend the probation by simple court order. Compressing five years of supervision into two will mean much quicker turnover and much smaller caseloads. With smaller caseloads, POs will have time to get to know each offender and to provide far more detailed reporting to judges and parole boards. The two-year term makes POs more accountable to offenders and offenders more accountable to POs.

2. Use savings from shortened sentences to expand access to treatment courts. Drug courts, veterans' courts, and mental health courts pair a wider array of services with more immediate accountability in the form of weekly or monthly meetings with a judge. Most importantly, treatment courts are collaborative. POs do less of what they're untrained to do and turn the treatment portion of offender rehabilitation over to licensed counselors. As drug laws continue to soften, addicts are more likely to end up in the court system as a result of crimes committed to fuel their addiction as opposed to drug offenses themselves. As drug courts serve a population whose addiction feeds increasingly risky behavior, the benefits of keeping addiction in check will be felt not only in the offender's improved physical and mental health but also in violent- and property-crime rates.

3. Establish a "transition year" for parolees by rolling parole dates for eligible inmates forward six months. Money saved on the early release—between $10,000 and $15,000

in most states—funds a year of rental vouchers so that no
one paroles to homelessness. Everyone comes out of jail
with a place to live and a treatment program if he wants it.

These ideas are only a start. On their own they probably won't do
enough to bring caseloads down to manageable levels. As a PO in New
Orleans, I spent 90 percent of my time on 50 of my 220 offenders, as
the department's risk/need assessment suggested I should. If the risk/
need assessment was understood to speak to department priorities, my
bosses were essentially advising me that more than three-quarters of
my caseload needed an hour or less of supervision *per year*. The Louisiana Department of Corrections, the world's leading incarcerator, was
indicating through internal accounting measures, if not through any
outward-facing policies or press releases, that most people on probation
and parole didn't pose a high enough risk for anyone to bother keeping
track of them at all.

Clearly the department believed in its assessment tool, but were
lower-risk offenders really less violent and addicted than higher-risk offenders, or were their low arrest numbers simply a product of fewer drug
tests and home inspections? It's an important question that's certainly
worth further study, but I can say for sure that the people who rated
high on the risk assessment got arrested by the police department—
that is, by entities other than their PO—far more often than medium-
or minimum-risk offenders. In New Orleans the assessment seemed
to get risk about right. We seemed to be spending most of our time
supervising the people who were likeliest to find their way into police
custody for serious crimes.

Just before I left, POs were authorized to place medium- and
minimum-risk offenders on "self-reporting" status, which amounted
to placing their cases in administrative mode and cutting off all contact
unless the offender got back in trouble. Like all new ideas, this one met
with some resistance. On occasions when the assessment and the PO
viewed the offender's risk level differently, there was sometimes pressure
from headquarters to make the move to self-reporting. In time POs
were granted the final say on whether or not an offender's probation
should be informally terminated three or four years ahead of schedule.

Because self-reporting amounted to a change in department policy rather than an amendment to sentencing law, it passed through the leadership quietly, the sort of minor adjustment that well-oiled government agencies are supposed to be able to make on the fly. Most of us came around to seeing self-reporting as a good thing, but we bitched about it anyway. It failed to address our central problem: lack of programming for the high-risk offenders on whom we were spending most of our time. In practical terms, self-reporting got rid of cases we weren't paying attention to in the first place. We still had no reliable way to get able-bodied offenders into decent jobs. Some of the best work on that front was being done at Angola, where reentry programming continued to flourish. Inmates learned lucrative trades like welding, HVAC, and auto repair. The prison arranged jobs for them before they got their parole.

In 2019 the reentry program is still being done on a very small scale, with offenders hand-selected by judges who see potential in them during court proceedings. Still, the early returns are extremely promising. Most inmates who successfully complete the Angola reentry program are serving ten-year sentences. The inmates are granted parole after two years instead of the standard four. Assuming they maintain the jobs that await them upon their release, as the overwhelming majority have done so far, years three and four of the sentence represent about $35,000 in taxpayer savings per offender. A full accounting of the program's success has to include the money the parolees contribute to the state coffers as payers of income and sales tax.

Reentry doesn't happen without commitments from business owners willing to overlook a criminal record as well as the growing pains common among people reacclimating to society after two years away. Employers who hire offenders straight out of prison do so with an understanding that the new employee might need a little extra care in the early going. The PO is there to help with that.

The reentry program allows POs to focus almost all of their energy on what they do best: going to the home and the job site and looking for tells. POs offer encouragement when warranted. If there are reasons for concern, they report them to the judge, who connects the offender with a treatment professional trained to meet the offender's needs. Reentry is the system as you would draw it up if you had unlimited time and unlimited money. All that Angola will say publicly about the costs of reentry is that they're too high to expand the program any faster than they're expanding it now, and the POs assigned to the reentry offenders don't have time to do much of anything else. Reentry offenders are treated as few of them have ever been treated before: as valued investments, to be checked up on at least once a week.

Good jobs will always be the single strongest crime reduction measure there is. When you take away need, most forms of risk don't know what to do with themselves. Companies that go out of their way to hire offenders—to recruit them rather than tolerate them—and that do so with an understanding of where many offenders are coming from, are doing a far greater service to public safety than any court or law enforcement officer.

New alternatives to prison are being thought up every day, and while many include a substance abuse component, the latest wave has looked at non-jail-based solutions for property crimes and even certain violent crimes. Nationwide, about 25 percent of inmates are locked up over a drug offense. The drug war is no longer the primary driver of the incarceration complex. Violent- and property-crime offenders make up the majority of prison sentences. Cutting the prison rolls by even a quarter, to three times what they were before the prison boom kicked off in the early eighties, would be hard to do without releasing some people who are serving time for crimes of violence.

Most of the reasons to be wary of this go without saying. We had fewer inmates before the prison boom, but we had a lot more violence. The murder rate in 1980 was nearly double the rate in 2017. Many criminologists now believe that surges of community activism—"self-policing," as it's sometimes known—were probably the main drivers of the violent-crime decline over the last forty years, but even the most vocal critics of mass incarceration acknowledge that the new prisons played a part. The next generation of criminal justice reformers have set themselves a challenging task: to preserve the substantial public-safety gains of the last four decades while weaning America off one of the primary instruments that helped bring them about.

I'm struck by how rapidly the academic thinking on so many

aspects of criminal justice reform has changed since I was an under-graduate minoring in sociology. In 2004, my senior year of college, "broken windows" policing was touted as the progressive answer to violent crime in American cities. The consensus seemed to be that local governments had allowed the physical disrepair of poor communities to seep into the social fabric. Many vulnerable people felt ignored, and crime was the result. In other words, the needier a place looked, the riskier the behaviors of the people who lived there.

Fifteen years later, many criminal justice scholars believe that the "broken windows" strategy's emphasis on prosecuting minor infractions, including possession-grade drug offenses, contributed to the criminal-ization of poverty. "Broken windows" policing reduced some harm, but not enough to justify the collateral damage. One way to interpret the rapid about-face in the prevailing criminal justice thinking is to con-clude that nobody knows what they're talking about. I've come to that conclusion often enough, but it's hard to deny that the current moment in the criminal justice system is one of once-in-a-generation engage-ment. Scores of talented people are striving to build a system that's safer, fairer, and more just. They're doing it by taking a close look at conven-tional wisdom, and they're not afraid to come forward with counterin-tuitive ideas, especially when it comes to reckoning with violence.

Michelle Alexander, arguably the criminal justice system's most decorated scholar, has become an advocate for the "restorative circle," a sort of controlled confrontation between a victim of violence and a perpetrator. The victim gets the chance to tell the perpetrator how the act changed his life. The perpetrator has to look the harm he's done in the eye. According to Alexander, a stunning number of repeat perpe-trators report feelings of remorse that prison, even long stretches of it, never induced in them. The victims report feeling what most people recovering from trauma ache to feel: that someone has heard them and recognizes their pain.

I'll admit, I rolled my eyes when I first read about the restorative cir-cle. People who victimize others often know exactly what counselors, judges, progressive researchers, and even victims want to hear. Remorse isn't that hard to fake. The victims who professed relief were not to be doubted, but I wondered how many victims of violent crime would really sign up for this. Here's the important part, at least for those of us with preconceived notions about what victims want and perpetrators need. Alternative sanctions don't have to work on every offender to be worth implementing. If restorative circles changed the behavior of only 5 percent of violent offenders—say, those convicted of isolated, first-time crimes of violence—hundreds of people who would otherwise go to jail could stay out. Government budgets are zero-sum. Keeping some violent people out of prison could help us fund programming to prevent other people from ever becoming violent.

---

When friends ask me what I think the future of criminal justice in America will look like, I say it'll look like a lot of different things. I believe restorative circles and other restitution-centric programming will have a role to play. Probation and parole can reduce their overall footprint while also taking on some of the duties currently under the purview of prisons. We still record about 17,000 murders a year in this country and more than 100,000 sexual assaults. It's hard to imagine a future without incarceration.

The topic of prison reform has produced many volumes and will produce many more before we arrive at a resolution. The gist of the research is that safe, clean facilities that provide inmates with educational, vocational, and treatment programming produce parolees more amenable to correction. The criminal justice system has more moving parts than a chain saw, but as the fallout from unjustified police shootings has demonstrated, a failure anywhere increases the chances of failures elsewhere. For better and worse, the courts and the jails and the cops and the POs and the treatment professionals are in it together.

In some of America's most violent cities—New Orleans, for one—it's common for fewer than half of murders to result in arrest. If the future justice system reallocates a certain number of resources from drug enforcement to enforcement of violent crime, some of the new arrests will probably be the sort that can be resolved only with prison. A justice system in which police have time and resources to focus on more serious offenses may also be a justice system in which jails are called upon to make room for more inmates.

If current trends continue, drug offenders will be vacating more and more space. Drug laws continue to be reconsidered across the US. Marijuana is legal in several states and functionally decriminalized in many more, and possession of small amounts of harder drugs is increasingly resolved with a fine or a misdemeanor charge rather than a felony sentence requiring probation. Consider the journey of the crack rock: once a ticket to prison, then to probation, now to a fine and misdemeanor. Making possession of personal-use quantities of drugs a non-felony offense has helped some jurisdictions bring down their community supervision populations, freeing POs to focus their attention on repeat offenders and offenders whose drug use spurs other forms of criminal activity: gun possession, theft, crimes of violence.

In 2016, my last year at the New Orleans District, second-degree battery, an offense that involves serious bodily injury to the victim, was frequently resolved with probation. On my own caseload, the results were predictable. The batterers who attended anger management counseling and, more importantly, accepted that such counseling was for their own good, learned to control their tempers and resolve disputes without violence. The batterers who wouldn't go to counseling or couldn't admit they had a problem soon struck again, and I asked their judges to send them to prison.

By then Louisiana, long the incarceration capital of the world, was getting aggressive about shedding the label. Courts were encouraged by the Department of Corrections to put more drug offenders through "diversion," a pretrial program with many of the same rhythms and features as drug court. Defendants who successfully complete diversion get their drug charges dismissed without further court proceedings and without spending any time in jail or on probation.

In 2017 a package of criminal justice reforms passed through the Louisiana legislature. They got conservative and liberal support and the backing of the state's district attorneys' association, usually a reliable holdout against any measures that could be viewed as soft on crime. Parole eligibility came sooner, felony thresholds were higher, and many 5-year probation sentences were reduced to 3. Seventy percent of the jail savings were required by law to be reinvested in reentry programming, to include job training and mental health and substance abuse treatment. Like the federal First Step Act that would pass through the US Congress a few months later and see to the release of certain inmates serving drug sentences, the reforms in Louisiana were marketed as only a beginning.

I've kept in touch with several of my former coworkers since I left, and while most of them are optimistic about the 70 percent promise, the essential structures of P&P in Louisiana are, for now at least, pretty much the same as they ever were. Most of the money is tied up in the prison system. For most offenders, the New Orleans District offers the same set of options it offered when I was new: Shape up or go to jail.

In 2018, judges weren't sending the New Orleans District's drug addicts upstate nearly as often as they used to, but as was usually the case when new ideas were implemented, unintended consequences abounded. With penalties for drug offenses growing lighter by the year and double probations becoming the norm, the dons were enjoying a golden age. Drugs remained illegal, so addicts had to go to drug dealers to get them, but the reduced penalties for possession and the courts' newfound reluctance to revoke probation over drug-related violations meant that drug dealers could make the same money as before but incur far less risk along the way. A lot of people at the New Orleans District were beginning to wonder whether the current moment in the drug debate represented a dangerous half measure in which drugs were still illegal enough to sustain a black market but not so illegal that dealers feared getting caught. To put it another way, the half measure approach gave up the drug war's greatest asset—fear among drug dealers that their profession could land them in prison—but without gaining the tax revenue or regulated product or sharp declines in black-market violence that were supposed to come with legalization. "Worst of both worlds" was how some POs came to describe it.

Less punitive drug laws were changing how police approached drug-related violence as well. It used to be that when you couldn't get anybody to testify against the gang member for the murders he'd done, you could put him away by catching him with drugs. Drug charges weren't scaring shooters anymore. My beloved drug court was taking some of the blame for this. Drug court was a great place for an addict to get clean, and it was a great place for a drug dealer to pass himself off as a drug addict—as a person with a disease—and apply for leniency. Shortly before I signed off from drug court in 2016, I watched a defense attorney convince a favorite judge to put an offender on triple probation. People around the office didn't believe it until I showed them the paperwork.

My last year on the job, I was always looking for a new approach to the drug problem. Some days I tried to handle drug addicts the way Charles did, with his reassurances and cool, cutting logic, and other days I wished I were more like Beth and Lamar, able to suggest that the person I was addressing had the wrong priorities or hadn't spent enough time considering the sweep of history. We could always turn back to the data that said that our demeanor didn't matter, but none of us really wanted to believe that. We all wanted to believe we had control. If we worked harder and paid closer attention, we could save more souls.

On my worst days I heard myself casually reminding drug dealers that not everyone who lived in their neighborhood or went to their high school had decided that selling heroin was an acceptable moral compromise for a poor person. I didn't say any of this the way Lamar might have said it, as an overture to a tough but fair dialogue about personal choice. I was blunt and sometimes insulting. I told offenders that people who lacked the will to participate in treatment had no standing to complain about their disease. I lectured offenders about phone calls I'd received from elderly neighbors who were tired of climbing over passed-out junkies on their way to the bus stop. I said things like "Nobody made you put that needle in your arm."

After two years of working with drug courts, I felt I knew addiction as well as I ever would, which is to say that I lost my capacity to be surprised by its cruelty. Addiction feasts on failure but it does a number on success, too. Travis and Hard Head both had dangerous relapses just as their fortunes were looking up.

Drug dealers remained the hardest people to handle. You always felt like you'd showed up too late to help. As long as the drug trade looked like the surest way out of poverty, some poor people were going to try it. Many appeared to be changed by the lifestyle, and the change sometimes manifested itself in violence. The hair-trigger sensibility that the drug trade had instilled in Damien and Javaron was difficult to unlearn, even in retirement. As I came to terms with all of this, I was working harder and staying later, and still nearly a third of the offenders on whom I was spending most of my time and effort turned up dead or back in jail. Two thousand and sixteen ended up being the worst overdose year on record, and I finally hit my bottom. I still believed the justice system was the institution where a public servant could have the greatest impact, but I needed to find a more suitable role.

I started thinking about that night out with the NOPD when I realized that solving crimes is a lot easier than solving people. When I talked to coworkers about leaving P&P for a more conventional law enforcement job, I always put it in terms of seeking my niche and finding the best use of my talents, but my fellow POs knew the truth. You left P&P because you wanted an easier life.

---

After years of hiring freezes, the federal law enforcement agencies were accepting applications. In the job interview I said that I viewed a federal law enforcement career as an opportunity to go after the big fish. I didn't mention that I also saw it as an opportunity to get away from drug addicts. To paraphrase my old friend, I worked hard and asked nicely and got what I wanted. Kristin and I got married. She was ready for a change, and she agreed to go wherever the feds sent me. They can send you worse places than New Jersey.

The bulk of my job duties nowadays involve going after white-collar criminals. Driven more often by greed than need, these are the people who steal your identity and tank your credit and cause you to pay a fortune in vehicle and health insurance. They live in mansions and drive cars that the dons of New Orleans can only dream of. Trying to unwind their schemes is every bit as gratifying as I'd hoped.

For the most part, the people I'm after now don't sell drugs, and they don't do violence. Many white-collar criminals end up on federal probation, where they have choices to make. If they want to go to detox or learn a new trade, the PO can help them. Offenders placed on federal probation receive extensive pre-trial and presentence screening, to include hours of interviews with counselors and treatment professionals. Federal presentence services look deeply at need before they assign a risk rating. The judge reads the report from cover to cover so that he or she knows not only the nature of the crime but also the nature of the individual, and can offer appropriate correction.

In the feds we have the two most important advantages: money and time. The federal probation system is tiny, less than 3 percent of the national P&P population, and in some jurisdictions nearly four times as costly per offender, but federal offenders, usually tracked into the federal system because they're the most sophisticated criminals around, reoffend about a third as often as offenders in Louisiana. The federal probation system is a marvel of government efficiency. By spending a little more money in the short term, federal probation saves the taxpayer a fortune over a lifetime.

As of this writing, my greatest fear is that the next round of national criminal justice reforms will be focused only on making cuts: smaller jails, smaller police departments, fewer resources all around. If the criminal justice system is to stop serving as the first line of defense against drug overdoses, the social safety net will have to fill the gap. For all their limitations, the treatments we supplied offenders at the New Orleans District were often the only forms of addiction counseling they'd ever received. Medicaid can provide rehabilitation services for addicts, but they have to know how to apply, and they to have the wherewithal to stay in the program's good graces once they get admitted.

Health care outreach is largely a state and federal matter, but local governments can still get involved. The city of New Orleans has made great strides in supporting its chronically poor and addicted. The New Orleans Mission is undergoing a major renovation, and Metropolitan Human Services District, state funded but administered locally, is taking walk-ins without a diagnosis. The mayor made good on his promise to get all the homeless veterans off the street, including Hard Head's tentmate.

The drug courts at Tulane and Broad have continued to adapt and expand, and offenders who commit to the program sometimes find it so effective that they don't want to graduate. People who've grown accustomed to weekly drug tests and counseling sessions to hold them in check fear losing their way without ongoing supervision. Are these offenders merely institutionalized, or are they rational people afraid of giving up the first tool that has provided them any relief? I don't have the answers to these questions, but I hope that as we try to decide how to address the drug problem in America, we'll consider as many approaches as possible. Even if the legalization movement prevails, I can't imagine that the criminal justice system will ever get out of the drug business. As long as drug use fuels property crime and violence, drug courts and detoxes and sober-living facilities will have a role to play in reforming criminal behavior.

As I did at P&P, I content myself most days with working on the micro level, but the trickle-down effect from systemic changes is sometimes surprisingly quick. I've left one of the toughest states in the nation on criminal justice matters for one of the most lenient. New Jersey has effectively eliminated cash bail. I was in favor of this but have been compelled to deal with the measure's unintended consequences.

Auto theft has long been a serious problem here. As the state justice system has gotten in the habit of granting many defendants immediate release on felony charges, the incentives to quit stealing cars seem to have disappeared. Recently, a crew of vehicle thieves stole the same car twice in a three-day period. When the victim called and told the police they ought to be ashamed of themselves, they said there was nothing they could do. Auto theft was a nonviolent crime, and jail wasn't the answer.

The prosecution of white-collar crime is going through similar growing pains. Many white-collar criminals do their work from behind a computer. Prison seems like a heavy-handed response to identity theft or bank fraud, but some white-collar criminals—more, probably, than the 16 percent of federal offenders whose probation gets revoked—get back to work the minute they return to their keyboards. As we move away from using prison to reform all violent crime, we should also accept that certain nonviolent criminals won't stop until we force their hands. The various binaries that we've relied on to this point—violent versus nonviolent, white-collar crime versus street crime, addict versus dealer—often give false impressions of risk and need. If we overestimate them, we take away a person's liberty, his chance to earn a living, and we waste a fortune in public money. If we underestimate them, the consequences run all the way to loss of life.

If you want to know a person's needs, there's no substitute for going to his house and having a conversation with him. Community supervision offers opportunities to understand risk that no other criminal justice measure can hope to provide, but if community supervision is to confront increasingly serious criminal activity, courts and parole boards will have to be willing to heed POs' reports and do the unpleasant work of revocation when incarceration is the only way to reduce harm. The most common complaint I get from friends at the New Orleans District these days is that in their enthusiasm to reduce incarceration, some judges have been too quick to move offenders from jail to probation. In honorable pursuit of a more equitable justice system with smaller jails, some judges have ignored warning signs that would have been obvious five years before. Preventable disasters are not being prevented.

It's easy for me to say. This book contains only a fraction of the misjudgments I made in my time as a professional assessor of risk and need. Community supervision may be the best assessment tool there is, but deciding how humans are going to respond to stimuli is anything but an exact science. When I left P&P, I thought I was trying to get away from addiction. It's clear to me now that I was also trying to get out of the business of assessing risk.

———————

For about six months after I left New Orleans, I did very little reflecting on my old job. There was another police academy to get through, and then an old apartment to pack up and a new one to turn into a home. There was the Northeast, with its hourlong commutes and staggering rents. Kristin and I liked our new jobs but missed friends and family. Even when I got homesick, I didn't spend much time thinking about P&P, and not because I believed I was a bad PO. If asked to score my overall performance, I would have rated myself about average for the New Orleans District, which is to say that I believed that in the final count, I undid more harm than I did.

I put a lot of people in prison. I kept a lot of people out. I never cast the only vote on an offender's fate, but I never abstained from the process, either. I had a hand in every sanction handed down or denied.

More than anything, when I thought about P&P, I was struck by the sheer magnitude of the authority I'd wielded, and the undeniable fact that half a decade after I made some of my decisions, their consequences had yet to be fully realized. I was gone, but my work, for better and surely also for worse, lived on.

Even as I tried to put P&P behind me, I found myself periodically evangelizing for it. When I fell into conversation about the state of the country, I argued that probationers and parolees were the Americans on whom poverty, addiction, and mental illness were doing their worst. Most started out as victims. Many became victimizers in time. An investment in them was an investment in public safety, and public safety was a cause everyone could get behind.

Depending on the crowd, I sometimes argued that giving second chances was the right thing to do. Most of the time, though, I just said that spending money on probationers and parolees was practical—a smart use of public funds—and it wasn't really a difficult case to make. Detox gets an addict clean for a little while—long enough, at least, to consider sobriety. A rental voucher gets a homeless person off the street. If we haven't discovered cures for all our social ills, we do know how to reduce the harm caused by many of them. Writing this book was a way to remember that.

When I needed a fact-check as I was drafting, I hit up Beth and Charles. The last time I got Charles on the phone, he told me about a veteran who overdosed on his watch. Charles had detoxed the offender once in jail, sent him to sober living, and offered drug court, but the young man had a death wish and fulfilled it soon enough.

"OD-wise," Charles said, "it was another rough year."

I'd heard him flustered, even outraged, but this was the first time he sounded exhausted. He was eighteen months from retirement, and he admitted he wished he could press the fast-forward button. It was a mortal certainty that some of the people on his caseload that day wouldn't be alive when he got his retirement papers—"my parole," he called them. Before Charles got out of the New Orleans District, there would be more harm to deal with.

Beth left not long after I did. She got on with a law practice and doubled her income. She says she couldn't have lasted one day longer than she did. "When it's time, it's time," she said. "People who can do that shit for twenty years are freaks."

Beth put in nearly seven years. I ended up logging four years and four months. Lamar has outlasted me by now. He claims he's in it for the long haul. He has time in the retirement system from his previous state employment and can probably tap out whenever he reaches his limit.

The old-timers in the lunchroom at the New Orleans District used to say that the one virtue you needed if you wanted to last was durability. Twenty years of ministering to the neediest people in one of the nation's poorest cities meant facing down dozens of overdoses and hundreds of prison sentences, and there was always at least a little blame for you, always a question of what else you might have done. Durability is an asset, to be sure, but I think grace is the one you really need, though Charles, like all graceful people, will never admit he has it.

A longstanding officewide code dictates that I never ask him for updates on the people I used to supervise. When you're gone, you're not allowed to keep tabs anymore. It's for your own protection, freeing you to hope for the best.

Sheila's baby is old enough to be walking, speaking, and trying her mother's patience in all the usual ways. Even if the boyfriend is providing Sheila with drug windfalls, young motherhood can't be easy. I hope Sheila hasn't returned to self-medicating. I hope that in the short time I knew her, I helped give her a chance at a safer, healthier life.

Damien and Travis paroled long ago. Kendrick should be eligible soon, if he hasn't been released already. Last I heard, the grant for offenders with co-occurring disorders is off to a strong start. Kendrick will walk out of prison with at least six months of meds and counseling behind him. He'll be enrolled in Medicaid and have his food stamps waiting and a prescription in pocket when he boards the bus out of prison, and an appointment scheduled at Metropolitan Human Services District a few weeks out. His address of record in the beginning will probably be the New Orleans Mission, safer and cleaner now, and by all accounts a more tolerable place to lay your head while you try to plan the next step. The landscape will look a little different to Kendrick—enough, I hope, to make a difference. With a little luck he'll look sufficiently run-down and defeated to catch the eye of Unity when the caseworkers pass through and get the help he needs to change his life.

By now Hard Head may be paying his own way for his Unity apartment. The last time I saw him there, he was less upbeat than usual. He was grateful for the housing voucher and the job and the support system he'd grown at Odyssey House and the Mission and Under the Bridge. He had friends now, the real thing—people he could run to when he felt his addiction stirring. He admitted that the Bible no longer spoke to him the way it once did, and he had yet to make the long-delayed call to his son on the West Coast. Even so, he hadn't felt loneliness—at least, not the way he used to feel it—in a while now. His big hang-up that day was time. Why couldn't he have gotten himself together sooner? Why didn't he get desperate for change when he was young?

"Other people had it worse," he said, "and didn't do half the dumb shit I did."

"They had more help," I said.

"Not all of them."

I told him this was a fool's trail and urged him to reflect on his surroundings and credit his own part in securing and sustaining them, but he wouldn't let it go. "Why did other guys figure it out and I stayed a mess?" he asked.

I was too tired to answer any way but honestly. "It's a mystery," I said, and took my leave of him. I was ready to be done with Hard Head. I was ready to be done with all of it. What aptitude I'd had for this work was spent, and everything good in me was threatening to sour. I didn't want to be around for another relapse, or worse. Help, in the form of a new job far away, seemed to be arriving not a minute too soon.

I'm sorry to say that time and distance haven't provided a more satisfying answer to Hard Head's question. All those people who take hardship in stride, who find ways to get by on their own—I can't account for them. I don't know how they do it.

I'll always wish I'd been kinder to Hard Head there at the end, but it didn't really matter. By then the work was done. He had a home and a community and a job he could be proud of. Three years after he walked out of prison, he was finally a free man.

# ACKNOWLEDGMENTS

Thanks first and foremost to my parents, who read and dutifully cor-
rected every essay, short story, and term paper from middle school
through my last semester of college. I was fortunate over the years to
find plenty of great readers who had no familial obligation to read my
stuff, first in creative-writing workshops at the University of Florida
and then in the MFA program at LSU.

Thanks to Farley Chase, who believed in this book long before
either of us knew what it would look like. So did Eamon Dolan, the
best editor I could have hoped for, who taught me how to write an
outline, a chapter, and, finally, a book. His energy, vision, and, above all,
his patience, are beyond measure.

Thanks to my former colleagues at the New Orleans District, who
taught me the job and talked me through my early lumps. Many of
you are still at it—still working long hours for low pay in the name of
changing the lives of the needy and the addicted and the mentally ill. I
truly believe you have the toughest job in the criminal justice system.
My fondest wish for this book is that it gets you more help.

And to all the probationers and parolees who wanted help but
didn't get it, I hope in the coming years we do better by you. We'll be
a safer and more equitable nation for it.

Finally, my deepest thanks to my wife, Kristin, who agreed to move
1,200 miles so that I could take my dream job, and who, after we got here, was
often left to her own devices on nights and weekends so that I could write
this book. I don't have any idea how to repay you, but I hope you'll let me try.

# NOTES

## introduction

xiv  *There are about 4.5 million people:* "Probation and Parole in US, 2016," Bureau of Justice Statistics, http://www.bjs.gov/index.cfm?ty=pb detail&iid=6188.

xv  *Until 2018, when Oklahoma edged us out:* "Louisiana No Longer Leads Nation in Imprisonment Rate," Pew Charitable Trusts, https://www.pewtrusts.org/en/research-and-analysis/articles/2018/07/10/louisiana-no-longer-leads-nation-in-imprisonment-rate.

## PART ONE – need

### one: emergency

5  *The state was about 30 percent black:* "Racial and Ethnic Disparities in Prisons and Jails in Louisiana," Prison Policy Initiative, https://www.prisonpolicy.org/profiles/LA.html.

5  *Louisiana spent more than half a billion dollars:* Martin Kaste, "Violent Crime Stays Flat Nationally, Louisiana Still Leads States for Murder," NPR.org, Sept. 25, 2018, https://www.npr.org/2018/09/25/651521938/violent-crime-stays-flat-nationally-louisiana-still-leads-states-for-murder.

11  *inmate death rate:* Matt Sledge, "Brutal Federal Monitors' Report Says New Orleans Jail Is 'Critically Unsafe' Despite Slight Improvement," *New Orleans Advocate*, Jan. 18, 2018, https://www.theadvocate

.com/new_orleans/news/courts/article_8a69a4fa-fc81-11e7-a44d
-27e4aadc5534.html.


## two: a max case

22    *We were told that best practices recommended*: Matthew T. DeMichele, "Probation and Parole's Growing Caseloads and Workload Allocation: Strategies for Managerial Decisionmaking," American Probation and Parole Association, May 4, 2007.

24    *17,800 families received Section 8 vouchers*: Richard A. Webster, "HANO to Open Section 8 Wait List, Accept New Applicants," *Times-Picayune /New Orleans Advocate*/Nola.com, Feb. 25, 2016, https://www.nola .com/politics/2016/02/hano_to_open_section_8_wait_li.html.


## three: the idea

42    *Opioid inhibitors produced good results*: "How Effective Are Medications to Treat Opioid Use Disorder?" National Institute on Drug Abuse, https:// www.drugabuse.gov/publications/research-reports/medications -to-treat-opioid-addiction/efficacy-medications-opioid-use-disorder.

44    *There would be 72,000 overdoses*: "Overdose Death Rates," National Institute on Drug Abuse, https://www.drugabuse.gov/related-topics /trends-statistics/overdose-death-rates.


## four: ride or die

47    *The first waves of doctors who prescribed it*: David Armstrong, "Sackler Embraced Plan to Conceal OxyContin's Strength from Doctors, Sealed Testimony Shows," Pro Publica, Feb. 21, 2019, https://www.propublica .org/article/richard-sackler-oxycontin-oxycodone-strength-conceal -from-doctors-sealed-testimony#.

48    *Only 16 percent of federal offenders*: "Annual Report, 2016," United States Courts, Probation and Pretrial Services, https://www.uscourts.gov /statistics-reports/probation-and-pretrial-services-annual-report-2016.

48    *Forty-three percent of parolees in Louisiana*: "Recidivism in Adult Corrections," Louisiana Department of Public Safety and Corrections, June 20, 2018.

48 *A Vera Institute of Justice study*: Christian Henrichson and Ruth Delaney, "The Price of Prisons: What Incarceration Costs Taxpayers," Vera Institute of Justice, January 2012.

50 *The latest research on marijuana*: "Risks of Adolescent Marijuana Use," US Department of Health and Human Services, https://www.hhs .gov/ash/oah/adolescent-development/substance-use/marijuana /risks/index.html.

57 *In the 2014–15 school year*: Danielle Dreilinger, "New Orleans Public Schools Pre-Katrina and Now, by the Numbers," *Times-Picayune/ New Orleans Advocate*/Nola.com, Aug. 29, 2014, https://www.nola .com/education/2014/08/new_orleans_public_schools_pre.html.

## five: addicted to the lifestyle

63 *A study by the Data Center*: "The New Orleans Prosperity Index: Tricentennial Edition," Data Center, April 11, 2018, https://www.data centerresearch.org/reports_analysis/prosperity-index/.

64 *Many local criminologists believed*: Emily Lane, "For New Orleans Gangs, It's Kill or Be Killed, No Matter the Collateral Cost," *Times-Picayune /New Orleans Advocate*/Nola.com, Oct. 9, 2018, https://www.nola .com/crime/2018/10/new_orleans_gang_violence_cult.html.

65 *Louisiana had far too many people*: "Frequently Asked Questions," Louisiana Department of Public Safety and Corrections, https://doc.louisiana .gov/frequently-asked-questions.

71 *Arrest rates for murders*: Ken Daley, "We Are Completely Broken, NOPD Detective Says of Struggling Homicide Unit," *Times-Picayune/New Orleans Advocate*/Nola.com, April 14, 2017, https://www.nola.com /crime/2017/04/we_are_completely_broken_nopd.html#incart _river_mobileshort_home.

## six: homebody

73 *There were 7,000 offenders*: "Louisiana Department of Public Safety and Corrections Fact Sheet," Dec. 31, 2018, https://doc.louisiana.gov /briefing-book.

## seven: institutionalized

84    *According to Volunteers of America*: Patricia McKernan, "Homelessness and Prisoner Re-Entry," *Journal of Community Corrections*, Fall 2017, https://www.voa.org/homelessness-and-prisoner-reentry.

93    *The fact that some early architects*: Dan Baum, "How to Win the War on Drugs." *Harper's*, April 2016, https://harpers.org/archive/2016/04/legalize-it-all/.

## PART TWO – risk

## eight: ninety-day turnaround

102    *In the late fifties and early sixties*: "Mentally Ill Persons in Corrections," National Institute of Corrections, US Department of Justice, https://nicic.gov/mentally-ill-persons-in-corrections.

## ten: the descendants of masters

134    *A local newspaper story*: Jed Lipinski, "The Trials and Travails of a New Orleans Public Defender," *Times-Picayune/New Orleans Advocate/*Nola.com, March 30, 2016, https://www.nola.com/crime/index.ssf/2016/03/new_orleans_public_defender_trials_and_travails.html.

## twelve: removed from circulation

160    *A National Institute of Justice study*: "Do Drug Courts Work? Findings from Drug Court Research," National Institute of Justice, https://www.nij.gov/topics/courts/drug-courts/pages/work.aspx.

## thirteen: best of the worst

176    *Portugal decriminalized drug possession*: "Drug Decriminalization in Portugal: Learning from a Health and Human-Centered Approach," Drug Policy Alliance, Feb. 20, 2019, http://www.drugpolicy.org/resource/drug-decriminalization-portugal-learning-health-and-human-centered-approach.

176   *As US overdoses continued to soar*: Nicholas Kristof, "How to Win a War on Drugs," *New York Times*, Sept. 22, 2017, https://www.nytimes.com /2017/09/22/opinion/sunday/portugal-drug-decriminalization .html.


## PART THREE – harm reduction

### fourteen: the wait

188   *the USDA believes*: "How FNS fights SNAP Fraud, Waste, and Abuse," US Department of Agriculture, https://www.fns.usda.gov/snap/fraud.

189   *By most statistical measures*: Emma Brown, "Katrina Swept Away New Orleans School System, Ushering in New Era," *Washington Post*, Sept. 3, 2015, https://www.washingtonpost.com/news/education/wp/2015 /09/03/katrina-swept-away-new-orleans-school-system-ushering -in-new-era/?utm_term=.f6aa14765977.

190   *The expansion of the jail population*: "Probation and Parole in US, 2016," Bureau of Justice Statistics, http://www.bjs.gov/index.cfm?ty=pb detail&iid=6188.

192   *Many modern criminologists gave*: Patrick Sharkey, *Uneasy Peace: The Great Crime Decline, the Renewal of City Life, and the Next War on Violence* (New York: W. W. Norton, 2018).

192   *Of the first thirty-three inmates*: Jenna Moll, "Finding Hope in an Unexpected Place: Louisiana's Re-Entry Court," Oct. 5, 2016, https:// imdiversity.com/diversity-news/finding-hope-in-an-unexpected -place-louisianas-reentry-court/.

198   *Research had shown little*: "More Imprisonment Does Not Reduce State Drug Problems," Pew Charitable Trusts, March 8, 2018, https:// www.pewtrusts.org/en/research-and-analysis/issue-briefs/2018/03 /more-imprisonment-does-not-reduce-state-drug-problems.


### seventeen: constraints of time and place

232   *In addition to a 17 percent decrease*: Jeff Asher, "Why Did Murder in New Orleans Fall in 2013?," *Times-Picayune/New Orleans Advocate* /Nola.com, July 3, 2015, https://www.nola.com/news/crime_police /article_1decf6e2-e201-570e-b778-a4464cda3938.html.

## epilogue

241  *Nationwide, about 25 percent of inmates*: Wendy Sawyer and Peter Wagner, "Mass Incarceration: The Whole Pie 2019," Prison Policy Initiative, March 19, 2019, https://www.prisonpolicy.org/reports /pie2019.html.

242  *Michelle Alexander, arguably*: Michelle Alexander, "Reckoning with Violence," *New York Times*, March 3, 2019, https://www.nytimes.com /2019/03/03/opinion/violence-criminal-justice.html.

243  *We still record*: "Uniform Crime Report: Crime in the United States, 2017," US Department of Justice, Fall 2018, https://ucr.fbi.gov /crime-in-the-u.s/2017/crime-in-the-u.s.-2017 .

244  *In 2017 a package of criminal justice reforms*: Julia O'Donoghue, "Louisiana Starts Redirecting Prison Savings to Local Rehab, Training Programs," *Times-Picayune/New Orleans Advocate*/Nola.com, Oct. 18, 2018, https://www.nola.com/politics/2018/10/second_phase_of _louisianas_cri.html.

# INDEX